'From the scientific quest for immortality to the question of life on other planets, and from scientific cures for sadness to human gene editing, this fascinating survey of contemporary issues shows how science and religion are integrated into the warp and woof of human existence. The very words we use to describe the issues reveal our own worldviews. This well-researched and engaging narrative is thoroughly recommended for all those concerned about contemporary challenges to human flourishing.'
Denis Alexander, editor of *Has Science Killed God?*

'*Playing God* is a powerful and very readable survey of the confrontation between science and religion. The authors refute the claim that science has somehow defeated religion by repeatedly showing the idea is a form of superstition that ignores the true complexity and depth of our existence. For people who have ever found themselves in the midst of this argument, this is an essential read.'
Bryan Appleyard CBE, author of *The Brain is Wider than the Sky*

'*Playing God* could not be more timely. It shifts the question of where science and religion intersect and sometimes collide away from the traditional and rather sterile arguments over creation and cosmology to the pressing debates about cutting-edge technologies that blur the boundaries of the human and which pose urgent ethical and societal dilemmas. Open-minded, thoughtful and humane, the book shows how religious perspectives can genuinely contribute to public dialogue on science and technology - and vice versa!'
Philip Ball, author of *How To Grow a Human*

On this deeply polarised issue, the norm is crude generalisation. In contrast, *Playing God* sheds light and brings nuance. An insightful book on a deeply important topic.
Philip Goff, author *of Why? The Purpose of the Universe*

Can anything new be said in the perennial debate between science and religion? Probably not; but every now and then we need a new guide to the current state of the argument; and for our generation this magnanimous and comprehensive narrative is exactly what we need.
Richard Holloway, author of *A Little History of Religion*

An accessible, engaging and satisfying engagement with some of the big questions of our time.
Alister McGrath, author of *Why God Won't Go Away*

It is sometimes said that debate on life's big questions boils down to anthropology. What is it to be human? And which of the available accounts of our nature in the marketplace of ideas is most robust? Nick Spencer and Hannah Waite have much to say from a Christian standpoint about science–religion dialogue – and especially about AI – that is of great relevance to the health of twenty-first-century society. They also voice prophetic warnings about where and how things may go disastrously wrong. Accessible as well as shrewd, *Playing God* deserves a large audience among believers and secularists alike.
Rupert Shortt, author of *Outgrowing Dawkins*

'Nick Spencer has made a timely and powerful contribution to the science versus religion debate by rebutting the dogma that they are opposite ways of knowing about the world. Rather, they address two different, but overlapping aspects of human existence: its material basis and its purpose. Not only do most people not perceive a binary opposition between science and religion, even today, but it breaks down philosophically, as soon as one asks the question not who created the world, but what humans are for.'
Robert Skidelsky, FBA, author of *The Machine Age: An Idea, a History, a Warning*

'*Playing God* is a compelling exploration that ventures beyond the conventional discourse into the realms where science and faith converge clash and coalesce. With clarity and insight, the authors navigate the intricate dance between two of humanity's most profound endeavours. Spencer and Waite do not shy away from contentious issues; instead, they invite us into a thoughtful and nuanced conversation about what it truly means to be human in an era of unprecedented scientific advancement. Whether you are a person of faith, a science enthusiast, or simply someone who ponders the big questions of existence, *Playing God* is a richly rewarding read.'
John Swinton, FBA, FRSE, co-author of *Struggling with God*

'A highly intelligent, well-informed and perceptive analysis of the frontiers of science-faith conversations in the twenty-first century. The authors provide an accessible, nuanced and theologically grounded analysis of the implications of scientific advance challenging traditional understandings of what it means to be human. Ranging from life extension, alien and artificial intelligences, gene editing and psychoactive medication, Spencer and Waite argue that we have a unique responsibility through advancing science to re-present God's love to his creation. In place of a cautious conservatism, Christians should embrace the positives. We are here to play God.'

John Wyatt, co-editor of *The Robot Will See You Now*

Nick Spencer is Senior Fellow at Theos, the religion and society think tank. He is the author of a number of books including *Magisteria* (Oneworld, 2023), *The Evolution of the West* (SPCK, 2016), *Atheists: The origin of the species* (Bloomsbury, 2014) and *Darwin and God* (SPCK, 2009). He is a Fellow of the International Society for Science and Religion, and the host of the popular *Reading Our Times* podcast, in which he engages with some of the biggest authors and most important books of the day, in the process exploring the key ideas that shape the world we live in.

Hannah Waite worked as a researcher of science and religion at Theos from 2019 to 2023. Hannah holds an MA in Psychology and a PhD in Theology, both from the University of Aberdeen. Her areas of research focus on the intersection of psychology, theology and psychiatry, and in particular on understanding the lived experience of stigma in the lives of Christians with significant mental health challenges. She is writing a book on stigma and mental health challenges that is being published in 2024 by SCM Press.

PLAYING GOD

Science, religion and the future of humanity

Nick Spencer and Hannah Waite

First published in Great Britain in 2024

SPCK
SPCK Group
Studio 101
The Record Hall
16–16A Baldwin's Gardens
London EC1N 7RJ

www.spck.org.uk

British Library Cataloguing-in-Publication Data
A catalogue record for this book is available from the British Library

ISBN 978–0–281–09003–7
eBook ISBN 978–0–281–09005–1

1 3 5 7 9 10 8 6 4 2

Typeset by Manila Typesetting Company
First printed in Great Britain by Clays Ltd

eBook by Manila Typesetting Company

Produced on paper from sustainable forests

Contents

Preface

The future has an irritating habit of not standing still. And that makes writing about it perilous. *Playing God* is about a future that is arriving daily in a blizzard of headlines. In the few months between our finishing the text of this book and signing off the final proofs, there was hardly a day when at least one of the topics on which we had written was not in the news.

We learnt how NASA's James Webb Space Telescope revealed the presence of methane and carbon dioxide on exoplanet K2-18, which might indicate life, or at least the potential for it, and how other astronomers had found what looked like 'the perfect solar system' for life, a hundred light years away from Earth. We read that there was a 'shocking' lack of evidence for the effect of antidepressants on chronic pain but also how 'Most people on antidepressants don't need them' anyway. (*The Economist*, 19 October 2022) We saw the UK medicines regulator approve gene therapy for sickle cell disease and beta thalassemia and we read reports of how a new gene editing treatment had shown signs of being able to reduce dangerous cholesterol levels. And, of course, we read story after story about AI predicting hurricanes, fighting wars, developing personality, needing regulation and failing to get regulation – to name only a tiny handful of stories.

We read these stories with fascination rather than fear. *Playing God* does not make sweeping predictions about the future so the book is unlikely to be disproved by a single new discovery, although contact with intelligent aliens who signed off their transmission with reference to the Holy Trinity would settle one or two issues raised in chapter 2.[1]

---

1 Aficionados of *The Simpsons* will recall that is exactly what the tentacular aliens Kang and Kodos do in the episode 'Gump Roast'.

Rather, the case we put forward in *Playing God* is that the kind of progress that science is making – from discovering potentially life-bearing exoplanets to discerning the genetic component of intelligence; from designing algorithms that imitate human thought to developing pharma-chemicals that can alter it; from extending human life and uploading human minds to assigning personhood to non-human animals, and defeating pandemics if only society 'follows the science' – this kind of progress raises precisely the kind of questions that science itself cannot answer.

Science is focusing the spotlight, with ever greater intensity, on ideas of human uniqueness, freedom, personhood, communication, the body, agency, autonomy, dependence and perfection. Such concepts are foundational to how we understand ourselves and our good, both personal and collective, and they open up scientific conversations to a whole range of humanistic disciplines.

This book is concerned with the religious dimension of those conversations. For too long, it argues, the science and religion conversation has snagged on neuralgic issues of evolution, the Big Bang, and miracles, with perhaps a bit of quantum theory thrown in for weird measure. Such debates, interesting as they can be, are largely absent from *Playing God*. Instead of evolution and cosmology, we focus on cryogenics, astrobiology, genetic engineering, pharmacology, primatology, cybernetics and obstetrics – disciplines that are rarely encountered in science and religion books.

Throughout we insist that the familiar warning against 'playing God' has no place in these debates. On the contrary, *humans are a God-playing species*, our uniquely communicative, imaginative, social and rational capacities giving us precisely the ability, and therefore the responsibility, to 'play God'. The question is not whether, but how: which version of God should we be playing, and how seriously? The news stories about AI, aliens, pandemics and pharmaceuticals do not change that question, except perhaps to make it more urgent than ever.

Nick Spencer and Hannah Waite
January 2024

Acknowledgements

This book is the product of a number of years' work on science and religion conducted in partnership with The Faraday Institute for Science and Religion. We would like to thank the entire team at Faraday and in particular Keith Fox, Paul Ewart and Alice Jackson.

The project was funded by Templeton Religion Trust to whom we also owe an enormous debt of thanks.

Part of the project involved interviewing over a hundred experts – scientists, philosophers, theologians, etc. This was a fascinating and educative experience, and even though their thoughts and words remain, for the most part, firmly under the bonnet of the text in this book, they proved invaluable and we would like to thank them for their time and engagement.

At the time of writing, both authors were working at the religion and society think tank Theos, and the feedback and encouragement of our colleagues throughout the whole project was extremely valuable. Different colleagues read and commented on different chapters, as did Andrew Davidson, John Wyatt, Mohammed Mohammed and Toby Hole. We are grateful to them for their time and expertise.

Both authors also have personal thanks they would like to register, Nick to Kate, Ellen, Jonny and his wider family, and Hannah to Barbara, Bryan, Cameron, Mackenzie, Abigail and her wider family and close friends.

A note on terminology

Writing about 'science' and 'religion' is perilous. We all know what those terms mean until we try to define them. At that point, they dissolve.

We have retained both words throughout most of this book, though we are acutely aware of the problems of doing so. In truth, this is less of an issue (for us) when it comes to 'science'. Each of the chapters in the book engages with a specific scientific discipline – astrobiology, genetic engineering, pharmacology, obstetrics, etc. These are not the usual fare for a science and religion book, but they are, at least, more precise than the generic 'science'. The reader will, we hope, be reasonably clear what kind of science we are talking about in these chapters.

Religion is more of a challenge. The authors' particular interest and expertise, such as it is, is on Christianity, and that remains our focus in the book. However, much of what we say could apply to the other Abrahamic faiths, and some of it to non-Abrahamic faiths. Referring constantly to science and Christianity risks making the arguments look more parochial and exclusive than they are intended to be. For that reason, we have usually stuck with the familiar, if generic, word 'religion', except for where we wanted to make more specific points.

Nick Spencer and Hannah Waite

Introduction

When science met religion

In 2000, Ian Barbour, Professor Emeritus of Physics and Religion at Carleton College in Northfield, Minnesota, published a book entitled *When Science Meets Religion*. Barbour argued that science and religion engaged with one another in a number of different ways and outlined a four-fold categorisation for the encounter: conflict, independence, dialogue and integration. Science and religion could be at loggerheads with one another, indifferent to one another, in casual conversation with one another, or in a kind of systematic and extensive partnership with one another. Barbour explored these categories and then proceeded to show what they looked like for a number of key areas within the debate – astronomy and creation, quantum physics, evolution, neuroscience, and divine action 'in a world of lawful processes.'[1]

Barbour's book was clear, learned, fair-minded and well received. In an already crowded field, it soon became respected as a seminal contribution. If you want to understand what happens when science meets religion, it is an important book to read. But it inadvertently gives the impression that when science meets religion it is primarily, perhaps even exclusively, to talk about issues like . . . astronomy, quantum physics, evolution, neuroscience, creation and miracles.

In this, it is not alone. The field of science and religion is not short of intelligent and erudite contributions. Whether coming from eminent believing physicists (such as John Polkinghorne), or eminent non-believing physicists (such as Paul Davies), eminent believing biologists (such as Francis Collins or Denis Alexander), or eminent non-believing biologists (such as Stephen Jay Gould), or that one-man science and religion

---

1 Ian G. Barbour, *When Science Meets Religion: Enemies, strangers, or partners?* (San Francisco: HarperOne, 2000), p. 150.

publishing industry, Alister McGrath, the shelves groan with books exploring the relationship between the two disciplines.

This is not one of those books. To be clear, we recognise that these are important and interesting subjects, but there is also something strange about the way in which they have come to dominate science and religion dialogue, almost to the exclusion of other topics. In essence, we think that the science and religion discussion is most relevant, most interesting and most important when it comes to the question of what it means to be human. If this is the case, the twenty-first century might just be the golden age for science and religion – if we can just get the parameters of dialogue right.

In order to explain what we mean by this, we need to delve into a little history.

A walk in the park

In 1927, the most famous scientist in the world took time out to go for a walk with a part-time lecturer in Brussels' Parc Léopold. Albert Einstein was attending the famous fifth Solvay conference in which the greatest physicists of the age were discussing quantum theory. His companion in the park was a cosmologist who was too junior to attend the conference but who had recently published a paper that was to prove highly influential.

The paper was entitled 'A homogeneous universe of constant mass and increasing radius accounting for the radial velocity of extra-galactic nebulae'. It had appeared in an obscure Belgian journal and argued, on the basis of Einstein's own theory of general relativity, that the universe was expanding. Furthermore, it posited that the speed of galaxies was in proportion to their distance, meaning that the further away they were, the faster they were moving. The apparent conclusion was disconcerting. At some point in the very distant past, all galaxies, all matter, all the universe had been in one place together. The universe had a 'beginning'.

Einstein could not fault the young man's mathematics, but he did not like the theory and judged the conclusion unsustainable. Others took a similarly dim view. The British cosmologist and atheist, Fred Hoyle, revolted against what seemed like an argument for a creator and coined the phrase 'Big Bang', allegedly in mockery of the theory.

Others would be more enthusiastic. After the Second World War, Pope Pius XII seized on the idea, newly confirmed by observational data, to argue that the universe had indeed been created. Addressing the Pontifical Academy of Sciences in 1951, the Pope said that 'present-day science . . . has succeeded in bearing witness to the august instant of the primordial *Fiat Lux* [let there be light]'. The conclusion was unavoidable. 'Hence, creation took place. We say: therefore, there is a Creator. Therefore, God exists!'[2]

The originator of the theory, Georges Lemaître, found himself in a difficult position between these contradictory interpretations. On the one hand, he was a Catholic. Indeed, not simply a Catholic, but a priest, educated at a Jesuit school and ordained in 1923. On the other hand, and in spite of what the Pope would conclude, he did not believe that his theory of the 'Primaeval Atom' (as he termed it) demonstrated the *Fiat Lux*, still less that it proved God's existence. He even intervened with the Pope's scientific advisor to prevent Pius from making such an assertion again.

Lemaître set out his underlying position for the *New York Times* a few years after he and Einstein had met. The biblical writers, he reasoned, had little interest in or exclusive knowledge about the dynamics of creation. 'Neither St Paul nor Moses had the slightest idea of relativity.' What interested them was the nature and fate of humanity. 'The writers of the Bible were illuminated more or less – some more than others – on the question of salvation. On other questions they were as wise or as ignorant as their generation.'[3]

In spite of Lemaître's assertion, the idea that cosmology and religious belief are somehow trapped in some combative, zero-sum game is curiously widespread. UK opinion polling makes it painfully clear that opposition between science and religion is the default position for the majority of the UK population, and that this opposition is driven by particular disciplines. When asked whether certain scientific subjects – like neuroscience, medical science, psychology, chemistry, climate science or geology – make it

2 Rodney D. Holder, 'Lemaître and Hoyle: contrasting characters in science and religion', *Science and Christian Belief* 24(2) (2012), p. 125.
3 Quoted in Pablo de Felipe, Pierre Bourdon and Eduardo Riaza, 'Georges Lemaitre's 1936 lecture on science and faith', *Science and Christian Belief* 30(1) (2015), p. 168.

harder to be religious, the majority of British adults say they do not. Cosmology, however, and in particular the idea of the Big Bang, is the exception: the only scientific discipline that people, on balance, think makes it hard to be religious.[4] According to this view, it's Genesis or cosmology . . . God or the Big Bang . . . science or religion. The whole relationship is caught up in a kind of intellectual Thucydides trap, in which one reigning but declining power (religion) is displaced by a new rising force (science). Once upon a time, religion explained how the universe began. Now science does. Such competing explanations cannot coexist. One must go.

The idea that science and religion were rival explanations for life and the universe was not completely unknown in the past, but it was certainly not common. For most of the time, science – or '(experimental) natural philosophy' as it was more commonly known – was a valued part of the wider intellectual endeavour of understanding reality in all its multi-layered complexity. There were disagreements aplenty, of course, as there are in any serious, live intellectual discipline. But the idea that science and religion were *competing* to explain the same thing would have struck most thinkers as most odd.

But if they weren't (and aren't) competing explanations, it's not entirely clear what they were, or are, doing. How did, how does and how should science and religion relate to one another?

Perhaps the best-known alternative to 'competing explanations' came from the pen of the late American evolutionary biologist, Stephen Jay Gould, who argued that, properly speaking, science and religion were NOMA or 'non-overlapping magisteria' – separate, discrete, and mutually disengaged territories or activities. By this logic, science covered the empirical realm. Its objective was to document 'the factual character of the natural world' and 'to develop theories that coordinate and explain these facts'. Religion, by contrast, operated in the 'realm of human purposes, meanings, and values'. In effect, science was 'what is the universe made of (fact)

---

4 According to the Theos/Faraday research 38% of UK adults say the Big Bang makes its hard to be religious, compared to 31% who disagree. Incidentally, this statement includes evolution, despite the oceans of ink spilled to suggest otherwise. The same survey found that 49% of adults agree that 'it is possible to believe in God and in evolution' compared to 23% who disagree. See Nick Spencer and Hannah Waite, *'Science and Religion': Moving away from the shallow end* (Theos, 2022); https://www.theosthinktank.co.uk/research/2022/04/21/science-and-religion-moving-away-from-the-shallow-end (accessed 22 November 2023).

and why does it work this way (theory)', and religion the realm of 'ultimate meaning and moral value'.[5] The result of this division was peace; each party retaining authority but only within its own, strictly delimited territory. 'If religion can no longer dictate the nature of factual conclusions residing properly within the magisterium of science, then science cannot claim higher insight into moral truth from any superior knowledge of the world's empirical constitution.'[6]

There is something appealing and convincing in the approach. Surely science *is* about facts and theories, and religion *is* about meaning and value. NOMA is certainly a much better reflection of reality than the idea that God and science are competing explanations for facts about the universe and life. Moreover, it's easy to quote plenty of examples of where NOMA makes good sense. Religion has nothing important to contribute to the structure of the periodic table, the second law of thermodynamics, the development of the Covid-19 vaccine, or the location of exoplanets.[7] Similarly, the scientific disciplines that are so competent in addressing these questions – chemistry, physics, biology or astronomy – have nothing to say about the understanding of the atonement, the reasoning behind 'just war' theory, the meaning of Jesus' parables, or the significance of the Latin mass. So far, so good: non-overlapping magisteria works.

The problem with it is that just as there are many topics, from scientific and from religious magisteria, where the logic of NOMA holds, so there are many where it does not. NOMA is predicated on the idea that 'facts' and 'values' are completely distinct and can be held entirely separate from one another. However, in reality, in a great many areas the magisterium of science (broadly understood) and the magisterium of religion (broadly understood) *do* overlap. And that is especially the case when it comes to the whole messy business of understanding human beings.

---

5 Stephen Jay Gould, *Rocks of Ages: Science and religion in the fullness of life* (New York, NY: Ballantine Books, 1999), pp. 2–6.

6 Gould, *Rocks of Ages*, pp. 4–5. Gould slightly modified the independence of NOMA in response to E. O. Wilson's *Consilience*. See Stephen Jay Gould, *The Hedgehog, the Fox, and the Magister's Pox* (Cambridge, MA: Harvard University Press, 2003); and Alister E. McGrath, 'A consilience of equal regard: Stephen Jay Gould on the relation of science and religion', *Zygon* 56(3) (2021), pp. 547–65.

7 Which is not, of course, to say religious commitments have been irrelevant in the history of chemistry, physics, biology or astronomy.

Partially overlapping magisteria

It was this conviction that lay behind Lemaître's comment to the *New York Times* that the writers of the Bible were illuminated more or less on the question of *salvation* but that on other questions they were as wise or as ignorant as their generation. When it came to understanding salvation – or, in less theological language, human identity, morality, responsibility, destiny – the writers of the Bible (and, Lemaître would have added, the tradition of the Church) were essential. When it came to understanding the formation and nature of the universe, or the constituent elements of matter, or the origins of life, the writers of the Bible had little to offer beyond the understanding of their times.

This was no modern innovation, not something that was forced upon people like Lemaître in the twentieth century as a result of science's unprecedented success. On the contrary, it was an ancient and venerable response to the ideas and progress of natural philosophy. Forty years before Lemaître met Einstein, the Anglican bishop, Charles Ellicott, wrote to the greatest mathematical physicist of the day, James Clerk Maxwell, asking him about his understanding of 'the creation of light' in Genesis 1. Maxwell replied with an answer of sorts but emphasised that his answer was in accordance with the science of 1876 'which may not agree with that of 1896'. He stressed that he would be very sorry 'if an interpretation founded on a most conjectural scientific hypothesis were to get fastened to the text in Genesis'. Maxwell was a devout evangelical, immersed in the Scriptures from a young age. He absorbed a serious understanding of sin and grace from the Bible, and was not the kind of Christian for whom the Bible was a leaf on every intellectual wind that blows. But he was also clear how far the Scriptures went, what they were *for* and *how* they should be used – and that wasn't to clarify or to be demonstrated by contemporary science.

A few centuries earlier, in 1615, just as the weather was beginning to turn for him, Galileo Galilei wrote a public letter to Grand Duchess Christina of Tuscany in which he defended Copernicanism. In it, he drew on an impressive range of theological sources to argue that 'with greater prudence' the authors of Holy Scripture had more or less ignored natural philosophy, not because it was unimportant but because it was of 'no use for eternal life'.[8] Ultimately, he famously asserted (actually quoting Cardinal Cesare Baronio) that 'the intention of the Holy Spirit is to teach us how one goes to heaven and not how heaven goes'.[9]

A full millennium earlier, John Philoponus of Alexandria, one of the most important philosophers of late antiquity, found himself arguing against those Christians in Antioch who believed that the Earth was flat (not a common position in late antiquity, but not unheard of). His text, *On the Creation of the World*, advocated the sphericity of the Earth without question and summarily dismissed his opponents' bad science – and their bad theology. Specifically, John dismantled the idea that Moses (then believed to be the author of Genesis) was writing about astronomy at all. 'No one considering the systematic treatment of nature by later writers is going to ask Moses' Scripture . . . what has been thoroughly researched on these subjects by specialists,' he wrote. 'That was not the excellent Moses' intent.' Excellent Moses, by John's reckoning, was 'chosen by God to lead people to knowledge of God', not of nature.[10]

Examples could be multiplied. The point is that, contrary to modern polemicists, these writers did not think science and religion were competing explanations, but also that, contrary to Stephen Jay Gould, neither did they think science and religion were non-overlapping magisteria. Rather, to coin a phrase, they seemed to gravitate to a kind of 'POMA' – partially overlapping magisteria – in which, for all that they were different enterprises, science and religion overlapped about the question of what it means to be human.

This helps explain a lot. It helps explain how the Christian faith has come to terms with the ever-changing scientific truths of the last two thousand years. Christianity found itself able to exist in a heliocentric system just as it did in a geocentric one. It found itself able to exist in a vast universe of innumerable galaxies just as it did in a unique and solitary solar system. It found itself able to exist in a universe that appeared (at least according to the reigning Aristotelian science, and later according to observational

---

8 Maurice A. Finocchiaro, *The Galileo Affair: A documentary history* (Oakland, CA: University of California Press, 1989), p. 94.

9 Finocchiaro, *The Galileo Affair*, p. 96.

10 Quoted in Pablo de Felipe, 'Curiosity in the early Christian era: Philoponus's defence of ancient astronomy against Christian critics', *Science & Christian Belief* 30(1) (2018), p. 46.

data) static and eternal, and then in a universe that was revealed to be expanding from a point of origin. It found itself able to exist in a universe made of atoms rather than one in which matter was continuous and indivisible. It found itself able to exist in a universe made up of four constituent elements – earth, air, fire and water – and then in one of dozens, eventually over a hundred. It found itself able to exist in a constrictively Newtonian cosmos and in an Einsteinian universe of relativity, in a mechanistic and apparently deterministic universe, and one that is unpredictable and apparently undermined at its deepest, quantum level. It found itself able to exist in a world of special creation and in one of Darwinian evolution.

It found itself able to exist in all these because, at the end of the day, the beliefs that lay at its core were not affected by the size, shape, composition, patterning or uniqueness of the planet, star system, galaxy or universe in which it found itself, any more than they were affected by the origin, development, constitution or capacities of life on Earth.

To be clear, such major shifts in scientific understanding were not always received well, and the history of science and religion did have some rough patches.[11] But in time, usually in short time, the vast majority of them were accepted and willingly accommodated. In short, many of the things that we focus on in science and religion debates even today, however stimulating they are, are essentially B-list topics, of interest but not of ultimate significance for religious belief itself.

There are exceptions, however: issues that did – and do – matter. Superficially, the existence of God should be top of the list here, but scientific proofs of God's (non-)existence have been rare, and most honest thinkers recognise that, however much indicative evidence might mount up either way, an earthly discipline like science is unlikely either to prove or disprove the existence of God.

The real point of entanglement came when science and religion engaged over the endlessly fascinating question of the nature of the human. And the real point of tension came when either science or religion laid claim to an understanding of the human that was authoritative, exclusive and incompatible with the view of the other.

---

11 Though it is also important to recognise that these rough patches often had as much to do with the science (in particular, the fact that such new developments were often poorly evidenced in the first instance) as they did with religion.

This was the reason why the church fathers disliked astrology (a serious science in its day): because it effectively denied the human freedom and agency that was necessary to their idea of humanity and salvation. This was why early modern Christians rejected the idea of life elsewhere in the universe: because it allegedly threatened the unique position and status of human beings within God's plan. This was why Enlightenment-era Christians impugned the conclusion that was drawn by some of the more adventurous French philosophers that 'man' was no more than 'a machine', with no 'soul' to save.[12] This was why (some) Christians in the nineteenth century baulked at geology, not so much because it showed the Earth was old but because in the process it appeared to obliterate the timeframe laid out by salvation history. This was why evangelicals of the same period had such a problem with phrenology (again, a serious science in its time): because if you genuinely could read someone's character and morality from the bumps in their skull, that would mean they had no true freedom. This was why many religious believers took issue with anthropology as it developed (from a notably Christian discipline) in the later nineteenth century: because it seemed to claim that some kinds of human were *intrinsically* inferior (and therefore not open to God's salvation), as well as claiming that all forms of religious practice and experience were illusory. This was why many Christians had a problem with Freudianism: because it appeared to destroy the scheme of guilt and grace that underlay salvation. And this, of course, was why many Christians objected (and still do) to evolution by natural selection: because they believe that it means that humans were *merely* evolved primates with no moral sense or spiritual identity; with no souls to save.

Time and again, this has been where science and religion have become entangled. This is where these different magisteria partially overlap. This has been where the conversation has got important as well as interesting. And this has been what's at stake: the nature, identity, dignity, purpose and destiny of the human.

---

12 See Julien Offray de La Mettrie, *Machine Man and Other Writings*, ed. Ann Thomson (Cambridge: Cambridge University Press, 1996).

'Human entanglement': a new agenda for science and religion

Science has never *not* been interested in the nature of the human, but its understanding – of humans, of others animals that show human-like traits, of planets that might contain human-like life forms, of artificial creations that might exhibit human-like characteristics – has progressed enormously over recent decades. Moreover, understanding has generated control (or at least the potential for control), and science and technology now boast the ability not simply to comprehend the human, but to extend, 'correct', modify, transform, and perhaps even save it from death. The twenty-first century has witnessed science park its tanks firmly on the lawn of what it means to be human, not only 'understanding' us better than ever before but also offering us the possibility of changing ourselves as never before.

This is most obviously the case with the rise of gene editing, in which we have the potential to reword the language in which we are written (that metaphor is explored in greater depth in the relevant chapter). It's the case in the breakneck speed of AI development, as ever more people ask whether AI might actually become intelligent, sentient, conscious, or indeed human – whatever that might mean. It's behind the scenes in the evolving field of radical life extension, as the rich pour billions into the dream of scientific longevity and immortality, in the process erasing the temporal boundary that has always been part of our humanity.

It's implicit in the massive pharmacological turn in our treatment of mental illness, which is increasingly understood not as a consequence of familial, social or economic troubles, still less a fundamental condition of our being human, but as a pathology that can be treated with drugs. It lies in the background of our enthusiastic search for extra-terrestrial life, as we scan the skies for signals or detect ever more Goldilocks exoplanets, and wonder how what we find – if we find anything – will shape what we think of ourselves.

It's there in the shadows of the movement for animal personhood, as campaigners wonder whether and why humans are unique in their qualification for personhood, and ask whether the same privilege should be extended to some animals. It's there in the way in which astonishing developments in obstetrics have allowed us to 'see', know and heal the unborn in an entirely unprecedented way. And it's even there in the vanguard of the next pandemic, as our ability to vaccinate ourselves into safety runs into questions over the proper authority of the state, in which religious believers play a prominent role. In short, many of the areas of scientific development in the twenty-first century are right in the area of partial overlap between science and religion – the question of what it means to be human.

This book explores those issues. It has its origins in a three-year project that the authors conducted, in partnership with The Faraday Institute for Science and Religion, funded by Templeton Religion Trust, conducted between 2019 and 2022, which explores popular and 'elite' understanding of and attitudes to science and religion in the UK today. The authors conducted in-depth interviews with over a hundred academics and also commissioned a very substantial public opinion survey of over 5,000 UK adults that was conducted by YouGov. This book is not a research report for this project (that is available online), and the data from this research remain firmly in the background of this book. But *Playing God* would not have been possible without hundreds of hours of fascinating conversations with scientists, philosophers, sociologists, theologians, journalists and commentators.

The dialogue between science and religion has not always been polite or constructive. Even when it has been, it has commonly gravitated towards cosmology, evolution, quantum theory, miracles, etc. There is nothing wrong with this. Such topics are stimulating, as are the science and religion dialogues that spin off from them. But the history of science and religion shows that the heart of the issue, the core area of concern and contention, has long been the nature and status of the human. This is where science and religion have become most entangled, most antagonistic and sometimes most fruitful. The seminal question turns out to be, 'What are humans?' and, more precisely, 'Are they the kind of entities that are envisaged in the beliefs and narratives of religions?'

The nature and status of the human will be an incalculably important area of debate in the twenty-first century. If the argument of this introduction, and indeed the book as a whole, is right, this is a debate that will not simply allow, but actively need a wide range of contributions, not least from religion and from science. It is our hope that the chapters in this book make one such helpful contribution.

1

How not to live forever

In as far as religion has any USP – 'Unique Selling Point' in marketing jargon; something that distinguishes it from other comparable phenomena and marks it out as worth investing in – it is surely the promise of eternal life. Marxism assures us of justice on Earth. Communism promises material equality. Liberalism gives us freedom, and nationalism a sense of belonging. Religion often gestures towards each of these goods, but it is its commitment to eternal life that really differentiates it.

'Eternal life' is an unhelpful phrase; vague to the point of misleading. The religious promise to conquer, circumvent or somehow cheat death comes in rather different flavours. Christians believe in the resurrection of the dead, exemplified by Christ, the redemption of creation, and an eternity of communion with a Trinitarian God. Jews look forward to 'the world to come', in which God will gather his people along with righteous Gentiles, resurrect the dead, restore his kingdom and inaugurate a new creation. Muslims anticipate a day of judgement, when each person is resurrected and reckoned. Hindus see humans as caught in a cycle of death and rebirth in which their soul is repeatedly reincarnated in a different body according to their moral balance in each life, until the point at which it is finally reabsorbed into Brahman or ultimate reality. Buddhists too envisage a cycle of rebirth until the point of nirvana, which affords final release from the suffering of life. Ancient Egyptians believed that humans had a life force that departed the body at death. Ancient Greek 'religion' (though the term is especially anachronistic here) spoke of an underworld to which the spirits of the dead slipped, except for a few heroic figures whose post-mortem existence brought them to Elysium. Ancient Roman religion had similar beliefs, which varied as the empire integrated localised cults.

'Eternal life' is a mixed bag of some very different ideas. It could be material or immaterial, universal or selective, joyous or bleak, and sometimes even downright painful. Moreover, not *all* religions have formal beliefs about eternity, still less ones that are precisely codified. Aside from a belief in the importance of deceased ancestors to whom the living owe piety, Confucianism is distinctly light on ideas about eternal life.

Religious beliefs and practices around death and eternity have also evolved over time, absorbing ideas from other traditions and drifting from foundational texts. They have been modified in the light of new ideas and challenged by heterodox interpretations coming from within the fold. Few religious traditions, even those with centralised texts, institutions or creeds, are completely univocal when it comes to eternal life.

Nevertheless, even with all these caveats in place, it is beyond serious doubt that ideas, teaching, practices and promises about the possibility of conquering death are a characteristic of religions; one not shared by other human ideologies or practices. For better or worse, the religious own 'eternal life'.

Or they did until recently. Because the ancient, arguably innate, human hope for eternal life has, over recent decades, caught the attention of scientists and billionaires alike. Immortality, whether biological, genetic, cryonic, cybernetic or digital, is now subject to serious scientific research, and serious money.

As is so often the case, where once religion first trod, there now science strides. Or, more polemically, where religion first stumbled, science now surges ahead. When it comes to eternal life, religion has failed to deliver the goods. No one has located Hades or Elysium. The day of judgement and the resurrection of the dead continue to elude us, in spite of frequent prophecies to the contrary. And the world to come has been endlessly postponed. Now, at last, in the face of all these failures, science promises to succeed where religion failed. Or so the argument goes.

The science of immortality

Around the world, as we write this, there are approximately 500 people who have paid good money to have their bodies pumped full of liquid nitrogen and stored upside down in a giant refrigerator for an unspecified period of time. A few have elected to be decapitated first, storing their head alone, 'neuropreservation' being a cheaper option than full body immersion. Some have even paid for their pets to join them, mainly dogs but on occasion cats and also, apparently, five hamsters, two rabbits and a chinchilla.[1]

Cryogenics, the science of preserving things at extremely low temperatures, is not without foundation. Freezers, after all, do a pretty good job of keeping our food edible. IVF, or In Vitro Fertilisation, depends on this technology. The idea that 'deceased' organs can be revivified is well attested. A 2019 paper in *Nature* reported how researchers, working with the severed heads of thirty-two pigs that had been killed for meat in a slaughterhouse, managed to 'revive the disembodied brains ... [up to] four hours after the animals were slaughtered'.[2] Another, published three years later, reported how the same researchers restored circulation and full cellular activity in the vital organs of pigs, including their brains, over one hour after the animals had died.[3] It has long been recognised that cells taken from brains can perform normal activities, such as making proteins, for some time after death. Death, it seems, may not be the end after all. As one of the pig researchers commented, 'For most of human history, death was very simple. Now, we have to question what is irreversible.'

Scientists are keen to downplay the implications of this for humans. Their caution is well advised. The science of neuropreservation is primitive. Researchers have seen no signs of the revival of coordinated electrical

---

1 Peter Wilson, 'The cryonics industry would like to give you the past year, and many more, back', *The New York Times* https://www.nytimes.com/2021/06/26/style/cryonics-freezing-bodies.html (accessed 17 November 2023).

2 Sara Reardon, 'Pig brains kept alive outside body for hours after death', *Nature* https://www.nature.com/articles/d41586-019-01216-4#:~:text=The%20researchers%20tested%20how%20well,systems%20seemed%20to%20be%20working (accessed 1 November 2023). This experiment apparently stopped short of 'restoring consciousness'.

3 Max Koslov, 'Pig organs partially revived in dead animals – researchers are stunned', *Nature* https://www.nature.com/articles/d41586-022-02112-0 (accessed 1 November 2023); 'Expert reaction to paper suggesting that cellular and tissue function can be restored in pigs after death', Science Media Centre https://www.sciencemediacentre.org/expert-re-action-to-paper-suggesting-that-cellular-and-tissue-function-can-be-restored-in-pigs-after-death/#:~:text=August%203%2C%202022-,expert%20reaction%20to%20paper%20suggesting%20that%20cellular%20and%20tissue%20function,occur%20in%20pigs%20after%20death (accessed 1 November 2023).

patterns or 'consciousness' in animal brains, and human brains are likely to be considerably more difficult to recover. The history of cryonics – the practice of freezing humans – is not without blemish. The first corpse to be cryonically frozen was in 1967, but the early years were marked by some unfortunate incidents, with poor preservation and insulation causing a few customers to thaw and refreeze, the most unlucky ones decomposing into a plug of fluids that had to be scraped off the bottom of the capsule and then 'buried'.[4]

It is no surprise, then, that Arthur Rowe, a former president of the Society of Cryobiology, which studies the effect of low temperatures on living tissues for legitimate procedures such as IVF, has claimed that 'believing cryonics could reanimate somebody who has been frozen is like believing you can turn a hamburger back into a cow'. The society itself has a bylaw that enables it to expel any member who takes part in 'any practice or application of freezing deceased persons in anticipation of their reanimation'.[5]

However primitive, speculative and downright ghoulish cryonics may be, though, it set the hares of 'scientific immortality' running. Perhaps science could enable us to defeat death, if not by cryonics then by some other approach?

The first step – that of delaying death – has been underway for well over a century. It is a remarkable fact that in Western Europe, average life expectancy has increased by over seven hours *per day* since 1900. People could expect to live until about 46 at the end of the nineteenth century. Today it is 81. The average Westerner has gained thirty-five years of life in the last 120 years.

Science can claim some credit for this – its ability to understand, diagnose and treat diseases being vastly greater today than it was a century ago – although much credit must also go to socially and politically driven improvements in hygiene, diet, work safety and public health infrastructure.[6] Either way, such success naturally gives credence to the idea that 'three score years and ten' is a wholly arbitrary figure and that the right

---

4 Tom Hartsfield, 'Horror stories of cryonics: the gruesome fates of futurists hoping for immortality', Big Think https://bigthink.com/the-future/cryonics-horror-stories (accessed 1 November 2023).

5 Wilson, 'The cryonics industry would like to give you the past year, and many more, back', *New York Times*.

6 All of which, of course, have roots in science.

science, mediated by the right politics, might extend life further and perhaps even indefinitely.

There are plenty of pseudo-scientific approaches available here. Life extensionism is the attempt to dramatically increase longevity by a 'scientifically tested' regime of vitamin and mineral supplements, calorie restriction, hormone replacement and programmatic exercise. In as far as it works at all, it doesn't appear to work very well, those embarking on the regime not noted for their Methuselan lifespans.

Only marginally more scientific – though what it gains in scientific credence it loses in gothic menace – is the practice of young-blood transfusion, sometimes called parabiosis. Parabiosis is the surgical joining together of different animals, the idea being that shared circulation of blood can benefit one or, possibly, both organisms. Scientists in the 1950s and 1960s found some sign of this when they conjoined young and old mice, but the results were small, questionable, and limited to rodents rather than humans. That has not stopped some companies, such as the hopefully named 'Ambrosia',[7] from selling young blood (at over $5,000 a litre) to those willing to give it a try – at least until the company stopped its 'trials' in 2019 in response to concerns from the United States Food and Drug Administration.

However ineffective these scientific approaches are, they are indicative of a mental reframing. Ageing, and perhaps even death, is now conceived as something unnatural and perhaps curable, rather than simply part of the natural order, about which we can do nothing. The World Health Organization's *International Classification of Diseases* (ICD), in its eleventh edition, has now included ageing (as opposed to age-related conditions, like dementia) in its compendium, giving it its own code – MG2A – and treating it as a disease 'associated [with] decline in intrinsic capacity'.

Understood in this way, ageing is not some kind of mysterious build-up of negative energy or loss of vitalist life force. It is, for want of a better phrase, a matter of wear and tear, accompanied by the rising costs of replacement. As the body ages, it becomes less adept (and less interested) in cleaning up or clearing out faulty or mutated cells, allowing the damage to build up to a critical level. Impaired cells create unhealthy tissue, leaving

---

7 Ambrosia was the food and drink of the Greek gods, alleged to confer longevity or even immortality upon those who consumed it.

organs increasingly less able to function. Moreover, with no potential (or need) to reproduce, the cost of the necessary repair seems to outweigh any comparable genetic reward. There's only so far you can drive your car, however carefully you look after it, before it becomes more economical to buy a new one.

Where that analogy breaks down, however, is in the fact that no car of any age produces perfect, shiny new car parts spontaneously. Humans do. The genetic material each of us inherits at birth is free of any age-related degeneration that might have affected our parents at the time. Both men and women are capable of having children after serious illness, and men in particular can breed way beyond their biological prime. Old bodies can generate young cells.

This opens up a more realistic approach to holding back age and death than that offered by ambrosia blood or life in the deep freeze. In 2012, the Nobel committee awarded the prize in medicine to Shinya Yamanaka, a Japanese biologist who had worked out how to 'reprogramme' mature cells so that they become young or, more precisely, 'pluripotent'. Pluripotent cells are 'stem cells' that are able to develop into a wide range of different cell types. In doing so, they are capable of repairing and rebuilding mature cells as they begin to decay. By 'bathing' mammalian cells in a series of four proteins, Yamanaka showed 'you could take any cell of any age from any part of the body and reprogramme it to go all the way back to zero age and zero state of identity'.[8]

Another death-defying medical approach, genetic rather than cellular in its strategy, relates to telomeres. Telomeres are the repeated DNA sequences found at the end of a chromosome, thousands of bases long in humans.[9] They act a bit like aglets – the plastic or metal tubes on the tip of a shoelace – preventing the ends of the chromosome from fraying and decaying, thereby protecting its information-carrying portions. Their protective function is not cost free, however, and whenever a cell divides, the telomeres are shortened. After a certain point, when they have become too short, the cell is unable to divide and dies.

8 Anjana Ahuja, 'Can we defeat death?', *Financial Times* https://www.ft.com/content/60d9271c-ae0a-4d44-8b11-956cd2e484a9 (accessed 1 November 2023).

9 A base is the basic unit of DNA, namely adenine (A), cytosine (C), guanine (G) and thymine (T).

This may not be an inevitable process, however. Telomerase is an enzyme that is expressed naturally in stem cells (and, curiously, in lobsters, which is why they keep growing through their long lives) but not in most mature, adult cells. It restores damaged telomeres, thereby prolonging the health and age of cells. The theory is that boosting the level of telomerase in the body might help protect telomeres and thereby slow cell senescence. More precisely, if the telomeres of T cells – white blood cells in the immune system – can be repaired by telomerase, it would allow the body to retain its ability to fight infections for longer than it presently does, hence extending both lifespan *and* health (sometimes helpfully elided into the word 'healthspan'). There is some evidence that this might be possible, although the jury is out on the matter, as indeed it is on the precise role of telomeres in ageing.

Other genetic possibilities have also been explored. Professor Cynthia Kenyon, a molecular biologist who has been working on the genetics of ageing for forty years, has worked out that it is possible to double the lifespan of the roundworm *Caenorhabditis elegans* by disabling a single gene.[10] If this sounds interesting but largely theoretical – roundworms being somewhat more distant from humans evolutionarily speaking than the compliant mice on whom we normally experiment for such matters – Kenyon has pointed out that studies have shown that humans who live to 100 are more likely to have mutations in daf-2, the relevant gene.[11] The idea of genetic medicine as a means of treating diseases is already a reality. If the ICD now classifies ageing as a disease, the idea of a genetic treatment for ageing, and possibly even death, is far from nonsensical.

In the light of all this, even those not given to hyperbole in such matters are open to the possibility of radical life extension. 'We are beginning to see early progress towards understanding the science of ageing,' remarked Reith lecturer and professor of biology, Tom Kirkwood, and it is now 'scientifically reasonable to begin considering what may one day become possible'.[12] Possible or not, should genetic longevity or immortality not appeal,

10 Kenyon herself began to avoid all sugar in her diet when she came to realise that sugar shortened the life of her worms by 'revving up the insulin pathway', which points back to the possible science behind 'life extensionism'.

11 Cynthia Kenyon, 'The idea that ageing was subject to control was completely unexpected', *The Guardian* https://www.theguardian.com/science/2013/mar/17/cynthia-kenyon-rational-heroes-interview (accessed 1 November 2023).

12 Ahuja, 'Can we defeat death?', *Financial Times*.

science may have another option up its sleeve, namely 'improving' humans by splicing them with technology.

It's worth noting that this is not so much science fiction as historical fact. Evidence for artificial body parts, such as legs, or aids, such as spectacles, dates back centuries. The quality and sophistication of artificial limbs has been improving for decades, and brain–computer (or brain–machine) interfaces, in which brain signals control external devices without using conventional neuromuscular pathways, have been the subject of intense research over the last twenty years, and have met with some success.[13] There can be no doubt that the technology will advance enormously in the twenty-first century, as much for its capacity to end life as to enhance it. 'Future wars will be won, not by those with the most advanced technology,' stated a 2021 UK government review into human augmentation, 'but by those who can most effectively integrate the unique capabilities of both people and machines.'[14]

Whatever the advances, the idea that human life can be prolonged indefinitely simply by replacing decaying bits of us with sophisticated tech is hardly more realistic than cryonic refrigeration. However remarkable and successful artificial hearts have become – people now survive years with them – the idea of an artificial brain is rather more far-fetched. That said, if the machine can't repair the human brain, perhaps it can recreate one.

Mind uploading, also sometimes known as 'whole brain emulation', is based on the idea that the brain can be deconstructed into the kind of digital information that computers process. The proposition here is that some form of ultra-high resolution scanning would allow scientists to create a complete map of the neural connections in the brain. This could then be copied, digitised and uploaded into a simulation, a kind of metaverse or virtual afterlife, and possibly then downloaded into a newfangled robotic human.

Fantastical and far-distant as this sounds, scientists point to the baby steps so far taken on the road. Artificial neural networks, inspired by biological ones, are well established, though they are vastly simpler than

---

13 Joseph N. Mak and Jonathan R. Wolpaw, 'Clinical applications of brain-computer interfaces: current state and future prospects', PMC, National Library of Medicine https://www.ncbi.nlm.nih.gov/pmc/articles/PMC2862632/#:~:text=The%2520most%2520common%2520example%2520of,without%2520using%2520conventional%2520neurom (accessed 1 November 2023).

14 Ministry of Defence, 'Human augmentation – the dawn of a new paradigm', GOV.UK https://www.gov.uk/government/publications/human-augmentation-the-dawn-of-a-new-paradigm (accessed 1 November 2023).

anything in the natural world. A complete connectome, the system of neural pathways in a brain, for the *Caenorhabditis elegans* has already been mapped in full, although the little creature does only have 302 neurons. Somewhat more ambitiously, the Blue Brain Project has, since 2005, been working to build 'the world's first biologically detailed digital reconstructions and simulations of the mouse brain'.[15]

Such successes have made some people inordinately enthusiastic about the possibilities allegedly on offer here, envisaging that some combination of brain scanning, artificial intelligence, digital uploading and human augmentation might one day 'save' and 'resurrect' or 'reincarnate' humans, thereby securing for us the immortality we crave.

The religious language is not inappropriate. Indeed, it is an intricate part of transhumanism, the title under which such efforts are known. Transhumanists talk openly about transcending earthly humanity and achieving eternal life. Articles breathlessly wonder whether transhumanism can 'save our species'[16] or whether it is 'savior of humanity or false prophecy'.[17] Ray Kurzweil, the St Paul of this movement, has proposed bringing his dead father back to life, albeit it as an avatar,[18] and has popularised the accompanying idea of the 'singularity', a kind of tipping point at which artificial intelligence surpasses that of humans and sends us plunging into a post-human future. Not without reason has it been compared to the idea of a cosmic Omega point, proposed by the Catholic priest and palaeontologist Pierre Teilhard de Chardin, or described as a kind of secular eschatological moment. Some new religious movements such as Raëlianism, a UFO religion, have enthusiastically embraced transhumanist ambitions. Other more traditional religions, or rather the murky corners of them, have even appropriated its ideas. The Christian Transhumanist Association, for example, believes, among other things, that 'the intentional use of technology,

---

15 EPFL, Blue Brain Project https://www.epfl.ch/research/domains/bluebrain (accessed 1 November 2023).

16 Celina Ribeiro, 'Beyond our "ape-brained meat sacks": can transhumanism save our species?', *The Guardian* https://www.theguardian.com/books/2022/jun/04/beyond-our-ape-brained-meat-sacks-can-transhumanism-save-our-species (accessed 1 November 2023).

17 Sachin Rawat, 'Transhumanism: savior of humanity or false prophecy?', Big Think https://bigthink.com/the-future/transhumanism-savior-humanity-false-prophecy (accessed 1 November 2023).

18 'Futurist Ray Kurzweil says he can bring his dead father back to life through a computer avatar', ABC News https://abcnews.go.com/Technology/futurist-ray-kurzweil-bring-dead-father-back-life/story?id=14267712 (accessed 1 November 2023).

coupled with following Christ, can empower us to grow into our identity as humans made in the image of God'.[19]

In short, if there were any sense that science and religion were non-overlapping magisteria, it would be demolished by a cursory glance at the more ambitious areas of the project for scientific immortality. The territory on which science stands is about as religious as it gets.

Who actually *wants* to live forever?

The quest for scientific immortality clearly does not want for enthusiasm. It needs it because the practical problems facing these attempts are almost incalculable and make the resurrection of Christ seem like a mere conjuring trick with bones by comparison.

Take transhumanism. The Blue Brain Project has now managed to map fully 1 cubic millimetre of mouse brain. They found that it contained more than 100,000 neurons with more than a billion connections between them, and that it required 2 petabytes of data (that is 2 million gigabytes) to store. The average human brain is around 1,400 cubic centimetres, and contains approximately 100 million neurons (of around 1,000 different types) and probably around 100 trillion synapses (contact points between neurons). We doubt whether there is a number big enough to describe the requisite storage space, let alone a computer for it.

Even if one were to solve such stupendous technical challenges, more theoretical ones would remain. The idea that mind can be reduced to information is questionable to say the least, based on a reductionism that is more ideology than fact. The idea that the mind is ever static enough to scan is equally doubtful, and raises questions about what age, what mood, what *kind* of mind you would be uploading.

The idea that the mind can exist without the body is equally dubious, as we explore in greater detail in a later chapter. Moreover, even were your uploaded mind to be subsequently downloaded into a reconstructed body, it would not be you, so much as a copy of you, not only endlessly replicable

19 Christian Transhumanist Association: Faith, Technology, and the Future, christiantrans-humanism.org (accessed 1 November 2023).

but, once reincarnated in its new robotic form, set off on a different experiential path. And quite beyond all of this, while a natural death may not be a consummation devoutly to be wished, it is surely more dignified than the prospect of death by power cut or accidental unplugging.

In short, such speculations would simply be fancy – scientific pie in the sky, so to speak – were it not for the fact that a number of extremely rich people are very interested in the whole affair at the moment, and are pouring considerable sums of money into it. Able to buy everything up to and including space flight, they have set their sights on eternal life.

All the big beasts are at the trough. Google's Sergey Brin invested $1 billion in an anti-ageing lab in 2016. His counterpart Larry Page helped launch Calico, short for California Life Company. Elon Musk's Neuralink is working on the possibility of mind-uploading. PayPal co-founder Peter Thiel has put millions of dollars into biotech companies focused on extreme life extension. Amazon's Jeff Bezos has invested heavily in Altos Labs, another biotech life extension company, while Oracle's Larry Ellison has also lent his fortune to anti-ageing research. Mark Zuckerberg helped set up the Breakthrough Prize in Life Sciences which honours 'transformative advances toward understanding living systems and extending human life', a prize that is sponsored by the personal foundations of several billionaires. The industry of life extension, which is already large, will be worth over half a trillion dollars by the mid-2020s. And it is not simply confined to humans. Loyal is a biotech start-up dedicated to extending the lifespan of dogs.

Money talks – and lots of money can shout – but it appears that it will need to shout very loudly to attract public opinion. When the Pew Forum asked Americans about their attitude to life extension in 2013, it found that fewer than four in ten US adults (38%) said they would want medical treatment that slowed the ageing process and allowed them to live for at least 120 years (more than half – 56% – said they would not). Fewer still wanted to live beyond 120, let alone 200. At the same time, 51% said that they thought medical treatments that allowed the average person to live to at least 120 would be a bad thing for society.[20]

---

20 'Living to 120 and beyond: Americans' views on aging, medical advances and radical life extension', Pew Research Center https://www.pewresearch.org/religion/2013/08/06/living-to-120-and-beyond-americans-views-on-aging-medical-advances-and-radical-life-extension (accessed 1 November 2023).

In a similar vein, seven years later, Theos/Faraday research found that only a fifth (19%) of Britons said they would 'want to live forever if scientists could engineer it', compared to three-fifths (60%) who did not. Perhaps not surprisingly, only 13% said they would want to be cryogenically frozen, compared with 72% who were not keen on the prospect.[21]

The *reasons* for this balance in public opinion are harder to discern, and will inevitably be complex and varied. Part of it is our instinctive resistance to cutting-edge technology of any kind. Had there been public opinion polls at the time of the development of the radio or the printing press, no doubt majorities would have seen them as against God and nature. However, to dismiss public opposition here as simply technophobia is unhelpful.

One academic study of people's attitudes to mind-uploading technology found that some factors – personality, values, 'individual tendencies towards rationality' – had no real impact on people's views, whereas others were more significant. It reported that (1) people who valued 'purity norms' and had 'higher sexual disgust sensitivity' were more inclined to condemn the technology; whereas (2) those who were 'anxious about death' were more accepting of it; while not surprisingly (3) those with 'higher science fiction literacy and/or hobbyism' were most likely to approve of it strongly.[22] The Theos study found that the younger were keener on scientific immortality than older people, and also that men were keener on it than women (a finding that is borne out by the fact that men outnumber women by almost three to one among clients at the Alcor Life Extension Foundation).[23]

The religious dimension within all this is complex. In the UK, the Theos study found that the more individuals participated in religious practices (attending religious services, praying, and reading holy texts), the less likely they were to want some kind of scientific immortality. In the USA, Pew found that white evangelical Protestants were among the least likely to

---

21 Hannah Waite and Nick Spencer, *Briefing Paper: The promise of scientific immortality – who wants to live forever?* (Theos, 2022); https://www.theosthinktank.co.uk/research/2022/05/20/briefing-paper-the-promise-of-scientific-immortality-who-wants-to-live-forever (accessed 1 November 2023).

22 'What makes people approve of condemn mind upload technology? Untangling the effects of sexual disgust, purity and science fiction familiarity', *Nature* https://www.nature.com/articles/s41599-018-0124-6 (accessed 1 November 2023).

23 The finding is also common in academic literature. See, for example, Michael D. Barnett and Jessica H. Helphrey, 'Who wants to live forever? Age cohort differences in attitudes toward life extension', *Journal of Aging Studies* 57(2) (2021).

want life extension (only 28% wanted it), whereas black Protestants (47%) and Hispanic Catholics (46%) were more divided.[24]

On the one hand, it should not be surprising to learn that religious attitudes to scientific attempts to cheat death are generally colder than the non-religious. After all, why pin your hopes on an imitation when you have the real thing to look forward to? On the other hand, we should not be surprised that there is a range of religious (in this case, Christian) opinions on the issue, from Christian transhumanists who find salvation (or at least hope) in technology, through those who approve of the possibility of radical life extension through genetic medicine, to those (a minority in our own time, but not in the past) who reject any attempt to cheat death through human ingenuity as a form of blasphemy. Christian believers do not appear to speak with one voice when it comes to the topic of scientific immortality.

Scientific immortality and religion in tension

There are various reasons for this polyphony of Christian voices about scientific attempts to cheat death. Some are bad – confusion, ignorance, indifference – but one is good. It is, in effect, that the Christian tradition itself does not speak with one voice here. There is a polyphony – or better still, a genuine, creative tension – at the heart of the Christian vision of life, death and immortality.

This will seem like a contentious claim, so it is important to be clear about what is and isn't being said here. We are *not* here making the (familiar) point that Christians themselves have held different views on this matter. They have, but that is hardly a surprise and can often be explained by confusion, ignorance or general indifference to doctrine. Popular Christianity has often slipped into a kind of implicit dualism in which the soul or spirit plays pretty much the same role as the uploaded mind of transhumanism. Therein, the belief goes, resides *me*: my essence, my core, my inmost being. Preserve that and you preserve all that too. An incorporeal soul, like love, is all you need.

---

24 See also William Sims Bainbridge, 'The transhuman heresy', *Journal of Evolution and Technology* 14(2) (2005). https://jetpress.org/volume14/bainbridge.html (accessed 1 November 2023).

However much individual believers or heterodox theologies have slipped into such dualistic beliefs, it does not change the orthodox position that, from the earliest days, Christians believed in the *bodily* resurrection from the dead, on the basis of Christ's own bodily resurrection from the dead. Eternal life, in Christian orthodoxy, was never spiritual in the disembodied, ghostly sense of the word. It was thoroughly physical, indeed *more* physical than physical life on Earth. At no time has this basic article of Christianity been abandoned, however frequently popular beliefs, images, hymns and practices have slipped back to a body–soul dualism.

In addition, there was never a question that this final bodily resurrection would be anything other than an act of God. However much Christians were charged to live as aliens in the world or as if time were short, there was no sense that their efforts would somehow effect the coming of the kingdom, as if they could twist God's arm into delivering on his promises.[25] History was not to be wound up, or eternal life to be achieved, by human endeavour. Eternal life wasn't something people deserved, or indeed something that necessarily happened because the human 'soul' (whatever that was) was necessarily immortal. Re-creation, like creation, was an action of divine grace, not a natural process or one based on human merit. In short, however much there has been confusion and tension within Christian minds, and debates on life, death and immortality, this is not what we are referring to. There is no polyphony here: orthodox Christian belief is that eternal life is (1) bodily and (2) a gift of God.

The polyphony or creative tension comes when we look at what this means for our attitude to life and death while on Earth. It would, for example, be easy to take the short step from acknowledging the beliefs just outlined to reaching the conclusion that believers should simply acquiesce in the face of death. The human condition is ineradicably mortal. Death cannot be defeated by anyone other than God, so there is no point in our fighting against it. Resignation in the face of the inevitable is the best option. Don't bother raging against the dying of the light. There's no point.

Were this the only voice, the response to scientific attempts to cheat death through biological, genetic or digital means would be straightforward. They are at best pointless, at worst wrong, blasphemous attempts to

---

25 1 Peter 1:17; 1 Corinthians 7:29.

achieve what only God can. In effect, such a response to scientific attempts to cheat death *permanently* would simply be a modern variant on the historic (though never mainstream) Christian view that scientific attempts to cheat death *temporarily*, through better medicine or sanitation, were an unacceptable usurpation of God's sovereignty.[26]

But it is not the only voice, as there is another that threads through the Christian Scriptures, which insists that death is not simply to be accepted without demur. On the contrary, the New Testament in particular is clear: death is the enemy, a dehumanising, alien and invasive force, a foe to be fought rather than an ally to be embraced. This is also the message (or at least *a* message) of the story of the Fall in Genesis chapter 3 (which, being a story, is open to multiple interpretations). Death and evil are intimately linked, but death is destined to be 'swallowed up in victory', as Paul writes in 1 Corinthians 15:54–55 (KJV), referencing the prophet Hosea by crowing 'O death, where is thy sting? O grave, where is thy victory?'

Herein lies the tension. On the one hand, death is the enemy, an attitude that inspires resistance (and hence, presumably, support for scientific attempts to cheat death). But on the other hand, victory over death is not in our gift, and death can only be defeated by the grace of God, an attitude that naturally breeds resignation (and hence at best suspicion of, and at worse hostility to, the cause of scientific immortality).

As an aside, it is interesting to note that this tension also affects contemporary secular attitudes to death. Take, for example, two recent well-received books on the topic. In *This Life: Why mortality makes us free* the Swedish philosopher Martin Hägglund argues that 'what I do and what I love can matter to me only because I understand myself as mortal'. It is death alone that gives humans meaning.[27] By contrast, in *The Case against Death*, another Swedish philosopher, Ingemar Linden, argues that death is a fundamental evil, resignation in the face of it intolerable, and that humans should pursue anti-ageing science and radical life extension with all

---

26 'Scientific' here includes public health measures. Hence the historical objection against covering open sewers to protect public health: how, now, would we know on whom God's judgement was justly falling?

27 Martin Hägglund, *This Life: Why mortality makes us free* (London: Profile Books, 2019).

their power.[28] It seems that secular philosophy is no more univocal on this than Christian theology, and arguably less so.

Community and transformation

What, then, is religion to make of this scientific quest for immortality? Does the programme of technological life-extension and immortality merit support (born of our resistance to death) or criticism (born of our resignation to it)? Navigating this question is far from straightforward but may be helped by two relevant but sometimes overlooked elements within the idea of 'resurrection': community and transformation.

Modern Western societies, being what they are, naturally approach the idea of eternal life in an individualistic way, as if what we are really talking about is the enduring existence of a single organism. Christians are hardly immune to this. Perhaps because the resurrection of the dead begins with one man, Christians are only too liable to conceive of eternal life in individuated terms. However, the New Testament claims that the resurrection of the Christ is the 'first fruit' of a general resurrection, the offering at the start of the harvest in which all is collected in. In this approach, eternal life is nothing if it is not communal.

We can glimpse something of this from the development of the idea of resurrection in the Old Testament. The chronology of this development is notoriously uncertain, but it seems that the earliest Hebrew texts have no concept at all of an afterlife. Here, the dead descend to Sheol where they dwell, if that is the right word, as insubstantial shades in eternal darkness. At some point, Israelites come to believe that the power and love of their God would not simply let his people disappear but would somehow return them to relationship with him. By the final pre-Christian centuries, this belief had morphed into the conviction that God would bodily resurrect his people when he finally came to restoring his kingship.[29]

Whatever the precise chronology, it does seem as if the later development of the idea of resurrection was tied to the idea that a people, who had been

---

28 Ingemar Patrick Linden, *The Case against Death* (Cambridge, MA: MIT Press, 2022).

29 That recognised, it is important to emphasise, as we see clearly in Jesus' interactions with various first-century Jewish sects and schools, that there was no single, accepted view on the matter even at that 'late' stage.

conquered and exiled, would be returned to their rightful land and to the rightful rule of their God.[30] Certain texts came to be interpreted (whether they were actually written to that end is more questionable[31]) as indicating that God would rescue his people from oblivion and recreate them anew in a restored kingdom. Ezekiel's vision of dry bones in chapter 37 imagined an almost medically vivid resurrection of the Israelite dead: 'I am going to open your graves and bring you up from them; I will bring you back to the land of Israel.'[32] The book of Daniel proclaimed: 'Multitudes who sleep in the dust of the earth will awake: some to everlasting life, others to shame and everlasting contempt.'[33] The prophet Isaiah declared that 'your dead will live . . . their bodies will rise – let those who dwell in the dust wake up and shout for joy'.[34]

Alongside these prophecies of *collective* resurrection, the prophet Isaiah developed the idea of a servant who would suffer and die for his people, before being vindicated: 'After he has suffered, he will see the light of life and be satisfied . . . '[35] This was not, however, a move towards an individualised post-mortem conception, as this figure was a representative of his people. As N. T. Wright has written, 'The either/or that has tended to drive a wedge between different interpretations of key passages (*either* "individual resurrection" *or* "national restoration") must be exposed as fallacious.'[36] Resurrection is a collective recreation of a people, not the ongoing survival of an individual. 'Resurrection hope is not like that of ancient Egypt, where life after death was thought of as a continuation of normal life by other means.'[37]

This connects with a second point: transformation. The problem with earthly humans is not simply that they are mortal, but that they are sinful. As such, the collective resurrection is not simply a matter of collective survival, but of re-creation. As Wright goes on to say, 'The [Hebrew] biblical

---

30 It seems likely that only a small percentage of the Israelite elite were taken into exile by the Babylonians – the nation was effectively decapitated – but the motif of exile was nonetheless used to describe, and came to characterise, the entire nation's experience.

31 Hosea 13:14 almost certainly was not.

32 Ezekiel 37:1–14.

33 Daniel 12:2–3.

34 Isaiah 26:19.

35 Isaiah 53:11.

36 N. T. Wright, *The Resurrection of the Son of God* (London: SPCK, 2003), p. 116.

37 Wright, *The Resurrection of the Son of God*, p. 122.

language of resurrection ... is not about discovering that Sheol is not such a bad place after all ... the language of awakening is not a new, exciting way of talking about sleep. It is a way of saying that ... Creation itself ... will be reaffirmed, remade.'[38]

In this way, religious immortality, or more precisely the kind that we have been speaking about in this chapter, is not and cannot be divorced from the idea of transformation. Eternal life is not only embodied and a gift of God (as we saw in the previous section), but it is relational, in a way that humans could be – or rather in the way that we *should* be but so rarely are. Eternal life – 'heaven' – is not so much a place, still less a reward, but a state of mutual love and gift, a state that we taste in this life but only fleetingly.

Resurrection involved not simply the defeat of death but also the defeat of sin, which is so often paired with it. Hence Paul's writing on the resurrection body in 1 Corinthians 15:44, where he is at pains to stress how that body is of a fundamentally different kind from our earthly bodies. Hence also his seemingly oxymoronic phrase that in the resurrection of the dead, the body 'is sown a natural body, it is raised a *spiritual body*' (emphasis added), meaning not a disembodied body (a genuine oxymoron) but a body that is powered by the Spirit of God rather than sinful, earthly concerns.

Eternal life, resurrection life, is life in community – community that remains unfractured by sin – which means it is necessarily transformed life. It is not simply the continuation of a particular organism, or even a group of them, but its/their re-creation. It may be helpfully understood qualitatively rather than quantitatively, an infinite extension of the quality of love and grace we experience, sometimes, on Earth rather than an infinite extension of the quantity of time we have here.

Stuck with being myself

It is telling that much of the commentary surrounding the scientific quest to cheat death homes in on the problems we would face were it to be, even partially, successful. What would a rapidly growing global population do to our natural resources? Would humans not simply find themselves in

---

38 Wright, *The Resurrection of the Son of God*, p. 127.

a catastrophic Malthusian trap, with ever more people seeking a limited supply of food?[39] How could humans cope with the changing parameters of their lives? 'Is it possible to stay happily married to the same person for 200 years?'[40] Could we even imagine working for our extended lives?[41] If not, what would we do? Would we (so to speak) die of boredom?[42]

If life extension therapy becomes routine, will refusal equate to suicide? Would we, if technically immortal, simply now live paralysed by the fear of the accident that could end our lives (after all, gene therapy won't stop you from falling in front of a bus)? Would an older world also be an intellectually more sterile one?[43] Would life extension simply exacerbate existing levels of inequality?[44] The questions are serious ones, before they even get close to thinking about mind uploading or the singularity.

In a sense, it is no surprise that such questions mount up. Eternal life unaccompanied by some corresponding transformation *of what it means to be human* is at best an uncertain and more likely a dismal and terrifying prospect. That might be one of the readings of the endlessly interesting and elusive story in Genesis chapter 3. Adam and Eve are banished from the garden and prevented from eating from the tree of life once they have rebelled against God, because living forever once you have 'known evil' (rather than only good) would be hell indeed. Eternal life without transformation may

39 'Maybe we need to define the sustainable carrying capacity of our planet and then ask some hard questions: if you take life extension drugs, should you have four kids?' Ahuja, 'Can we defeat death?', *Financial Times*.

40 Ahuja, 'Can we defeat death?', *Financial Times*.

41 'Do you really think that the longshoreman, the hard labourer, the person who works as a clerk in a store, at the age of 65 is going to say, "Great! I get to work for another 50 years!"' Jenny Kleeman and Emma Haslett, 'Big Tech and the quest for eternal youth: who wants to live forever?', *The New Statesman* https://www.newstatesman.com/podcasts/audio-long-reads/2022/04/big-tech-and-the-quest-for-eternal-youth-audio-long-reads (accessed 1 November 2023).

42 'If we could live forever, we might just drift aimlessly into near-eternity, like the alien cursed with immortality in Douglas Adams's *Life, the Universe and Everything*.' Emily Lawford, 'Billionaires want to abolish death. But do we really want to live forever?', *Prospect* https://www.prospectmagazine.co.uk/culture/38534/billionaires-want-to-abolish-death.-but-do-we-really-want-to-live-forever (accessed 1 November 2023).

43 In the words of Steve Jobs, 'Death is very likely the single best invention of Life. It is Life's change agent. It clears out the old to make way for the new.' Rupendra Brahambhatt, 'Will we ever cheat death and become immortal with mind uploading?', Interesting Engineering https://interestingengineering.com/science/cheating-death-and-becoming-immortal-with-mind-uploading (accessed 1 November 2023).

44 Max Anderson, 'Peter Thiel, N. T. Wright on technology, hope, and the end of death', Forbes https://www.forbes.com/sites/valleyvoices/2015/06/24/peter-thiel-n-t-wright-on-technology-hope-and-the-end-of-death/?sh=2a05c98f3848 (accessed 1 November 2023).

not be a prospect we actually desire. Or, put another way, the kind of transhumanism that only transcended our mortality, and not our sinfulness, would be a grim prospect indeed.

In the final chapter of Julian Barnes's novel, *A History of the World in 10½ Chapters*, the narrator wakes up in heaven. He has a wonderful time there. The food is great, the wine excellent, the sex sensational. He plays golf to his heart's content and gets impossibly good at it. Millennia tick by. Eventually, things begin to pale a little and he discovers that, in spite of heaven affording every pleasure anyone can think of, 100% of people who end up there decide, in the end, 'to die off'. People like him usually go first.

> People who want an eternity of sex, beer, drugs, fast cars . . . they can't believe their good luck at first, and then, after a few hundred years, they can't believe their bad luck . . . *they're stuck with being themselves*. Millennia after millennia of being themselves.[45]

He tries to find a solution by becoming the kind of person 'who never gets tired of eternity', but he is informed that people have tried it and it never works. 'You can't become someone else *without stopping being who you are* [and] nobody can bear that.'[46] Eventually, he acquiesces. 'It seems to me', he reflects at the end, 'that Heaven's a very good idea, it's a perfect idea you could say, but not for us. *Not given the way we are.*'[47]

The story is remarkably acute and relevant as a 'religious' perspective on the scientific quest to cheat death. Human life is a complex, multi-layered thing, at once biological and cognitive, communal and spiritual. Science may hold out some hope of being able to transcend some of those layers – the biological and perhaps even the cognitive – but (the religious perspective insists) humans are more than biological organisms or thinking machines. Being able to transcend and transform some layers or dimensions of our humanity, without touching others, may end up the worst possible option for us.

---

45 Julian Barnes, *A History of the World in 10½ Chapters* (London: Jonathan Cape, 1989), p. 306; emphasis added.

46 Barnes, *A History of the World in 10½ Chapters*, p. 308; emphasis added.

47 Barnes, *A History of the World in 10½ Chapters*, p. 309; emphasis added.

2

Is there anybody out there?

On 7 August 1996, President Bill Clinton stood on the South Lawn of the White House and gushed, 'If this discovery is confirmed, it will surely be one of the most stunning insights into our universe that science has ever uncovered.' There was still work to be done, he admitted, work that, even as it promised to answer 'some of our oldest questions', would pose 'others even more fundamental'. However challenging those questions might be, though, there was no mistaking the significance of this moment. '[The discovery's] implications are as far-reaching and awe-inspiring as can be imagined.'[1]

The discovery of which he was talking was a meteorite – Allan Hills 84001 – or, more precisely, what scientists claimed was inside the meteorite. Discovered in the Allan Hills in Antarctica in 1984, the rock was identified as a four-billion-year-old piece of Mars that had arrived on Earth in a meteorite shower about 13,000 years ago. Scientists examining it in 1996 detected 'possible relic biogenic activity' within the rock, in effect what appeared to be micro-fossils of tiny Martian nanobacteria.[2] The world went nuts.

It's worth noting that only a year earlier, the discovery of 51 Pegasi b had also captured headlines. 51 Pegasi b was not the first exoplanet, a planet outside our solar system, to be identified, but it was the first to be found in orbit around a Sun-like star.[3] The planet – a Jupiter-like gas giant, closer to its star than Mercury is to ours, with a four-day solar orbit, and a 'surface'

1 President Clinton Statement Regarding Mars Meteorite Discovery, Jet Propulsion Laboratory, NASA https://www2.jpl.nasa.gov/snc/clinton.html (accessed 2 November 2023).

2 David S. McKay et al., 'Search for past life on Mars: possible relic biogenic activity in Martian meteorite ALH84001', Science https://www.science.org/doi/10.1126/science.273.5277.924 (accessed 2 November 2023).

3 Pat Brennan, 'What's out there? The exoplanet sky so far', NASA https://exoplanets.nasa.gov/news/1673/whats-out-there-the-exoplanet-sky-so-far (accessed 2 November 2023).

temperature of around 1,000 degrees centigrade – was no Eden, and there was no suggestion that life could ever survive on it. But its very existence hinted at the possibility of many more exoplanets, some possibly bearing life. In the mid-1990s, nearly 2,000 years after the birth of Christ, humans were finally getting confirmation that they were not alone in the universe.

Alas, it wasn't so. Even at the time, many scientists were sceptical of the conclusions reached about Allan Hills 84001, and twenty years on, few believe it confirms the existence of Martian proto-life.[4] Nevertheless, speculation continues. The number of exoplanets rises inexorably, as does our ability to analyse their atmospheres. Humans have sent numerous probes to Mars, including one that launched in 2020 equipped with a rover and a helicopter to traverse the barren surface, dig through rock, analyse the results, and look for indications of water and life. All the while, humans were busy scanning the skies for signs of electromagnetic radiation that might be a tell-tale sign of alien communication, at the same time occasionally broadcasting our own messages, some intentional, more unintentional, that confirmed our own existence.[5]

However disappointing Allan Hills 84001 may have turned out to be, the search for extra-terrestrial life and intelligence merely intensified in its wake. And however unjustified Bill Clinton's initial enthusiasm was, in a more general sense he was spot on. Discovering signs of life, let alone intelligent life, elsewhere in the cosmos would be perhaps the most remarkable scientific discovery in human history, one with huge implications – not least for religious belief. In the words of one of the expert interviewees in the Theos/Faraday research: 'If we came across another intelligent species from another part of the galaxy, what God would they believe in? Where does God fit into that? Would they have religious deities, would these be great people? Would they have souls? . . . Things that would leave religion struggling a bit.'[6]

---

4 Charles Q. Choi, 'Mars life? 20 years later, debate over meteorite continues', Space.com https://www.space.com/33690-allen-hills-mars-meteorite-alien-life-20-years.html (accessed 2 November 2023). One of the criticisms levelled at the conclusion was that the 'wormlike features that resemble fossils could actually have been uneven patches in the coating used to prepare the samples for electron microscopy' – a somewhat mundane objection which helpfully reminds us of the mundanity of much scientific research.

5 'If an extraterrestrial civilization has a SETI project similar to our own, could they detect signals from Earth?', SETI https://www.seti.org/faq#obs11 (accessed 2 November 2023).

6 Interview no. 37.

The long search

Our interest in alien life massively predates our ability to look for it. Ancient philosophers speculated about (what for many centuries was known as) a 'plurality of worlds'. Some were positive about the prospect. Democritus and Epicurus argued that there was a 'principle of plenitude' within nature and that we should expect to find 'Earths' elsewhere supporting life. Others were less enthusiastic. Plato argued (on philosophical grounds) and Aristotle (on physical) that Earth, standing at the centre of the universe, was unique. There was much speculation on the subject in the Middle Ages, but it was after Copernicus elevated Earth to the heavens,[7] and the heavens themselves began to yield their wonders to the telescope, that speculation really took off.

The first 'scientific' proposal for communicating with extra-terrestrial life came in the early nineteenth century. The mathematician Carl Friedrich Gauss suggested planting an enormous forest in Siberia, in the shape of a Pythagorean triangle, that would signal human intelligence to any observing aliens. Nothing came of the idea but, half a century later, a similar message seemed to come from above when the Italian astronomer Giovanni Schiaparelli thought he saw a network of suspiciously straight lines on the surface of Mars, which he termed *canali* or 'channels'. The word was mistranslated into English as 'canals', and the discovery stoked decades of speculation about Martian civilisation, until closer inspection revealed the 'canals' to be an optical illusion.

By this time, the development of wireless technology led some to favour radio contact of some kind, and by mid-century SETI – the Search for Extra-Terrestrial Intelligence – was underway, deploying radio telescopes to detect unusual signals. There have been few to write home about, although on 15 August 1977, the American astronomer Jerry Ehman detected an unusually intense burst of activity that lasted for seventy-two seconds coming from the direction of the Sagittarius constellation. He scrawled the word

---

7   The idea that Copernicus demoted the Earth by suggesting a helio- rather than a geocentric system is one of the myths that dogs the history of science and religion and is dealt with in Nicholas Spencer, *Magisteria: The entangled histories of science and religion* (London: Oneworld, 2023), ch. 6.

'Wow!' in the margins of the printout, and although the signal remains un-explained to this day, it also sadly remains unrepeated.

While scientists listened, they also looked, in particular for planets that might sustain life. The first evidence for a planet beyond our solar system was found, but overlooked, as early as 1917, and it was not until the early 1990s, only a few years before Bill Clinton's speech, that any were formal-ly confirmed.[8] Since then, however, the sky has been the limit. As we write this, the existence of 5,535 exoplanets has been confirmed, and NASA rec-ognises a further 9,913 as candidates.[9] Planets come in all different sizes, and although larger gas-giants are easier to detect, at least 100 Earth-sized ones have been found.[10] Astronomers have further identified an increas-ing number of exoplanets in the habitable 'Goldilocks' zone around their stars, warm enough to sustain liquid water and cool enough to sustain life.

In addition to the Goldilocks zone, there are also Goldilocks stars, mean-ing ones that are not too hot, not too cold, not too violent and not too short-lived – in other words, that have the conditions to allow life to get going. Sometimes, all the factors combine. In October 2022, NASA announced the discovery of LP 890-9 c,[11] in NASA's own words, a 'super-Earth': rocky, 40% larger than our own planet, and in the habitable zone of its star.[12] In truth, not quite all the factors combine here as LP 890-9 c is on the edge of the habitable zone and it orbits a red-dwarf star, a type that, although long-lived, is liable to expose nearby planets to levels of X-ray and ultravio-let radiation that would kill off life. But the principle of genuinely possible life-supporting planetary candidates is now well established.

---

8   Elizabeth Landau, 'Overlooked treasure: the first evidence of exoplanets', NASA https://
    exoplanets.nasa.gov/news/1467/overlooked-treasure-the-first-evidence-of-exoplanets
    (accessed 2 November 2023).

9   Exoplanet Exploration: Planets beyond Our Solar System, NASA https://exoplanets.nasa.
    gov (accessed 2 November 2023).

10 Most of the Earth-sized planets so far detected are orbiting red-dwarf (as opposed to Sun-
    like) stars, which are smaller, dimmer, have more limited habitable zones, and are seemingly
    less hospitable to life, especially in their early years, when '[p]owerful flares tend to erupt
    with some frequency from their surfaces'. 'The habitable zone', NASA https://exoplanets.
    nasa.gov/search-for-life/habitable-zone (accessed 2 November 2023).

11 There can be no doubt that wherever else they were deficient, ancient and early modern
    astronomers were better at naming heavenly bodies.

12 Pat Brennan, 'Discovery alert: a rocky "super-Earth" in the habitable zone', NASA
    https://exoplanets.nasa.gov/news/1712/discovery-alert-a-rocky-super-earth-in-the-habit-
    able-zone (accessed 2 November 2023).

In reality, the habitability of a planet depends at least as much on its atmospheric composition as its solar orbit, and this is far harder to determine at a distance. Telescopes are increasingly able to peer into exoplanetary atmospheres and detect the presence of key elements, and of water, but at the moment the data are piecemeal.[13] Either way, it seems clear that the ingredients – carbon, hydrogen, nitrogen, oxygen, phosphorus and sulphur – are common in the universe, as are the kind of planets on which they might synthesise life.

All of which begs the question, how likely – or how common – is life in the universe? Calculations have been thrown at this question for at least half a century without any gaining consensus. In 1961, the American astrophysicist, Frank Drake, developed an equation that calculated the number of civilisations in our Milky Way with which we could, in theory, communicate. It did so by providing estimates for all the relevant factors: the average rate of star formation, the fraction of stars that had planets, the fraction of planets that could support life, the fraction of life that was intelligent, the fraction of these intelligent civilisations that would develop the requisite technology, and the length of time their detectable signals would take to travel to us. What the Drake equation gained in its accurate breakdown of relevant factors, it lost in the inevitably vague estimations that were necessary at each level. Estimating civilisations is effectively guesswork.

More recently, it has been calculated that as many as a fifth of Sun-like stars could have an Earth-size planet orbiting in their habitable zones. Given that, of the estimated 100 billion stars in our galaxy about a quarter could fall into the 'Sun-like' category, that would mean somewhere in the order of 5 billion potentially habitable planets in the Milky Way alone. And, given that there are, at best current estimates, well over 100 billion galaxies in the observable universe, the result is a truly stupendous number of candidate planets.

The sheer (potential) abundance of such exoplanets strongly suggests that the universe is positively teeming with life. And yet, because no one really knows how life got started on Earth, it's hard to know what the probability of it starting anywhere else is. Had Allan Hills 84001 delivered the

---

13 'Hubble traces subtle signals of water on hazy worlds', NASA https://science.nasa.gov/missions/hubble/hubble-traces-subtle-signals-of-water-on-hazy-worlds (accessed 2 November 2023).

goods, all bets would have been off. Two planets out of the two examined testing positive for life would have meant that life was pretty much everywhere. Even discounting Martian life, however, and operating on a sample of one, the fact that life on Earth seems to have begun relatively quickly – perhaps even as soon as it could – does gesture in the direction of a fertile universe.

Having said that, we should not underestimate the strength of the counter-argument in our breathless excitement at the prospect of alien life. Given the complexity of even the simplest form of life and the range of conditions necessary for it to get going in the first place – the right kind of planet, with the right chemical conditions, in a habitable orbit around a Goldilocks star with sufficient longevity – the chances of life are always going to be low. And that is life, not intelligence. For that, we would also need to factor in the evolutionary bottlenecks, extinction events, historical accidents, bellicose tendencies, and the apparent willingness of an 'advanced civilisation' to poison its own resources or blow itself up – all of which rather lengthens the odds of intelligent civilisations reaching out peacefully across the cosmos.

There is, in other words, a balance here: a very low possibility of (intelligent) life combined with a very high number of planets on which it might be possible. How the two weights on the scale balance up is anyone's guess, although one of the cosmologist interviewees in the Theos/Faraday research said, 'You can make a strong argument that there could be on average one civilization per galaxy at any one time'.[14] As far as our Milky Way is concerned, we might be as good as it gets.

If our interviewee's estimation were right – and admittedly it is a big 'if' – it might provide an answer to the famous 'Fermi Paradox', named after the Italian-American physicist Enrico Fermi who asked, if extra-terrestrials do exist, where is everybody? Perhaps the rarity of the kind of life that can and wants to communicate with other similar kinds of life, and has the ability and the patience to listen for such communication – combined with the sheer distance such communication would have to travel – means that 'everybody' is eternally just out of earshot.

---

14 Interview no. 77.

The great early modern Dutch scientist Christiaan Huygens made a similar suggestion in the late seventeenth century, in the process arguing that this isolating distance signified how God had intended such different beings not to know one another. Not many cosmologists would adopt that line of argument in the twenty-first century, but the elements underlying his assertion – of alien life, of human status and of belief in God – remain live ones today.

The alien threat

Pretty much every church father who voiced an explicit opinion on the question came down against the plurality of worlds.[15] No less a figure than St Augustine argued, in *City of God*, book 11, chapter 5, against 'Epicurus' dream of innumerable worlds'. Eight hundred years later, Aquinas asked himself in *Summa Theologica*, 'Whether there is only one world', and answered that although *in theory* God, being omnipotent, could have created many, in reality, and in line with what Aristotle taught, he had not.[16] With theologians of this stature throwing their weight on one side of the debate, speculation on the other felt dangerous.

For all that early modern Christian thinkers such as Huygens might speculate positively about life elsewhere, sceptics saw an opportunity to ridicule the faith. 'Though it is not a direct article of the Christian system that this world is the whole of the habitable creation,' wrote Thomas Paine in *The Age of Reason* in 1794, it has, nonetheless, more or less become dogma. The creation story, the tale of Eden, the idea of the incarnation, and the crucifixion: they all seemed to point towards – indeed, to require – a unique Earth. The cosmic perspective afforded by a plurality of worlds (and of life) rendered 'the Christian system of faith at once *little and ridiculous*'.[17] Without adducing actual reasons, Paine's dismissal is a telling one. A *plurality* of worlds and the *particularity* of the Christian religion make uncomfortable

---

15 Marie I. George, 'The early church fathers on the plurality of worlds', quoted in Michael Crowe (ed.), *Extraterrestrial Life Debate, Antiquity to 1915: A source book* (Notre Dame, IN: University of Notre Dame Press, 2008), p. 15.

16 Aquinas, *Summa Theologica*, Pt I, Q. 47, art. 3.

17 Thomas Paine, *The Age of Reason* (London: Barlow, 1794); emphasis added.

bedfellows. They 'cannot be held together in the same mind', and 'he who thinks that he believes both has thought but little of either'.

The whole truth was, as usual, a bit more complex. The church fathers did, as a rule, oppose the plurality of worlds, but some, such as Origen, John Chrysostom, Athanasius, Basil and Ambrose, thought that God could have created other worlds had he so chosen.[18] Speculation on the plurality of worlds was rife in the later Middle Ages, with some of Christendom's most gifted thinkers exploring the issue and concluding, as Nicole Oresme did, that 'God can and could in His omnipotence make another world besides this one or several like or unlike it'.[19]

By the mid-eighteenth century, the general census of opinion was that life beyond Earth was not only possible but likely, with religious thinkers being no more hostile to the prospect than others. Interestingly, as Michael J. Crowe has observed, the three new religions that were founded between 1760 and 1820 – the Church of the New Jerusalem (also known as Swedenborgians), the Church of Jesus Christ of Latter-Day Saints (aka Mormons) and the Seventh-day Adventist Church – all paid serious attention to the idea of extra-terrestrial life.[20] When the theologian and scientist William Whewell published his *Of the Plurality of Worlds: An essay* in 1853, in which he pointed out that, theological approval or not, the actual scientific evidence for alien life was precisely zero, he was considered rather unpopular.

As then, so now. US research, conducted by the Pew Forum, reports that religious Americans are generally less likely to believe in intelligent life beyond Earth, although this is primarily an Evangelical phenomenon, with Catholics and non-Evangelicals being no more hostile than the national

---

18 In reality, those who rejected the plurality of worlds did so because the doctrine was associated with the materialistic philosophies of the atomists, which were judged as fundamentally incompatible with belief in God. Hippolytus, *Philosophumena*, book I; Eusebius, *Praeparatio Evangelica*, xv; Theodoret, *Graecarum Affectionum Curatio*, sermon IV. See Grant McColley, 'The seventeenth-century doctrine of a plurality of worlds', *Annals of Science* 1(4) (1936), pp. 385–430.

19 Although he added, 'of course, there has never been nor will there be more than one corporeal world'. Quoted in Crowe (ed.), *Extraterrestrial Life Debate*, p. 26.

20 Michael J. Crowe, 'The plurality of worlds and extraterrestrial life', in Gary B. Ferngren (ed.), *The History of Science and Religion in the Western Tradition: An encyclopedia* (New York, NY: Routledge, 2000), p. 343.

average.[21] That said, this does not equate to feeling threatened by the prospect of alien life. Research conducted by Ted Peters in 2011 concluded that across the different religious traditions,[22] 'the vast majority of believers . . . see no threat to their personal beliefs', in contrast to those who identified themselves as non-religious, of whom 69% thought the discovery would cause a crisis for world religions.[23] In other words, aliens were judged to be a religious threat by the non-religious rather than by the religious. As Peters observed, 'respondents who self-identify as non-religious are far more fearful (or gleeful?) of a religious crisis than are religious'.[24]

The perceived threat of aliens to religious belief – or at least to believers – seems, therefore, to be somewhat overblown. That recognised, it would be dishonest to dismiss it altogether. Perhaps Tom Paine was on to something. Whatever else the discovery of (intelligent) life 'out there' would do, it would surely pose a number of serious questions – particularly, as we shall presently see, to Christianity. And even if those questions have been profitably discussed since the Middle Ages, that doesn't diminish their gravity.

Little green atonement

In the early fifteenth century, the French theologian William Vorilong speculated about whether, if there were other planets, Christ would have been incarnated on them. Vorilong was sceptical about whether this would have been necessary. The 'men' on other worlds, not being descended from Adam, would not have been tainted by sin, and therefore would not have *needed* the salvation offered by Christ. Be that as it may, he went on to argue that 'as to the question whether Christ by dying on this earth could redeem the inhabitants of another world, I answer that he is able to

---

21 Becka A. Alper and Joshua Alvarado, 'Religious Americans less likely to believe intelligent life exists beyond Earth', Pew Research Center https://www.pewresearch.org/short-reads/2021/07/28/religious-americans-less-likely-to-believe-intelligent-life-exists-on-other-planets. Rather pleasingly, white evangelicals and atheists unite in being the least likely groups to say that UFOs reported by people in the military are evidence of intelligent life outside Earth. Perhaps there is hope in the culture wars after all.

22 Roman Catholics, evangelical Protestants, mainline Protestants, Orthodox Christians, Mormons, Jews and Buddhists.

23 Ted Peters, 'The implications of the discovery of extra-terrestrial life for religion', *Philosophical Transactions: Mathematical, Physical and Engineering Sciences* 369(1936) (2011), pp. 644–55.

24 Peters, 'The implications of the discovery of extra-terrestrial life for religion', p. 645.

do this even if the worlds were infinite', although he concluded by saying that 'it would not be *fitting* for Him to go into another world that he must die again.'[25]

Vorilong's speculations appear to have been the first on a topic that has kept theologians busy ever since. Four hundred years later, the endlessly energetic Scottish theologian, economist and minister, Thomas Chalmers, mused in his *Astronomical Discourses* that just as time did not diminish the effects of the cross on Earth, so distance was irrelevant, the power of Christ's sacrifice rolling outward in space just as it rolls forward in history. For all we know, he said, 'the plan of redemption may have its influences and its bearings on those creatures of God who people other regions'.[26]

Today, there are, broadly speaking, four responses to the question Vorilong raised. The first is that Jesus' incarnation, Passion and resurrection constitute(d) a single and unique salvation event, rescuing earthly humans alone of all possible intelligent (alien) species, either because others do not exist or they do not need saving (as Vorilung thought). The second is that Jesus' unique sacrifice did indeed save the whole cosmos, including non-human intelligent aliens in space. The third is that the second person of the Trinity became incarnate on other planets, adopting the form of other alien species, just as the Word did as a human on Earth, in order to effect their salvation. This is sometimes, rather nicely, called the 'little green Jesus' hypothesis, but was rejected by Vorilong as unfitting. Finally, there is the idea that God adopted a variety of different approaches to salvation, each tailored to the particular, intelligent species that needed it, but which are inaccessible to us humans.[27]

Such debates are liable to be dismissed by the non-religious – and indeed by many of the religious – as a matter of angels on pins. Whichever answer you choose, it is completely unfalsifiable and presumably largely irrelevant to most people's lives. No one is going to lose their faith over the status of the atonement for aliens. But the specific nature of this debate is situated within a bigger question, one that lies behind Tom Paine's withering

---

25 Quoted in Crowe (ed.), *Extraterrestrial Life Debate*, p. 27; emphasis added.

26 Quoted in John J. Davis, 'Search for extraterrestrial intelligence and the Christian doctrine of redemption', *Science & Christian Belief* 9(1) (1997), p. 26.

27 For a good overview on this, see Joel L. Parkyn, *Exotheology: Theological explorations of intelligent extraterrestrial life* (Eugene, OR: Pickwick, 2021).

dismissal of the Christian faith, in the light of the plurality of worlds, as 'little and ridiculous'.

The idea that Copernicus's heliocentric ideas devastated human ego-centricity is a myth, popularised by Sigmund Freud, with pretty much no historical basis to it.[28] That said, the idea that the entire universe is teeming with life, on perhaps billions of planets, did and does risk making humans, and everything they do, including their story of divine salvation, seem *smaller.* Opening up the cosmic vista to incorporate alien life did (and does) pose questions about salvation, as noted above, but it does so primarily by posing questions of the humans that participated in it.

The discovery of alien life – particularly if it were more sophisticated than our own – would cast doubt on human uniqueness and significance. Some have argued that such intelligent life would put human achievements into humbling perspective. What a piece of work is a human being? Well, the truth may end up being not as impressive a piece of work as an alien, with its nobler reason and super-infinite faculty. Along similar lines, others have reasoned that any such super-intelligent beings would either have no use for religion or would espouse religious beliefs far in advance of those on Earth, whatever that might mean.

Either way, the point is that intelligent alien life would relativise our lives and stories on Earth, and make them seem smaller and perhaps more ridiculous. In the searching, but not hostile, words of the physicist Paul Davies, '[I]f God works through the historical process, and if mankind is not unique to his attentions, God's progress and purposes will be far more advanced on some other planets than they are on Earth . . . we would be at a stage of "spiritual" development very inferior to that of almost all of our intelligent neighbour aliens.'[29]

As an aside, this is surely one of the reasons why many people have often seen aliens as vaguely salvific, a kind of secular version of redemption and deliverance from the heavens. Intelligence has got us so far on Earth: out of caves and into cities. But only super-intelligence will enable us to transcend our all too palpable problems and achieve – immortality? happiness? perfection? As the British cosmologist, Sir Fred Hoyle, pointed out as long

---

28 As is explained in Spencer, *Magisteria*, ch. 5.
29 Paul Davies, *Are We Alone? Implications of the discovery of extraterrestrial life* (New York, NY: Penguin, 1995), p. 33.

ago as 1949, at least some of the motivation for believing in the existence of extra-terrestrial intelligence was 'the expectation that we are going to be saved from ourselves by some miraculous interstellar intervention'.[30]

In the light of this, how can we – anything we do or any stories we tell, however great – still claim cosmic significance? Why would God be bothered with us, given what we are now learning about our cosmic *insignificance*? Or, to revert to Shakespeare, humans are naturally preoccupied with our 'strange eventful history', with its exits and entrances. We imagine it important, even ultimate. But when we discover that *every* world is a stage, not just ours, full of (super-intelligent?) players, it might just make our own plot seem like childishness and mere oblivion.[31]

What does it mean to be special?

This is the heart of why (intelligent) alien life is – or at least appears to be – such a threat to the Abrahamic faiths and especially to Christianity. The idea of humans made in the image of God, sinning by falling out of communion with God, and then being redeemed when God takes human form and dies as a human, invests the human with a significance that feels harder to sustain when placed against a background of billions of other life-bearing planets. Why is what happens on this rock so special? Indeed, what makes humans special at all?

The idea that humans *are* special – an idea that lies at the root of all humanist philosophies – is indeed fundamental to the Abrahamic understanding of the world. Any attempt to downplay it by countersigning the fashionable view that humans are 'nothing but' or 'basically just another' animal is unsustainable. (It is also unsustainable in the face of common sense and vast reams of zoological evidence, but that is another matter.) But there are different forms of special. Specifically, there is being special by merit (or desert), and there is being special by grace.

Humans *are* special because of their particular range and depth of capabilities. For all that birds communicate, crows think, dolphins remember, dogs understand, elephants grieve, chimpanzees learn, octopuses take

---

30 Fred Hoyle, 'On the cosmological problem', *Monthly Notices of the Royal Astronomical Society* 109 (1949), pp. 365–71.
31 See Jaques's famous speech in *As You Like It*, Act II, Scene vii.

revenge, and macaques have a sense of justice, no species on Earth combines all these characteristics, and others, to the extent that humans do.[32] Humans are special because of their capabilities, if not quite as incomparably special as we used to think. We can legitimately call ourselves special because our capabilities merit the epithet – though it is worth underlining that, by this reckoning, we can also call chimpanzees, crocodiles, emus, snails and every other species on Earth 'special'. Indeed, to be a species is, by definition, to be special; the two words share the same linguistic root.

However, if something can be special for intrinsic reasons – because there is something about it that marks it out as different from comparable things – it can also be special on account of being chosen or treated in a particular way. A toddler will often have a special teddy bear; a child, a special pet; a teacher, a special pupil; or an adult, a special holiday destination. These choices aren't necessarily arbitrary. Indeed, they almost always reflect some intrinsic quality about the object, pet, person or place in question. However, what makes that object, pet, person or place special is not only its intrinsic qualities – the fluffiness of the teddy, the calmness of the pet, the diligence of the pupil or the beauty of the resort – but also the fact that someone has, for their own reasons, chosen them. Things can be special on account of grace conferred on them from without, as well as merit, earned by them 'from within'.

Discovering (intelligent) alien life would certainly cast doubts on the human sense of being special by merit, not least because humans tend to use that sense of special actually to mean superior. If we base our sense of specialness on being better than other comparable creatures ('better' meaning more intelligent, more rational, etc.) then the discovery of more intelligent, more rational creatures elsewhere in the universe would indeed dent or even destroy that specialness.

But it is wrong to imagine that the Christian approach to humans is based only on that sense of special-by-intrinsic-merit. It is sometimes claimed that the opening chapters of Genesis are univocal on human specialness. The true picture is more complex. As Old Testament theologian Chris Wright has argued, '[A]t point after point the Bible tells us that we have more in common with the rest of the animate creation than in

---

32 For examples of all these and more, see the work of the primatologist Frans de Waal.

distinction from it.' Humans are blessed and told to multiply and fill the Earth, as are fish, birds and insects.[33] They share a day of creation with livestock and creepy-crawlies.[34] They are in-spired (literally in-breathed) by God, but share the breath of life with other creatures.[35] The idea that humans uniquely have a soul because God breathed life into human nostrils 'and the man became a living being' is misleading as the Hebrew word sometimes translated as 'soul' – *nepesh* – is used repeatedly of other creatures.[36] As Wright concludes, any serious dispassionate reading of the creation narratives in Genesis would come to the conclusion that 'we are animals among animals'.[37]

This is not to say that there are *no* differences. The creation stories say two things of humans that they don't of other creatures: they are instructed to rule, and they are made in the 'image of God', albeit an image that becomes battered and bruised. That phrase, endlessly parsed and defined, indicates that humans are different and, in that sense, special.

Having recognised but downplayed this idea of humans as intrinsically different – special-by-merit – it is important to recognise that there is also a strong sense of special-by-grace that runs through the biblical story.

Shortly before the 1987 UK General Election, the BBC broadcaster John Humphrys tried to catch Margaret Thatcher out in an interview by asking her what she thought was 'the essence of Christianity'. Humphrys had expected to trick her into 'mumbl[ing] something about morality or love' (though Thatcher never really mumbled anything). Without missing a beat she replied 'Choice'.[38] Humphrys was wrong-footed but latterly impressed. Thatcher's answer was, in truth, a rather partial interpretation of Christianity because, although the motif of choice does play a role in the Bible (albeit not as central a role as Thatcher seemed to think), most of that choosing is done by God. Moreover, it is exercised *not* because the person or group chosen deserved to be chosen but often, explicitly, because they didn't.[39]

---

33 Genesis 1:22.

34 Genesis 1:26.

35 Genesis 2:7; 1:30.

36 Genesis 2:7.

37 Chris Wright, *Old Testament Ethics for the People of God* (Leicester: IVP, 2004), pp. 117–8.

38 John Humphrys, *Devil's Advocate* (London: Arrow Books, 2000), pp. 261–2.

39 Deuteronomy 30:11–20 is the obvious exception when it comes to the significance of human choice.

Thus, God chose Abraham to be a blessing to the world despite his obscurity. He chose Moses to lead his people despite his protestations, his inability to speak well in public, his cowardice and his murderous temper. And he chose David to be king in spite of his Clinton-like eye for attractive women. Perhaps most pointedly, God chose his people Israel to be 'his treasured possession', not, as he emphasised, 'because [they] were more numerous than other peoples', but simply because he loved them and wanted to keep his oath.[40] Indeed, as he repeatedly reminded them, they were a 'stiff-necked' people, obstinate, difficult to lead, obstructive and sinful. That the people of Israel are special, according to the Scriptures, is not in doubt. But they are special because they are chosen – special-by-grace – rather than because they had something intrinsic about them that merited, still less necessitated, a special status.

There is a similar motif in the farewell discourses in John's Gospel. Having called and invited his disciples at the start of his mission, Jesus assembles them near the end. 'You did not choose me, but I chose you,' he tells his newly named 'friends', before going on to say, '[I] appointed you so that you might go and bear fruit – fruit that will last . . . '[41] In other words, the disciples' specialness is not down to their own merits (not that the Gospel writers leave us in any doubt about that) but to God's act of grace.

The implications of this are hinted at in a confrontational moment early in the Gospels, when John the Baptist finds himself faced with Pharisees and Sadducees at the River Jordan. Infuriated by their failure to fulfil the role to which they had been called as part of God's 'treasured possession', he berates them violently, saying, 'Do not think you can say to yourselves, "We have Abraham as our father."' 'I tell you', he says bluntly, 'that out of these stones God can raise up children for Abraham.'[42]

The implications of John's words are in line with much else within the biblical narrative. Humans *are* different from other species, in the same way as the people of God are different from the surrounding nations – although in both cases there is also much that is shared and common. However, that difference – that specialness – does not reside simply in some intrinsic (and therefore inalienable) quality they possess. That specialness is

40 Deuteronomy 7:6–8; 14:2.
41 John 15:16.
42 Matthew 3:9.

also due to an act of grace, of divine choice, of calling. It is a specialness given, not earned.

Aliens and theocentric humanism

One of the greatest and most important humanist texts of the twentieth century was written by the French Catholic Thomist philosopher, Jacques Maritain, in the mid-1930s. *Integral Humanism* draws an important distinction between what Maritain called 'anthropocentric humanism' and 'theocentric humanism'. Both humanisms have – as the name suggests – a high view of the human, replete with dignity, agency, morality and rationality. However, the former grounds that view in natural human capacities. Anthropocentric humanism 'believes that man himself is the centre of man, and therefore of all things. It implies a naturalistic conception of man and of freedom.'[43] By contrast, theocentric humanism grounds its high view of human identity not in the capacities of 'man' but in the grace of God, or as Maritain puts it elsewhere, in human 'openness to the world of the divine and superrational'.[44]

Maritain's concern, writing at the time he was, was that anthropocentric humanism was highly vulnerable to doctrines that showed that humans were not in fact as capable or important as we like to think we are. Under the gaze of Darwin and Freud, 'the well-regulated dignity of our personal conscience appears as a deceitful mask', and 'this proud anthropocentric personality . . . has quickly crumbled to dust'.[45] By contrast, theocentric humanism was resilient in the face of external threats because it said humans were special and of worth because they were loved by God.

This distinction speaks to our contemporary discussion of the impact that discovering (intelligent) alien life would have on humans. Belief that humans are special because we are more rational or intelligent than other species would be liable to take a fatal hit were (intelligent) life discovered elsewhere. A species that reached out to us before we did them would,

---

43 Jacques Maritain, *Integral Humanism* (London: Geoffrey Bles, 1938; first published as *Humanisme integral* (Paris: Fernand Aubier, 1936)), in *The Collected Works of Jacques Maritain*, vol. XI, ed. Otto Bird (Notre Dame, IN: University of Notre Dame Press, 1996), p. 169.

44 Jacques Maritain, *Scholasticism and Politics* (London: Geoffrey Bles: The Centenary Press, 1940), p. 7.

45 Maritain, *Integral Humanism*, p. 170.

in all likelihood, be more technologically sophisticated, and perhaps more civilised than ourselves. It might even be more spiritually advanced. Our pride would take a fall.

However, the belief that humans are special because they are loved by God and charged by him with certain responsibilities in our local garden that is the Earth would not be so harmed by the discovery of superintelligent life elsewhere. In essence, we might, on first contact, first feel rather insecure and a little hostile, like a toddler whose parents bring home a newborn. But we might also then reflect that the presence of another being in the house does not diminish a parent's love.

Tellingly, this is close to the idea reached by one of the most creative medieval theologians who pondered the possibility of alien life in the fifteenth century. Nicholas of Cusa imagined a plurality of worlds, on which life was abundant, as well as a universe in which there was no centre or boundary. He did not, of course, deny human specialness but argued that this specialness derived not from the Earth's physical centrality but from the proximity of human relationship to the Creator.[46] His was, in effect, a humanism that had God at its centre, and not human (or earthly) attributes.

So, let's imagine another press conference on the White House lawn in which a future president, flanked by the director of NASA and the SETI Institute, confirms, to an expectant world, that cosmologists have received irrefutable communication from an alien civilisation on the other side of the galaxy. The president gushes, the cosmologists explain, and the world wonders.

It seems that the galaxy and, by implication, the universe is indeed teeming with life, in much the same way as does the Earth. Some of that life appears, through a process of reproduction and selection, to have navigated its way to civilisation and, with it, an apparent desire to reach beyond its planet and explore what lies beyond. The species, so far as we are in a position to judge, is very different from us – though perhaps not as different as we are from octopuses, a species separated from us by 500 million years of evolution but that seems to have developed intelligence and possibly even consciousness too.

---

46 Nicholas of Cusa, *On Learned Ignorance*, III.1–4. See also Thomas F. O'Meara, *Vast Universe: Extraterrestrials and Christian revelation* (Collegeville, MN: Liturgical Press, 2012), p. 76.

Religiously, well, we know nothing yet of our cosmic interlocutors' faith, or lack thereof. Nobody has yet found evidence that they meditate daily on St Paul's letter to the Martians, and few think they cross themselves and utter a Trinitarian prayer in moments of reverence or distress. And as for the idea of an incarnate God, well . . .

And so the sceptics channel their inner Paine and go to work. The existence of extra-terrestrial super-civilisations shows that humans are not so special after all. All that 'image of God' stuff was basically a nursery rhyme to make us less afraid of the dark. There is no more evidence of a Fall up there than there is down here. And no Fall means no (need for) redemption. The cosmic drama unravels. It seems we're not on the main stage, after all. We're probably not even on the fringe. Nothing here *really* matters.

And yet, what NASA scientists have been looking for (and have now found) is, in their own words, a 'communicative, technological species'.[47] Indeed, given that our aliens will have had to master and manage planetary resources in order to reach out across the cosmos and make contact, they are, by definition, both technological and communicative – and that combination may sound vaguely familiar.

After all, the two distinguishing characteristics of humans outlined in the Genesis story are of a species that (1) has the responsibility of working, tending and ruling God's patch[48] – i.e. exercising art and skill to reorder nature – and that (2) is made in the image of a God who, we are repeatedly told, has just spoken creation into existence.[49] Indeed, the two qualities are linked. As Oliver O'Donovan has noted, 'God's own lordship is exercised not by keeping his own to himself, but by "communication."'[50] Our aliens are indeed utterly foreign, but they seem to occupy the same conceptual space as us – ordering their environment, communicating with one another, searching for communication beyond themselves with others.

And perhaps the same existential space too. For, although the sceptics are right – there is no more evidence for an exoplanetary Fall than an earthly one – our aliens, being communicative as they are, necessarily exist

---

47 Pat Brennan, 'Life in the universe: what are the odds?', Exoplanet Exploration: Planets beyond Our Solar System, NASA https://exoplanets.nasa.gov/news/1675/life-in-the-universe-what-are-the-odds (accessed 3 November 2023).

48 Genesis 2:15; 1:28.

49 Genesis 1:3, 6, 9, 11, 14, 20, 22, 24, 26, etc.

50 Oliver O'Donovan, *The Ways of Judgment* (Grand Rapids, MI: Eerdmans, 2005), p. 244.

in relationship to one another and so are morally conscious, cognisant of what each owes the other and how they fail.

It's all pure, wild, baseless speculation, of course. We may never make contact because there is no one to contact. Or we may never make contact because our neighbours are simply too far away. Or we may find telling traces of conducive atmospheres. Or even signs that the galaxy is teeming with bacterial life, a fascinating discovery that does little to combat our sense of cosmic loneliness. Even were we to make some kind of contact with some kind of intelligent alien life, we might find them so different from ourselves – perhaps, as we glimpsed in the chapter on immortality, digitised, data-cleaned, uploaded and re-embodied – that all bets would be off and all comparisons found wanting.

One of the joys of writing about alien life is that the possibilities are always bigger than you can imagine, and no one can tell you you're wrong. Whatever transpires, the idea that finding life, intelligent or otherwise, would knock out the keystone of the Christian (indeed Abrahamic) faith is a result of anthropocentric, rather than theocentric, humanism. It would do no such thing.

It would, however, stimulate much science and religion debate, underlining once again how the two disciplines overlap. As religiously interested (if not religiously inclined) physicist Paul Davies observed in his book *Are We Alone?*:

The search for alien beings can thus be seen as part of a long-standing religious quest as well as a scientific project. This should not surprise us. Science began as an outgrowth of theology, and all scientists, whether atheists or theists, and whether or not they believe in the existence of alien beings, accept an essentially theological worldview . . . [the separation between science and theology] is really only skin-deep.[51]

51 Davies, *Are We Alone?*, pp. 90–1.

3

Anti-vaxxers, or how we need political theology to save the world

Surely one the greatest reasons for celebration in 2020 – a year largely devoid of reasons for celebratory moments – was the speed and success with which scientists developed a vaccine for Covid-19.

Good news or not good news?

Astonishingly, the complete genetic sequence of SARS-CoV-2, or Severe Acute Respiratory Syndrome Coronavirus 2 to give it its full name, was decoded and shared by 11 January 2020, long before most people had even heard of the virus. Unprecedented effort from, and collaboration between, pharmaceutical companies, governments, university research groups and international health organisations resulted in the rapid development of vaccines, which were trialled within months, and licensed by the end of the year – despite the fact that the World Health Organization had initially estimated that the process would take at least eighteen months. According to one study, the vaccination programmes prevented somewhere between 15 and 20 million deaths in 2021 alone (and that's not counting China where reliable data were not available).[1] At the time of writing, nearly 5.5 billion people had received at least one vaccination, weakening the pandemic's impact and removing the need for years of government lockdowns (except, again, in China). This was good news indeed.

In the light of this, it is a source of profound embarrassment to many believers that the *rejection* of this particular good news became associated with people of 'the good news'. Anti-vaxxers are disproportionately

---

1   Oliver J. Watson et al., 'Global impact of the first year of COVID-19 vaccination: a mathematical modelling study', *Lancet Infection Diseases* 22(9) (2022), pp. 1293–302.

Christian, and many have deployed 'Christian' arguments against this life-saving scientific endeavour. To be clear – as we will explore in this chapter – it isn't *only* Christians who rejected the vaccine, and the vaccine isn't rejected *only* for 'theological' reasons. But the association is nonetheless there, a contemporary example of the longstanding conflict between science and religion, at least for those with ears to hear it that way.

This is not simply a little local difficulty. 'How Covid raised the stakes of the war between faith and science' is a headline one might have expected from the *New York Times*.[2] But *POLITICO* magazine also wrote about 'Science vs. religion as Greek priests lead the anti-vax movement',[3] while the Berkley Center for Religion, Peace and World Affairs at Georgetown University provided a lengthy analysis of 'Anti-science, mistrust, and anxiety in the Orthodox world'.[4]

What made this 'science vs religion' reading of the story so much more credible was the fact that we have been here before. Covid-19 was not the first time vaccination appeared in the much-trumpeted conflictual history of science and religion. In 1896, the historian Andrew Dixon White published his massive *History of the Warfare of Science with Theology in Christendom*, which devoted an entire chapter to the 'theological opposition to inoculation, vaccination and the use of anaesthetics'.[5]

White talked about how French theologians of the Sorbonne in the eighteenth century solemnly condemned the early practice of inoculation, while English divines preached sermons with titles like 'The Dangerous and Sinful Practice of Inoculation' or 'Inoculation, an Indefensible Practice'.

---

2 Tish Harrison Warren, 'How Covid raised the stakes of the war between faith and science', *The New York Times* https://www.nytimes.com/2021/11/07/opinion/faith-science-covid. html (accessed 3 November 2023).

3 Nektaria Stamouli, 'Science vs. religion as Greek priests lead the anti-vax movement', *POLITICO* https://www.politico.eu/article/science-vs-religion-greece-priests-anti-vaccine-coronavirus-movement (accessed 3 November 2023).

4 Hermina Nedelescu, 'Anti-science, mistrust, and anxiety in the Orthodox world', Georgetown University https://berkleycenter.georgetown.edu/responses/anti-science-mistrust-and-anxiety-in-the-orthodox-world (accessed 3 November 2023).

5 Andrew Dixon White, *History of the Warfare of Science with Theology in Christendom* (London: Arco, 1955), vol. 2, ch. xiii, sect. x, pp. 55–63. The words 'vaccination' and 'inoculation' are commonly used interchangeably to mean the practice of introducing an infective agent into an organism to stimulate the body's autoimmune response. Inoculation can, however, have a broader meaning: to implant a microorganism (such as a bacteria, virus or amoeba) into a foreign environment. The word 'immunisation' is often used as a synonym for vaccination or inoculation, but it really refers to the result of vaccination or inoculation.

In 1803, Revd Dr Ramsden thundered against vaccination in a sermon before the University of Cambridge, mingling scripture texts with attacks against pioneering vaxxer Edward Jenner. Over eighty years later, a small-pox outbreak in Montreal killed more Catholics than Protestants because their clergy forbade vaccination. White did not need more evidence. Theology was at war with science and the result was many needless deaths.

The religious anti-vaccination movement of the 2020s is, therefore, just a little bit of history repeating itself. But it is of more than merely historic interest. SARS-CoV-2 came out of the blue for (most of) the world, which had not experienced a comparable crisis since the so-called Spanish Flu pandemic after the First World War. There is good reason to believe, however, that we may not need to wait a hundred years for another such disaster. One recent study of pandemics drew on historic evidence of the scale and frequency of comparable disease outbreaks and on data for 'the increasing rate at which novel pathogens such as SARS-CoV-2 have broken loose in human populations in the past 50 years'. It came to the conclusion that 'the yearly probability of occurrence of extreme epidemics [could] increase up to threefold in the coming decades', with the probability of experiencing a pandemic similar to Covid-19 in one's lifetime currently standing at about 38%.[6]

'Spanish Flu' was famously caused, in part, by significant population, especially troop, movements in the wake of the First World War. In the twenty-first century, the global population will near 10 billion. Many hundreds of millions will be on the move. Globalisation, the effects of climate change, the potentially huge numbers of environmental and economic migrants, combined with 'increasing rates of disease emergence from animal reservoirs associated with environmental change', all mean that the twenty-first century risks much higher levels of pandemic disease than the twentieth.

And if, as the Pew Forum research contends, the twenty-first century is set to become more rather than less religious, any religious resistance to vaccination is liable to have disproportionately serious consequences. Anti-vaccination is an area for science and religion dialogue, and a rather important one.

---

6 Michael Penn, 'Statistics say large pandemics are more likely than we thought', Duke University   https://globalhealth.duke.edu/news/statistics-say-large-pandemics-are-more-likely-we-thought (accessed 3 November 2023); Marco Marani et al., 'Intensity and frequency of extreme novel epidemics', PNAS https://www.pnas.org/doi/10.1073/pnas.2105482118 (accessed 3 November 2023).

The Christian anti-vax movement

When it comes to vaccination, numbers really matter, so it is important to get as clear a picture as possible about the true level of religious anti-vaccination sentiment. Historical data are always piecemeal and speculative, but there is good reason to think that the idea of blanket religious (i.e. Christian) opposition to vaccination, intimated by White's account, is a bit of a myth.

White had a story to tell. His history conformed to its controlling metaphor, and if it didn't, it was made to. By his reckoning, however, it was *theology* that was bad. Religion, properly understood, was not a problem. So it was, he explained, that the Church of the nineteenth century 'was far more honourable' in the struggle against disease than the Church of previous centuries, simply because theology (which treated illness as punishment from God and rejected vaccination as immoral) had declined, whereas religion (which involved caring for the sick and needy) had advanced. When theology dominated, people died, White argued. When religion dominated, they survived, or at least died with greater dignity.

> On the religious side few things in the history of the Roman Church have been more beautiful than the conduct of its clergy in Canada during the great outbreak of ship-fever among immigrants at Montreal about the middle of the present century. Day and night the Catholic priesthood of that city ministered fearlessly to those victims of sanitary ignorance; fear of suffering and death could not drive these ministers from their work; they laid down their lives cheerfully while carrying comfort to the poorest and most ignorant of our kind: such was the record of their religion.[7]

Even with this clarification, however, his narrative was a bit uneven. From the earliest days, White admitted, 'some churchmen . . . [were] giving battle on the side of right reason' on this matter. Cotton Mather, the leading Puritan clergyman, 'had been among the first to move in favour of inoculation' – though White failed to mention that Mather had learned

---

7 White, *History of the Warfare of Science with Theology in Christendom*, p. 60.

of the treatment from his African slave, named Onesimus.[8] White wrote that it was 'to the honour of the Puritan clergy of New England' that so many were strong supporters of Dr Zabdiel Boylston, who promoted inoculation in the early 1720s. He mentioned – how could he not? – the great pioneer of vaccination, Edward Jenner, but failed to make reference to his equally great piety. Even in the bad old 'theological' days, it seems that the story of religious anti-vaccination was complex.

What about today? Well, there are innumerable anecdotes that support the case for the prosecution. Many American evangelical church leaders proudly proclaimed their church 'anti-mask, anti-social distancing, and anti-vaccine', in the words of Tony Spell from Life Tabernacle Church in Baton Rouge, Louisiana.[9] Some went as far as Rick Wiles, a Florida pastor and broadcaster, who condemned vaccinations as part of a 'mass death campaign'.[10] Nor is this simply a US problem. In Canada, Derek Sloan, a Conservative MP and Seventh-day Adventist, sponsored a parliamentary petition arguing that 'bypassing proper safety protocols means Covid-19 vaccination is effectively human experimentation'. It received over 40,000 signatures.[11] In Greece, priests such as Vasileios Voloudakis preached against government and doctors for 'treat[ing] the churches the same way they do gyms', closing them as if they were commonplace, secular distractions.[12] In Romania, Teodosie Petrescu, Romanian Orthodox Archbishop of Tomis, spoke out against vaccinations, and some sects, such as the Old Calendarist Romanian Orthodox Church, have made vaccine opposition an official position.[13] And so on and so forth.

8 Erin Blakemore, 'How an enslaved African man in Boston helped save generations from smallpox', HISTORY https://www.history.com/news/smallpox-vaccine-onesimus-slave-cotton-mather (accessed 3 November 2023).

9 Monique Deal Barlow, 'Christian nationalism is a barrier to mass vaccination against COVID-19', The Conversation https://theconversation.com/christian-nationalism-is-a-barrier-to-mass-vaccination-against-covid-19-158023#:~:text=A%20study%20earlier%20this%20year,ignoring%20precautionary%20behaviors%20regarding%20coronavirus (accessed 3 November 2023).

10 Michael Coren, 'How the Christian right is driving the anti-vax movement', New Statesman https://www.newstatesman.com/international-politics/society-international-politics/2021/12/how-the-christian-right-is-driving-the-anti-vaxx-movement (accessed 3 November 2023).

11 Coren, 'How the Christian right is driving the anti-vax movement', New Statesman.

12 Stamouli, 'Science vs. religion as Greek priests lead the anti-vax movement', POLITICO.

13 Marcel Gascón Barberá et al., 'Religious strain of anti-vax grows in CEE', Balkan Insight https://balkaninsight.com/2021/01/19/religious-strain-of-anti-vax-grows-in-cee (accessed 3 November 2023).

However, anecdote can be fought with counter-anecdote. Prominent US evangelical leaders and groups, including Revd Russell Moore of the Southern Baptists, Franklin Graham and the National Association of Evangelicals, spoke out vigorously in favour of vaccination. In Greece, the church leadership officially supported vaccination, with Archbishop Ieronymos saying that he 'would [have] be[en] the first to go and get vaccinated if I had not been sick' (with Covid!). In eastern Europe, the influential Polish conservative Catholic group Ordo Iuris openly promoted vaccination. And so forth, again.

Getting to the heart of the religious response to vaccination requires survey work. The historic or generic anti-vax survey data here are not encouraging. In 2017, the Pew Research Center found that more than 20% of white evangelicals in America – more than any other group – believed that 'parents should be able to decide not to vaccinate their children, even if that may create health risks for other children and adults'.[14] The Theos/Faraday research found that, while only 4% of the UK population thought the risks of vaccination outweighed its benefits, and only 3% of self-designating Christians felt that way, that figure rose to 13% of biblical textual literalists.[15]

Specific Covid surveys report a similar balance of opinion. The case of the USA is probably best known. Surveys have repeatedly shown that white evangelicals are the group most resistant to vaccination. According to the Pew Forum, as of September 2021, white evangelicals were the religious group least likely to have been vaccinated, with 57% having received at least one shot, compared to 70% of Black Protestants, 86% of Hispanic Catholics and 90% of atheists.[16] Similar results have been reported by the US Public

---

14 Brian Kennedy, 'Majorities in all religious groups support requiring childhood vaccination', Pew Research Center https://www.pewresearch.org/short-reads/2017/02/07/majorities-in-all-major-religious-groups-support-requiring-childhood-vaccination (accessed 3 November 2023).

15 This group is commonly referred to as 'fundamentalists', but we feel that term is both vague and increasingly rendered unhelpful by its careless and often highly judgmental usage. In this instance 'textual literalist' refers to people who agree that the Bible is 'the actual word of God and to be taken literally, word for word'. It should be noted that this is a relatively small sample (3%) of UK adults.

16 Cary Funk and John Gramlich, '10 facts about Americans and coronavirus vaccines', Pew Research Center https://www.pewresearch.org/short-reads/2021/09/20/10-facts-about-americans-and-coronavirus-vaccines (accessed 3 November 2023).

Religion Research Institute[17] and the Associated Press-NORC Center for Public Affairs Research.[18] In the UK, by comparison, according to the Office for National Statistics, vaccine hesitancy was higher for adults identifying as Muslim (14%) than those who identified as Christian (4%), with no statistically significant difference among any other religious groups.[19]

These might still be minority positions; after all, Pew data show that even among US evangelicals, more have heard church leaders encourage vaccination than discourage it.[20] Nevertheless, the point is that these figures still tend to be above the secular mainstream, and it doesn't take a large minority of people to reject vaccination for the majority to be at risk.

Is there any wider, global or universal pattern in the data? Small, early localised studies were divided and unclear.[21] Some showed that religious people defied and ignored governmental recommendations on protective behaviour during the Covid-19 pandemic.[22] Some showed the link between vaccine hesitancy, low trust in science, and fundamentalism – a

17 'The highest rates of resistance [are] among Republicans who most trust far-right news sources (42%), multiracial Americans (31%), and white evangelical Protestants who regularly attend religious services (30%).' See 'Religious identities and the race against the virus: American attitudes on vaccination mandates and religious exemptions (wave 3)', PRRI https://www.prri.org/research/religious-identities-and-the-race-against-the-virus-american-attitudes-on-vaccination-mandates-and-religious-exemptions (accessed 3 November 2023).

18 '40% of white evangelical Protestants said they likely won't get vaccinated, compared with 25% of all Americans, 28% of white mainline Protestants and 27% of nonwhite Protestants.' David Crary, 'Vaccine skepticism runs deep among white evangelicals in US', AP News https://apnews.com/article/coronavirus-vaccine-skepticism-white-evangelicals-us-32898166bbb673ad87842af24c8daefb (accessed 3 November 2023).

19 It is well recognised that the Christian self-identification in the UK is a weak one. 'Coronavirus and vaccine hesitancy, Great Britain', Office for National Statistics https://www.ons.gov.uk/peoplepopulationandcommunity/healthandsocialcare/healthandwellbeing/bulletins/coronavirusandvaccinehesitancygreatbritain/9august2021 (accessed 3 November 2023).

20 Justin Nortey and Mike Lipka, 'Most Americans who go to religious services say they would trust their clergy's advice on COVID-19 vaccines', Pew Research Center https://www.pewresearch.org/religion/2021/10/15/most-americans-who-go-to-religious-services-say-they-would-trust-their-clergys-advice-on-covid-19-vaccines (accessed 3 November 2023).

21 'Some studies have demonstrated that religious people have defied and ignored governmental recommendations on protective behavior during the COVID-19 pandemic . . . Some studies also demonstrated the negative influence of religiosity on COVID-19 vaccination intention . . . However, other studies have shown that religion does not significantly affect COVID-19 vaccination acceptance or that it even affects vaccination positively . . . the association of religiosity with COVID-19 vaccination remains unclear.' Radosław Treowski and Dariusz Drążkowski, 'Cross-national comparison of religion as a predictor of COVID-19 vaccination rates', *Journal of Religion and Health* 61 (2022), p. 2198; Springer Link https://link.springer.com/article/10.1007/s10943-022-01569-7 (accessed 3 November 2023).

22 M. A. Milligan et al., 'COVID-19 vaccine acceptance: influential roles of political party and religiosity', *Psychology, Health & Medicine* (2021), pp. 1907–17.

combination that fits perfectly into the science and religion conflict narrative.[23] Some demonstrated a clear negative influence of religiosity on Covid-19 vaccination intention.[24] But others contended that religion did not significantly affect Covid-19 vaccination acceptance[25] or even that it affected vaccination positively.[26] In short, at least initially, 'the association of religiosity with Covid-19 vaccination remain[ed] unclear'.[27]

By mid-2022, a clearer picture was emerging. Drawing on data from ninety countries, representing 86% of the world population, a study published in the *Journal of Religion and Health* was able to evaluate accurately the impact of religiosity alongside variables such as sex, culture, and economic and social development, in order to achieve a 'Cross-national comparison of religion as a predictor of Covid-19 vaccination rates'.[28]

The study found that Christianity *was* negatively related to vaccination. It reported that only Christianity was predictive of the actual vaccination rates in country-level analyses, and that the proportion of Christians in a given country was negatively related to the vaccination rates after accounting for socio-economic and cultural factors. No such effects were observed for other religions or other religion-related variables.[29]

In effect, the anecdotal stories and (some of) the local surveys were pointing in the right direction. As the global study remarked, impassively, 'The finding that only Christianity is associated with vaccination hesitancy suggests that specific mechanisms related to a particular religion may

23 M. Linke and K. S. Jankowski, 'Religiosity and the spread of COVID-19: a multinational comparison', *Journal of Religion and Health* 61 (2022), pp. 1641–56.

24 J. Murphy et al., 'Psychological characteristics associated with COVID-19 vaccine hesitancy and resistance in Ireland and the United Kingdom', *Nature Communications* 12(1) (2021), pp. 1–15.

25 S. Sherman et al., 'COVID-19 vaccination intention in the UK: results from the COVID-19 vaccination acceptability study (CoVAccS), a nationally representative cross-sectional survey', *Human Vaccines & Immunotherapeutics* 17(6) (2021), pp. 1612–21.

26 J. P. Guidry et al., 'Willingness to get the COVID-19 vaccine with and without emergency use authorization', *American Journal of Infection Control* 49(2) (2021), pp. 137–42.

27 Trepanowski and Drążkowski, 'Cross-national comparison of religion as a predictor of COVID-19 vaccination rates', p. 2199.

28 Trepanowski and Drążkowski, 'Cross-national comparison of religion as a predictor of COVID-19 vaccination rates'.

29 Such as 'the importance of religion and freedom of expression and belief... Although... positive correlations between freedom of belief and vaccination rates have been observed, most become non-significant after introducing socio-economic and culture variables into the regression model.' Trepanowski and Drążkowski, 'Cross-national comparison', p. 2204.

explain this relationship . . . [in other words] there may be specific anti-vaccination attributes of Christianity'.[30]

The official positions

This conclusion, however, invites a perplexed question – one to which the authors of the global study nodded. 'Our findings that Christianity is negatively related to the vaccination rates are notable as *the official stance of most Christian denominations is either in favor of vaccination or, at the very least, not against it.*'[31] Pretty much every mainstream Christian church or denomination's teaching on vaccination is unequivocally positive.

Many years before Covid, the Pontifical Academy for Life issued a statement on vaccination, specifically offering 'moral reflections on vaccines prepared from cells derived from aborted human foetuses'. The topic was revisited in the 2008 Instruction *Dignitas Personae*, and again in a Note in 2017. Following a further enquiry for guidance in 2020, the Congregation for the Doctrine of the Faith stated clearly that 'when ethically irreproachable Covid-19 vaccines are not available[32] . . . *it is morally acceptable to receive Covid-19 vaccines that have used cell lines from aborted fetuses in their research and production process*.'[33] This, note, was advice with particular regard to those vaccines developed from cell-lines originating from an aborted foetus in the 1980s, not vaccines *per se* about which there was no question to be answered. Catholic bishops' conferences worldwide echoed this guidance, as of course they would, including the US Bishops' Conference, despite (or perhaps because of) some resistance among American

---

30 Trepanowski and Drążkowski,'Cross-national comparison', p. 2205.

31 Trepanowski and Drążkowski, 'Cross-national comparison', p. 2205; emphasis added.

32 Meaning 'in countries where vaccines without ethical problems [i.e. vaccines that have not been prepared from cells derived from aborted human foetuses] are not made available to physicians and patients, or where their distribution is more difficult due to special storage and transport conditions, or when various types of vaccines are distributed in the same country but health authorities do not allow citizens to choose the vaccine with which to be inoculated'.

33 'Note on the morality of using some anti-Covid-19 vaccines', Congregation for the Doctrine of the Faith; emphasis original; https://www.vatican.va/roman_curia/congregations/cfaith/documents/rc_con_cfaith_doc_20201221_nota-vaccini-anticovid_en.html (accessed 3 November 2023).

Catholics.[34] More personally, but no less influentially, both Pope Francis and Pope Emeritus Benedict were open about getting vaccinated, Francis in particular being a staunch and loud advocate of the vaccine, even calling it a 'moral obligation'.

The Church of England issued a similar statement explaining the moral validity of any vaccine developed using foetal cell-lines.[35] Senior Anglican figures have been vaccinated and none (to the best of our knowledge) has spoken out against vaccination. Anglican primates called for Covid-19 vaccines to be made available to the world's poorest people.[36] The Anglican Alliance has been active in 'addressing reasonable concerns and questions' in order to counter vaccine hesitancy.[37]

In Russia, the Orthodox Church rebuked people who had refused vaccination, urged everyone to receive it, and stated that anyone who refused and then fatally infected someone else was committing 'a sin for which they will have to atone throughout their lives'.[38] The Sretensky Theological Seminary, the leading Orthodox higher education institution in Moscow, publicly advocated vaccination, rejected conspiracy theories and addressed the foetal-cell-line objection, while pointing out that the Russian Orthodox Church (ROC) had supported vaccination against smallpox from as early as the nineteenth century.[39] In an interview in August 2021,

34 'Memo to bishops on vaccines for COVID-19', United States Conference of Catholic Bishops https://www.usccb.org/resources/memo-bishops-vaccines-covid-19 (accessed 3 November 2023).

35 'We concur with the Pontifical Academy for Life's conclusions that the morality of voluntary abortion and the morality of using aborted foetal material are not conjoined so that "we believe that all clinically recommended vaccinations can be used with a clear conscience and that the use of such vaccines does not signify some sort of cooperation with voluntary abortion".' Quoted in David Pocklington, 'Vaccines and religion', in Law & Religion UK, 16 December 2020, https://lawandreligionuk.com/2020/12/16/vaccines-and-religion (accessed 3 November 2023).

36 'Global Anglican leaders call for "equitable" Covid-19 vaccine roll-out to world's vulnerable', Anglican Communion https://www.anglicancommunion.org/communications/press-and-media/press-releases/global-anglican-leaders-call-for-equitable-covid-19-vaccine-roll-out-to-worlds-vulnerable.aspx (accessed 3 November 2023).

37 'Overcoming Covid-19 vaccine hesitancy. Part 1 – addressing reasonable concerns and questions', Anglican Alliance https://anglicanalliance.org/overcoming-covid-19-vaccine-hesitancy-part-1-addressing-reasonable-concerns-and-questions (accessed 3 November 2023).

38 'Vaccinate or repent, Russian church says amid hundreds of daily COVID-19 deaths', Reuters https://www.reuters.com/world/europe/vaccinate-or-repent-russian-church-says-amid-hundreds-daily-covid-19-deaths-2021-07-05 (accessed 3 November 2023).

39 Alexander Agadjanian and Scott Kenworthy, 'Resistance or submission? Reactions to the COVID-19 pandemic in the Russian Orthodox Church', Georgetown University https://berkleycenter.georgetown.edu/responses/resistance-or-submission-reactions-to-the-covid-19-pandemic-in-the-russian-orthodox-church (accessed 3 November 2023).

the Ecumenical Patriarch of Constantinople said that 'the refusal of vaccination and other protective measures is irrational and unjustified by theological or scientific criteria'.[40] The Greek Orthodox Church reprimanded bishops for inciting resistance to Covid vaccinations.[41] The Romanian Orthodox Church 'saluted the good news' of the vaccines.[42]

Even in evangelical America, ground zero for Christian anti-vaxxers, most of the highest-profile figures, as we have noted, explicitly endorsed the vaccination, claiming biblical warrant. Jesus Christ would advocate vaccination, Franklin Graham told his Facebook followers, drawing on the ever-flexible parable of the Good Samaritan to make his point.[43] In short – and with no disrespect to the Old Calendarist Romanian Orthodox Church – no significant Christian denomination or church of any size opposed – biblically, theologically, doctrinally, institutionally or personally – the Covid-19 vaccination.

So, one might legitimately ask, what is going on? Why is there a statistically significant relationship between Christian religiosity and anti-vax sentiments? What on earth is Christian anti-vaxxers' problem? To understand this, it is necessary to examine the actual 'religious' reasons for vaccine hesitancy, both current and historic.

What is your problem?

As a rule, we do not protect someone from burning to death by roasting their fingers. We do not prevent people from drowning by pouring water down their throat until they gag. And so, safeguarding a person against a disease by infecting them with a bit of that disease is, to put it mildly, a little bit counterintuitive.

---

40 Nedelescu, 'Anti-science, mistrust, and anxiety in the Orthodox world', Georgetown University.

41 Jonathan Luxmoore, 'Greek bishops reprimanded over resistance to Covid vaccinations', *Church Times* https://www.churchtimes.co.uk/articles/2021/10-september/news/world/greek-bishops-reprimanded-over-resistance-to-covid-vaccinations (accessed 3 November 2023).

42 Barberá et al., 'Religious strain of anti-vax grows in CEE', Balkan Insight.

43 Franklin Graham post, 24 March 2021, Facebook https://www.facebook.com/FranklinGraham/posts/the-internet-is-full-of-articles-theories-data-and-opinions-concerning-the-covid/276922917136643. For the ever-flexible parable see Nick Spencer, *The Political Samaritan: How power hijacked a parable* (London: Bloomsbury, 2017).

It is worth remembering this when we look back at early 'religious' objections to immunisation. Rather than being irrational or ignorant, many objections were simply based on common sense. And indeed on *scientific* sense, because, in the eighteenth century, medical opinion was deeply divided on the efficacy of immunisation. As White himself acknowledged, when the practice emerged 'ultra-conservatives *in medicine* took fright'. The fiercest opposition to Zabdiel Boylston's experiments came from a Scottish physician by the name of Dr Douglas. 'Perhaps the most virulent of Jenner's enemies was one of his professional brethren, Dr Moseley'.[44] The Anti-vaccination Society in Boston 'was formed by physicians and clergymen'.[45] In short, when clerics thundered against the new practice, they usually did so on the basis of medical advice.

Usually – but not always – because there were distinctively theological or religious justifications deployed against vaccination. These varied but can be profitably divided into four categories. First, vaccination was seen as denying God's sovereign authority or as White put it 'flying in the face of Providence' and 'endeavouring to baffle a Divine judgment'. According to this logic, smallpox was 'a judgment of God on the sins of the people', and 'to avert it is but to provoke him more'.[46]

Second, the practice of vaccination was seen as unethical. When, in 1721, Dr Boylston 'made an experiment in inoculation' by infecting his own son, clerics (and indeed many others) were outraged and denounced him as immoral.[47] Third, some preferred to see disease as a 'spiritual' rather than a 'material' battle, to be fought with prayer and Scripture rather than medical treatment. During the 1885 epidemic in Montreal, particularly virulent among Catholics who refused vaccination, 'the faithful were exhorted to rely on devotional exercises of various sorts . . . [and] a great procession was ordered with a solemn appeal to the Virgin'.[48] Finally, there were examples of biblical proof texting, in which divines plucked verses, 'most [of them] remote from any possible bearing on the subject', to justify medical

---

44 White, *History of the Warfare of Science with Theology in Christendom*, pp. 55–8; emphasis added.

45 White, *History of the Warfare of Science with Theology in Christendom*, p. 58.

46 White, *History of the Warfare of Science with Theology in Christendom*, p. 56.

47 White, *History of the Warfare of Science with Theology in Christendom*, p. 56.

48 White, *History of the Warfare of Science with Theology in Christendom*, p. 60.

inaction. 'He hath torn, and he will heal us,' as the prophet Hosea said; 'he hath smitten, and he will bind us up.'[49]

Providentialism, morality, spirituality and biblical proof texting: it is possible to find examples of each of these historic 'justifications' among contemporary Christian vaccine sceptics today. When it comes to providentialism, although we have not been able to identify any examples of pastors saying explicitly that God was using Covid to execute judgement on the ungodly – that line of argument at least seems to have died out[50] – some Christian responses have been marked by a sense of fatalism, a kind of providentialism minus vengeance.[51] With regard to moral concerns, these have been obviated by the rather more rigorous and ethical processes of testing vaccines today, although they remain, as we have seen, in anxieties around the use of foetal cell-lines. When it comes to 'spiritual' responses, a handful of church leaders, such as the Romanian Orthodox Archbishop of Tomis, have opined that 'the thing that cures the most is praying, much more than any vaccine'.[52] And with regard to proof texting, while we have not found anyone quoting the prophet Hosea at the virus, 'the mark of the beast' from the book of Revelation, which acts as a kind of biblical wild card for the paranoid, has been deployed against Covid vaccination.[53]

In short, it is possible to trace a thread from early Christian anti-vaxxers to their 'descendants' today. However, that thread is gossamer thin because when you explore the more prevalent 'religious' reasons for anti-vax beliefs today, neither providentialism, nor spirituality, nor biblical proof texting, nor (foetal cell-lines excepted) morality is especially visible. Instead,

---

49 White, *History of the Warfare of Science with Theology in Christendom*, p. 56.

50 Or nearly died out: '[there are] monastic circles who interpret the deaths from the virus "mystically", blaming it on God's wrath and apostasy.' Pantelis Kalaitzidis, 'Russian Orthodoxy and the endangered "symphonia" model in the age of COVID-19', Georgetown University https://berkleycenter.georgetown.edu/responses/russian-orthodoxy-and-the-endangered-symphonia-model-in-the-age-of-covid-19 (accessed 3 November 2023).

51 'We are going to go through times of trials and all kinds of awful things, but we still know where we are going at the end,' commented one 75-year-old Christian interviewee for an Associated Press report into white evangelical vaccine scepticism. 'Heaven is so much better than here on Earth. Why would we fight leaving here?' Crary, 'Vaccine skepticism runs deep among white evangelicals in US', AP News.

52 Barberá et al., 'Religious strain of anti-vax grows in CEE', Balkan Insight.

53 Carla Hinton, 'No, the COVID vaccine is not the "mark of the beast". Here's what an Oklahoma Bible prophecy expert says', *The Oklahoman* https://eu.oklahoman.com/story/news/religion/2021/01/25/the-covid-vaccine-not-the-mark-of-the-beast-here-is-what-an-edmond-bible-prophecy-expert-has-to-say/323205007 (accessed 3 November 2023).

you are cast into the world of politics or, more precisely, of assumed political theologies.

But what is *really* your problem?

This is, all too often, an overlooked dimension of science and religion debates. However, if, as the underlying thesis of this book argues, the liveliest area of science and religion discourse centres on the nature of the human, this political dimension should not surprise us. Humans are, after all, political animals. To be human is to agonise over how to live together with others in justice and truth. Science and religion is, therefore, necessarily, a political conversation too.

Within this framing, Christian anti-vax sentiments today can be profitably divided into two positions – positions that stand at opposing ends of a spectrum, but which, horseshoe-like, end up being remarkably close to one another: Christian libertarianism and Christian nationalism.

Evangelicals were, as we have noted, among the least likely to be vaccinated against Covid-19. Saliently, however, they were also among the most hostile towards basic, government-mandated anti-Covid measures. Early on during the pandemic, in July 2020, the Pew Forum found that 18% of evangelicals said that their place of worship should be 'open to the public and holding services in the same way as before the outbreak', compared to 18% who said they should not be open. The only other group reporting a comparable opinion was Republicans, with 19% vs 16%.[54] Social distancing and mask wearing were heavily resisted by this group. White evangelicals were also the least likely to support state restrictions on business and public activities during the pandemic. In effect, vaccine resistance was a piece of wider resistance to all government measures that threatened to restrict individual liberty on account of Covid. However much evangelical

---

54 Sixty-four per cent said they should be 'open to the public for services, but with changes as a result of the outbreak'. Nortey and Lipka, 'Most Americans who go to religious services say they would trust their clergy's advice on COVID-19 vaccines', Pew Research Center.

attitudes to science might have shaped vaccine resistance, it was their distrust of, indeed antipathy towards, the state that drove it.[55]

It is important to emphasise that this was not a uniquely evangelical, Christian or even religious response to the crisis. R. R. Reno, editor of the Conservative Catholic magazine *First Things*, wrote an excoriating editorial just as lockdown measures were being imposed, complaining about how anti-Covid measures were an 'ill-conceived crusade against human finitude and the dolorous reality of death'.[56] Meanwhile, in the UK, the former Supreme Court justice, Jonathan Sumption (no religious believer), came to prominence for his strong criticism, on civil libertarian grounds, of the government's lockdown measures.[57] Evangelicals do not have the monopoly on (civil) libertarian objections to Covid measures. It's just that some went a bit further in applying those objections to the vaccine itself rather than just to practical government measures to limit the virus.

If libertarianism stands at one end of Christian anti-vax movements, nationalism stands at the other. In theory these two ideologies are opposites. Libertarianism favours the individual over any collective grouping, whereas nationalism places value precisely in the collective group of the nation. However, in the case of the USA – with liberty so deeply embedded in the nation's identity – the two ends of the spectrum end up nearly touching.

Christian nationalism has been defined as 'an ideology that idealizes and advocates a fusion of American civic life with a particular type of Christian identity and culture'.[58] Advocates believe that America 'was founded as a Christian nation' and that the nation holds a special place in God's plan for

---

55 It's worth noting that this isn't ubiquitous distrust. US evangelicals as a rule trust their church leaders, as do other religious Americans, even though only 4% of evangelicals say they have heard their clergy *discourage* them from getting the vaccine. It was distrust of the state, a state seemingly intent on taking away their liberties. Nortey and Lipka, 'Most Americans who go to religious services say they would trust their clergy's advice on COVID-19 vaccines', Pew Research Center.

56 R. R. Reno, 'Say "no" to death's dominion', First Things https://www.firstthings.com/web-exclusives/2020/03/say-no-to-deaths-dominion (accessed 3 November 2023).

57 'If we hold politicians responsible for everything that goes wrong, they will take away our liberty so that nothing can go wrong.' Jonathan Sumption, 'Set us free from lockdown, ministers, and stop covering your backs', *The Sunday Times* https://www.thetimes.co.uk/article/set-us-free-from-lockdown-ministers-and-stop-covering-your-backs-kvwrnk9ww (accessed 3 November 2023).

58 The definition is from Andrew L. Whitehead and Samuel L. Perry's book *Taking America Back for God: Christian nationalism in the United States* (New York, NY: Oxford University Press, 2020), pp. ix–x.

the world; its global pre-eminence explicable through some kind of divine, providential protection and favour.

There is, on the surface of it, no good reason why such an ideology should orient anyone *away* from a vaccination programme. After all, one might equally say that God exercised his providential care for America, and via America the world, by granting it the scientific and technological ability and economic power to develop and deploy life-saving vaccines in record time.

However, the argument doesn't tend to work that way and there is increasingly good evidence to show that 'Christian nationalism is one of the leading predictors of vaccine hesitancy'.[59] Christian nationalism is a strong predictor of believing that vaccines in general 'cause autism', that 'children are given too many vaccines' and that vaccines do not 'help protect children'.[60] Other studies have shown a correlation between conservative evangelicalism and higher levels of overall vaccine hesitancy, lower rates of vaccine uptake and lower levels of vaccine knowledge.[61] Not surprisingly, therefore, early studies show that these views are being carried into the age of Covid. In the words of one paper, 'Christian nationalists are less likely to view Covid-19 vaccines as safe and effective and less likely to have received or plan to receive a Covid-19 vaccine.'[62]

Christian nationalism is also correlated with pandemic 'incautious' behaviour, such as gathering in large groups when advised not to, refusing to

59 Katie E. Corcoran, Christopher P. Scheitle and Bernard D. DiGregorio, 'Christian nationalism and COVID-19 vaccine hesitancy and uptake', *Vaccine* 39(45) (2021), pp. 6614–21; PMC, National Library of Medicine https://www.ncbi.nlm.nih.gov/pmc/articles/PMC8489517 (accessed 3 November 2023).

60 Andrew L. Whitehead and Samuel L. Perry, 'How culture wars delay herd immunity: Christian nationalism and anti-vaccine attitudes', *Socius* 6 (2020).

61 Note: although conservative evangelicalism and Christian nationalism are closely related, they are not quite the same thing. According to one estimate (Andrew L. Whitehead and Samuel L. Perry, *Taking America Back for God: Christian nationalism in the United States* (New York, NY: Oxford University Press, 2020), approximately half of US evangelicals are Christian nationalists. According to a second (Samuel L. Perry, Andrew L. Whitehead and Joshua B. Grubbs, 'Culture wars and COVID-19 conduct: Christian nationalism, religiosity, and Americans' behavior during the coronavirus pandemic', *Journal for the Scientific Study of Religion* 59(3) (2020), p. 407), this figure rises to 75% for *white* evangelicals. There is, therefore, a considerable overlap, but the two are not coterminous. Historically, however, many studies have tended to treat evangelicalism as the measurable variable rather than Christian nationalism. Conservative (and especially white) evangelicalism in the USA may be taken as an indication of Christian nationalism, but with caution.

62 Corcoran et al., 'Christian nationalism and COVID-19 vaccine hesitancy and uptake', *Vaccine* 39(45) (2021), pp. 6614–21.

wear a mask and refusing to sanitize hands.[63] The parallel here with Christian libertarianism is obvious. However, the difference is that Christian nationalism's antipathy towards the state is born of a sense of its failure or, more accurately, its misplaced and ungodly priorities. Christian nationalists commonly hold the view that, precisely because God has a special dispensation towards the nation, he will protect it – *if* that nation calls upon and turns to him. The fact that it persistently refuses to do so means that Christian nationalists also tend to agree with the statement that 'the nation is on the brink of moral decay', and that, therefore, the truest and best response to a crisis such as Covid is repentance.[64] In the words of one academic paper, as far as Christian nationalists are concerned, 'the solution to the crisis is *not* to take behavioral precautions like hand-washing, mask-wearing, or social distancing, but to increase America's collective devotion, attending religious services and repenting of national sins (e.g., abortion, homosexuality, general lawlessness)'.[65]

Thus far, this politically coloured Christian antipathy to vaccination might seem like a quintessentially American phenomenon. America has a disproportionately large problem with Christian anti-vaxxing and also a disproportionately large evidence base by means of which we can interrogate this. However, this does not appear to be the case, as Christian anti-vaccination sentiments in a very different country (Russia) with a very different religious tradition (Orthodoxy) illustrate.

As with American Christians, those Orthodox Russians who (loudly) refuse vaccination do so for a number of reasons.[66] Alexander Agadjanian and Scott Kenworthy have rightly pointed out that, in spite of the Western tendency to think otherwise, the Russian Orthodox Church is not 'a monolith' but, rather, 'internally diverse, both as an institution and as a faith

---

63 Samuel L. Perry et al., 'Culture wars and COVID-19 conduct: Christian nationalism, religiosity, and Americans' behavior during the coronavirus pandemic', *Journal for the Scientific Study of Religion* 59(3) (2020), pp. 405–16.

64 Corcoran et al., 'Christian nationalism and COVID-19 vaccine hesitancy and uptake', p. 6614.

65 Perry et al., 'Culture wars and COVID-19 conduct', p. 407. This is one of those moments when we can see the link between forms of current Christian anti-vax thinking and those of the past, which recommended personal penitence as a means of winning what it judged to be essentially a spiritual war.

66 Among them being concerns about foetal cell-lines.

community' – a diversity that has been exacerbated by Covid.[67] That diversity recognised, libertarian and nationalist stances are prominent among the reasons for Orthodox vaccine resistance.

With regard to the former, in spite of the much-trumpeted Byzantine model of *symphonia*, in which the Church and State work together harmoniously for the good of the people, a number of Russian clergy and believers have been highly sceptical about state restrictions placed on religious practice – insisting that churches are not amenities to be closed like bars or theatres, or to be sanitised like gyms – and have been similarly sceptical about the state-mandated vaccination programme. The state, for all its alliance with the Church since 1991, is not fully trusted or trustworthy. 'It seems that, for many Orthodox Christians, the deep distrust of the state stemming back to the Soviet period runs even deeper than sympathies for Putin's conservative and patriotic regime.'[68] Some believers have resisted vaccines on just these grounds.

At the same time, there has also been resistance to vaccination on Christian nationalist grounds. Some clerics and more believers in Russia, and indeed in Greece, central Europe and the Balkans, have come to see the vaccination programme and, of course, state-mandated lockdowns and restrictions as part of a wider assault on nations that have historically, and should still be, purely and authentically Orthodox. By this reckoning, vaccination and restrictions are part of the programme of Western liberalism and globalisation, threatening the unique Orthodox culture, and grounded in a secular, scientific worldview that made modernity – and atheism – possible.[69] As in America, authorities are denounced in sermons for being godless and for failing to recognise the true problem and the true solution to the crisis. As with American

---

67 See Scott M. Kenworthy and Alexander S. Agadjanian, *Understanding World Christianity: Russia* (Minneapolis, MN: Fortress Press, 2021). 'The pandemic has revealed or exacerbated many of these tensions, which lie between the church and the state both at the federal and local levels; between the patriarchal administration and local bishops, monasteries, and clergy; and between believers and the institutional church'. Agadjanian and Kenworthy, 'Resistance or submission? Reactions to the COVID-19 pandemic in the Russian Orthodox Church', Georgetown University.

68 Agadjanian and Kenworthy, 'Resistance or submission? Reactions to the COVID-19 pandemic in the Russian Orthodox Church', Georgetown University.

69 Kalaitzidis, 'Russian Orthodoxy and the endangered "symphonia" model in the age of COVID-19', Georgetown University.

Christian nationalists, the only principled response to the pandemic is seen to lie in a full-scale national repentance, a turning of the people and the state to the God who called and formed and blessed the nation, together with a wholesale rejection of atheistic, sexually deviant, Western lifestyles.[70]

As in America, with its evangelical divides on this matter, this is emphatically not a universal or unchallenged view among the Orthodox. Indeed, in some instances, the Russian Orthodox Church authorities have come down very hard on dissident priests or monks who have taken the anti-vax lead.[71] However, where there has been outspoken Orthodox resistance to vaccination, as in America, it has taken its cue both from this kind of theologically justified nationalism, with its simultaneous elevation and critique of the holy and blessed nation, and from a theologically justified libertarianism, with its resolute suspicion of any state interference with individual liberty. When it comes to vaccination, science and religion meet in politics.

Vaccination and the need for political theology

Shifting the focus in this debate to politics and to political theology is not to deny that there is a more narrowly scientific problem at play. Although the alleged hostility of evangelicals to science can be rather overdone,[72] it is nonetheless true that Christian nationalists do have comparatively low levels of trust in science and in scientific expertise, and are significantly more likely to reject evolution, to view scientists as hostile to faith, and

---

70 Kalaitzidis, 'Russian Orthodoxy and the endangered "symphonia" model in the age of COVID-19', Georgetown University.

71 For example, the so-called 'Covid-dissident' priest-monk Sergii Romanov, who was particularly outspoken in his criticism of the measures against the pandemic, was defrocked and excommunicated from the Church altogether, and then arrested. In all fairness, however, Sergii had already been removed from his position as abbot in 2005 because of his scandalous behaviour. Cyril Hovorun, 'COVID-19: a challenge for the Russian symphony', Georgetown University https://berkleycenter.georgetown.edu/responses/covid-19-a-challenge-for-the-russian-symphony (accessed 3 November 2023).

72 As Elaine Howards Ecklund and colleagues have repeatedly shown. See, for example, Elaine Howard Ecklund and Christopher P. Scheitle, *Religion vs. Science: What religious people really think* (New York, NY: Oxford University Press, 2018).

to respond incorrectly to scientific questions on religiously contentious topics.[73] Treating religious vaccine hesitancy as a political issue is not to deny the reality of science antagonism, let alone scientific ignorance.[74] The only defence here is that the religious world does not have the monopoly on ignorant or crazy anti-vax theories.

What this shift in emphasis does is clarify and disambiguate the correlation, described earlier, between Christianity and vaccine resistance. Those studies that have controlled for political views have found that Christian religiosity itself is either unrelated or even positively correlated to vaccination views. In the words of one paper, '[W]e find that religious service attendance is, in fact, positively associated with Covid-19 vaccine confidence and uptake.'[75] The same applies to positive behaviour during the pandemic. '[Not only was] religious commitment . . . completely unrelated to incautious behaviors in our full models . . . [but] once we account for Christian nationalism, devout Americans are more likely to alter their behavior and wash hands or sanitize more often, wear a mask, and avoid touching their face.'[76]

This point is of more than academic or merely reputational significance. Returning to where we started this chapter, if, as is predicted, the twenty-first century sees an increased probability of global pandemics, it will also see an increased dependence on successful vaccination programmes, and vaccination programmes are vulnerable to even relatively small groups of people opting out. It is, therefore, essential for all our sakes to recognise *why* such groups are opting out, in order to formulate a coherent response. Simply putting such resistance down to 'being religious' or

---

73 Samuel L. Perry, Joseph O. Baker, Joshua B. Grubbs, 'Ignorance or culture war? Christian nationalism and scientific illiteracy' (2021), Sagepub https://journals.sagepub.com/doi/abs/10.1177/09636625211006271 (accessed 3 November 2023).

74 Such as Bishop Porfirii's arguments, made on (and then rapidly removed from) YouTube that the Covid vaccines genetically alter the person into something that potentially damages the 'image of God' in them. Agadjanian and Kenworthy, 'Resistance or submission? Reactions to the COVID-19 pandemic in the Russian Orthodox Church', Georgetown University. Or, indeed, the synod of the Orthodox Church of Moldova, a semi-autonomous part of the Russian Orthodox Church, which issued a statement claiming that the vaccine allows 'the global antichrist system to inject microchips into people's bodies in order to control them using 5G technology'. Kalaitzidis, 'Russian Orthodoxy and the endangered "symphonia" model in the age of COVID-19', Georgetown University.

75 Corcoran et al., 'Christian nationalism and COVID-19 vaccine hesitancy', p. 6619.

76 Perry et al., 'Culture wars and COVID-19', p. 414.

'anti-science' is not only inaccurate but ultimately harmful. In the words of one paper:

> social scientists, pollsters, and those in the media need to employ greater nuance when explaining why so many Americans are resistant to governments implementing and/or maintaining sweeping social distancing restrictions. The answer is not political partisanship or evangelicalism *per se*, but much of it has to do with the pervasive ideology that blends Christian identity with conceptions of economic prosperity and individual liberty even at the expense of the vulnerable.[77]

It is only by identifying the problem correctly that we can address it – and that problem is political theology. 'Pollsters and studies have utilized imprecise measures that might misattribute patterns to religious affiliations or religiosity *per se* rather than Americans' *specific political theologies or conceptions of public religion*, which . . . are likely far more important.'[78] And, we might add, having looked at the responses in Orthodox lands, this applies not just to Americans.

Precisely *how* to address this is an altogether bigger issue. Christianity has baptised quite a range of political theologies over the years and, perhaps more relevantly, American evangelicals or Russian Orthodox believers caught up in an apparently all-consuming culture war are unlikely to take kindly to being told that their political theology is all wrong.

That said, some perspective might make this task a bit more hopeful. First, no one is suggesting that what we need here is to bring believers to the complete knowledge of the one true, perfect, saving political theology. Christians have disagreed, and ever shall disagree, on the proper function of the state, not least in an age when the historically rather circumscribed responsibilities of states have expanded enormously. We don't need consensus on this intractable issue to avoid the worst excesses of bad answers. The task is simply to draw people away from those political theologies that

77 Samuel L. Perry, Andrew L. Whitehead and Joshua B. Grubbs, 'Save the economy, liberty, and yourself: Christian nationalism and Americans' views on government COVID-19 restrictions', *Sociology of Religion: A Quarterly Review* 82(4) (2021), p. 441. https://academic.oup.com/socrel/article/82/4/426/6054784 (accessed 3 November 2023).
78 Perry et al., 'Culture wars and COVID-19 conduct', p. 406; emphasis added.

act as deterrents to government vaccination programmes. This may not be easy, but it shouldn't prove impossible.

Second, we should recall, as we emphasised earlier, that the vast majority of religious believers, church leaders and theological guidance is on the right side of the fence on the vaccination issue. Catholic, Anglican, Orthodox, evangelical: the mainstream and majority counsel is all pretty much unambiguously pro-vaccination. We are not pushing at a closed door here, so much as one that is already nearly fully open.

Third, there is good evidence that flocks do listen to and trust their pastors on this matter. A 2021 Pew report found that 'most Americans who go to religious services say they would trust their clergy's advice on Covid-19 vaccines'. Much of the time that advice is pro-vaccine. The Pew study found that, of US churchgoers, 39% claimed that their clergy had encouraged them to be vaccinated against Covid-19, compared to only 5% who said they had been discouraged. The real issue appears to have been that over half (54%) had not heard anything much either way from their church leader on the matter. This is a problem, but crucially it is a solvable problem. Influencing the general population is always difficult because governments need to know not only what information to convey but, crucially, by which means. What channels and which authoritative voices will reach and persuade people? In societies that are becoming ever more antagonistic towards all forms of authority, this is an ever-growing challenge. The fact that connections of trust already exist between pew and pulpit cannot be underestimated in this task.

Fourth, and finally, the biblical foundations on which all these political theologies ultimately build can be marshalled against the various forms of Christian libertarianism and Christian nationalism that are at the heart of the problem here.[79] The Bible contains within it a number of distinct and apparently conflicting political impulses. Drawn together they provide the raw materials for a subtle, flexible and intelligent attitude to individual, nation and state, simultaneously respectful towards but sceptical about the exercise of earthly power.

---

79 The following paragraphs are adapted from Nick Spencer, *Freedom and Order: History, politics, and the English Bible* (London: Hodder, 2011).

One key impulse is to freedom, and in particular the 'negative' freedom *from* political constraints.[80] Ideas of negative freedom have been derived from the story of the exodus, which became *the* icon of political liberation. They have been drawn from the strict conditions placed upon kings in the Old Testament law. They have been drawn from the origins of Israelite kingship in all its ambiguity. They have been drawn from the various tales of wicked Old Testament kings who angered God and were (sometimes) punished for their sins. They have been drawn from the subservience of all earthly kings before the King of kings, who would one day judge them for the way in which they discharged the obligations of their office. They have been drawn from Jesus' rather contemptuous attitude to the Roman authorities in Palestine. If the biblical thrust towards this kind of freedom has a proof text it is Acts 5:29, on which many a Christian radical through history has seized: 'We must obey God rather than human beings!' Taken in isolation, this becomes the foundation stone for libertarianism. I must always obey God (whose views my church, or my reading of Scripture, or my conscience alone can discern) rather than humans (and whatever structures of authority they form).

The other impulse is to value 'the people' as called, judged and disciplined by God. This impulse has been drawn from God's calling of Israel to be a blessing to all the world. It has drawn on his salvation of that people from slavery, on his gift of the law to them, on his judgement of the people, and in particular of their ordained kings. The position has also taken its cue from the way in which early Christians were judged to be a distinct and separate people, called by God to carry his message into the world. If this biblical thrust towards political nationalism has a proof text it is either Deuteronomy 28:9 – 'The LORD will establish you as his holy people, as he promised you on oath, if you keep the commands of the LORD your God and walk in obedience to him.' Or perhaps 1 Peter 2:9 – 'you are a chosen people, a royal priesthood, a holy nation, God's special possession'. Taken in isolation, this becomes the foundation stone for Christian nationalism and authoritarianism. God alone knows and governs this people, choosing their leaders and demanding their allegiance.

---

80 It also has a strong impulse to positive freedom *to* enable the fulfilment of inherent human potential, which is discussed at greater length in the introduction to Spencer, *Freedom and Order*.

These imperatives are deeply and profoundly embedded in the Christian narrative. However, there are other views within the Scriptures to temper and balance them.

When it comes to the first, alongside the emphasis on political freedom, there was a strong emphasis on respecting political authority. Old Testament kings were anointed, thereby sanctifying them with the very authority of God. Jesus recognised that Caesar had a right to what he was due. The early Christians had a high level of respect towards the authorities, and Paul famously wrote, 'Let everyone be subject to the governing authorities, for there is no authority except that which God has established'.[81] The Bible's stress on political freedom is balanced by an emphasis on political order and respect for authority.

In a similar way, while the Bible does obviously have a particular interest and respect for the nation of Israel or the people of God, it is a unique one, not to be appropriated by other nations. The tendency of some Protestant countries to view themselves as the 'new Israel' or of certain Orthodox churches to hitch their creed and culture to an ethnic nationalism (a heresy known as phyletism and condemned by an Orthodox council of 1872) makes the cardinal mistake of applying God's particular treatment of Israel (or the Church) to ordinary, contingent, modern nation-states.[82] Straightforwardly applying the criteria used of Israel to any modern nation is unjustified by the scriptural terms on which it is allegedly based.

This brief detour into political theology is not intended to lay out every argument needed to counter the kind of Christian libertarianism and Christian nationalism that lie at the heart of Christian anti-vax sentiments. Rather, it is intended to show that there are resources to do so. Just as it is sometimes said that the solution to bad religion is not no religion but good religion, so the answer to the Christian libertarianism and Christian nationalism that dog the vaccination issue is not to dismiss political theology altogether but to draw on the full resources available here. Christian libertarians need to hear that the state and political authorities are to be respected, without simultaneously abandoning all rights to criticism. Christian nationalists need to hear that their own nation has no special,

---

81 Romans 13:1.
82 David Koyzis, *Political Visions and Illusions* (Downers Grove, IL: InterVarsity Press, 2003), pp. 97–123.

chosen status under God, without its simultaneously abandoning all rights to loyalty.

If we are to ensure the success of large-scale vaccination programmes in an age when they are likely to be increasingly necessary, it will be important to try to answer people's concerns about them on their own terms. And that means that this particular but vital corner of the science and religion conversation will be drawn into the fascinating and endlessly contestable arena of political theology.

4

My personhood and other animals

The sad story of Happy

In June 2022, a New York court had to decide whether Happy was a person. Happy was a 51-year-old female Asian elephant. She had been resident in Bronx Zoo for most of her life. She was, by all accounts, an impressive animal; sensitive, intelligent and the first Asian elephant unambiguously to have passed the mirror test.[1]

Happy's case had been brought on her behalf by the Nonhuman Rights Project (NhRP), a US organisation dedicated, in its own words, to 'challeng[ing] an archaic, unjust legal *status quo* that views and treats all non-human animals as "things" with no rights'.[2] NhRP had argued that the legal principle of habeas corpus, intended to prevent unlawful detention, applied to Happy. Drawing on expert zoological witnesses, they contended that Happy, like many elephants, had the capacity for 'self-awareness, long-term memory, intentional communication, learning and problem-solving skills, empathy, and significant emotional response', as well as 'autonomy' in as far as she could 'direct [her] behavior based on some non-observable, internal cognitive process, rather than simply responding reflexively'.[3] That being so, holding her in captivity was no more defensible than imprisoning an innocent human being. Happy should, legally speaking, be treated as a 'person' with all the rights that accrue to personhood.

---

1 On which more below.
2 www.nonhumanrights.org.
3 State of New York Court of Appeals, *Nonhuman Rights Project, Inc., &c., Appellant, v. James J. Breheny, &c., et al.*, 52opn22-Decision.pdf; https://www.nycourts.gov.

The argument had failed to impress five appellate justices in a lower Manhattan court two years earlier and it did no better on appeal.[4] Although publishing two dissenting opinions, the court found against NhRP. It did so, however, on narrowly legal grounds: 'It is not this court's role to make such a determination.'[5] The serious philosophical and anthropological issues raised by the case were deemed just too significant for the court to pronounce on. Granting legal personhood to nonhuman animals would have huge implications 'for the interactions of humans and animals in all facets of life',[6] and create 'an enormous destabilizing impact on modern society'. The case of Happy was not heard and found to have failed, but heard and found to have been too difficult.

Happy's plea gained global attention, but it was not unique. The NhRP's 'clients' (their word) have included Tommy, Kiko, Hercules and Leo – all male chimpanzees – and Beulah, Karen and Minnie – Asian and African elephants. In addition, the organisation demands 'recognition of the legal personhood and fundamental right to bodily liberty' for dolphins and whales held in captivity. They have set up or collaborated with legal working groups in the UK, Spain, France, Sweden, Finland, Switzerland, Portugal, Israel, Turkey, India and Australia. And they have even met with some success in Pakistan,[7] India[8] and Argentina, where Cecilia the chimpanzee is now considered a 'non-human legal person' with 'inherent rights'.[9]

---

4   Holly Honderich, 'Happy the elephant is not a person, New York court rules', BBC News https://www.bbc.co.uk/news/world-us-canada-61803958 (accessed 9 November 2023).

5   'The use of habeas corpus as a vehicle to extend legal personhood beyond living humans is not a matter for the courts.'

6   Such as risking the disruption of property rights, the agricultural industry (among others) and medical research efforts, and calling into question 'the very premises underlying pet ownership, the use of service animals, and the enlistment of animals in other forms of work'.

7   'Owais Awan on the legal fight for Kaavan's freedom', Nonhuman Rights Project https://www.nonhumanrights.org/blog/the-legal-fight-for-kaavans-freedom (accessed 9 November 2023).

8   'In April 2013, the Ministry of Environment and Forests of the Government of India declared that all cetaceans (especially dolphins) are highly intelligent and sensitive and, as such, should be seen as "non-human persons" with their "own specific rights".' See Vishrut Kansal, 'The curious case of *Nagaraja* in India: are animals still regarded as "property" with no claim rights?', *Journal of International Wildlife Law & Policy* 19(3) (2016), pp. 256–67. https://doi.org/10.1080/13880292.2016.1204885 (accessed 9 November 2023).

9   Lauren Choplin, 'Chimpanzee Cecilia finds sanctuary: an interview with GAP Brazil', Nonhuman Rights Project https://www.nonhumanrights.org/blog/chimpanzee-cecilia (accessed 9 November 2023).

The campaign to recognise animal personhood is not some little local eccentricity. It is serious business.

Quite how serious is indicated by the comparisons and precedents NhRP cite for their work. The US Supreme Court, they point out, once excluded black people from legal personhood on the basis that they were 'beings of an inferior order'.[10] The California Supreme Court once called Chinese people 'a race... whom nature has marked as inferior'.[11] Perhaps most relevantly, they point out, when, in June 1772, Lord Mansfield, the Chief Justice of the Court of King's Bench, ruled for the enslaved man James Somerset against his 'owner' Charles Stewart, thereby effectively prohibiting slavery in Britain, he did so on the basis of habeas corpus.[12]

In that instance, it had been Somerset's godparents who had applied to the King's Bench for a writ of habeas corpus. Somerset had recently been baptised, and the belief that enslaved people were made legally as well as spiritually free at baptism was widespread in England at the time. The abolitionists would make good use of habeas corpus in their campaign against slavery. Mostly evangelicals and Quakers, the abolitionists were repelled by the idea that some human beings did not qualify as legal persons, and were at the forefront of the fight for their rights.

Two hundred and fifty years later, this new, would-be abolitionist cause is rather less likely to be spearheaded by religious believers. In the USA, a 2015 Gallup poll showed that 32% of Americans believe 'animals deserve the exact same rights as people from harm and exploitation', but with Republicans being half as likely to agree as Democrats (an imperfect but instructive cipher for religious opinion in America).[13] The religious are more likely than the non-religious, in the UK and elsewhere, to see benefits in animal research.[14] More generally, polling in the UK and the US consistently

---

10 *Dred Scott v. Sandford*, 60 U.S. 393, 407 (1857).

11 *People v. Hall*, 4 Cal. 399, 404 (1854).

12 In that case, Mansfield, alert to the magnitude of what he was being called to adjudicate upon, had initially tried to prevent the case being heard in court. But he eventually acquiesced, declaring boldly, 'If the parties will have judgment, *fiat justitia ruat coelum* [let justice be done though the heavens fall].' The comparison between Mansfield and the judges of the New York court will not, we suspect, be lost on the Nonhuman Rights Project.

13 Rebecca Riffkin, 'In U.S., more say animals should have same rights as people', Gallup https://news.gallup.com/poll/183275/say-animals-rights-people.aspx (accessed 10 November 2023).

14 Nick Spencer, *Science and Religion: The perils of misperception* (London: Theos, 2019), p. 90.

shows that it is the idea that humans and apes share a common ancestor, or that humans (as opposed to other species) evolved, that most vexes evolution deniers, especially religious ones. In short, maintaining a clear division between humans and other animals may not be the preserve of religious believers, but it is certainly more prevalent among them.

There is clearly potential for tension between science and religion here. Indeed, given that the origins and premises of the nonhuman animal rights movement lie in loosely anti-Christian ethical foundations, as we shall note below, and that its energies come from our growing knowledge of nonhuman animal capacities, from fieldwork and laboratories, there appears to be considerable potential for conflict here.

However it is framed, this is not an issue that is going to disappear any time soon. As the New York Court of Appeal's Justice Eugene M. Fahey remarked in a chimpanzee rights case brought by the NhRP in 2018, 'The issue [of] whether a nonhuman animal has a fundamental right to liberty ... is profound and far-reaching ... Ultimately, we will not be able to ignore it.'

Getting emotional about animals

The Nonhuman Rights Project was launched as the Center for the Expansion of Fundamental Rights in 2007, but its roots go back to the 1970s when its founder, Steven Wise, who was newly qualified as a lawyer and seeking a social justice cause, read *Animal Liberation* by the Australian philosopher Peter Singer.

Widely credited as the founding text of the animal rights movement, *Animal Liberation* adopted Singer's unflinching utilitarianism and applied it across what he deemed to be the arbitrary boundary between humans and other species. It was not that there were no differences between humans and other animals but rather that the simple taxonomic distinction between species A and species B was *ethically* less salient than their different (or rather similar) capacities to suffer. If an animal from species B could think, feel and suffer as much as an animal from species A, why should we necessarily accord it different (or no) rights? In effect, Singer asked, why should we evaluate human pain or grief in a qualitatively different way from that of chimpanzees or other mammals that show apparently comparable sensitivity? If animals can suffer just as much as humans, our indifference towards, or minimisation of, their status and condition becomes untenable in any ethically just system.

Singer was clear that at least part of the reason for our current injustice was Christianity. This was not simply the familiar, if overdone, point that Christianity sanctioned the mistreatment of the natural world by giving humankind dominion over it. Singer did make that point but recognised that the world into which Christianity was born was quite happy to massacre thousands of exotic animals (and a good few humans) merely for public entertainment.[15] Christianity had no monopoly on undervaluing or mistreating nature.

Rather, his was the more specific point that Christianity 'brought into the Roman world the idea of the uniqueness of man, which it inherited from the Jewish tradition', and then 'insisted upon [it] with still greater emphasis because of the importance it placed on man's immortal soul'.[16] In this way, and for all that Singer acknowledged the 'very progressive' impact of Christian ethics when it came to human beings, he asserted that the idea of a *fundamental qualitative difference* between the worth of humans and other animals was ultimately a Christian one.

There is much truth in Singer's narrative, although not as much as he initially placed in it.[17] First, as theologian David Clough has noted when commenting on Singer's arguments, 'it is not the case that a group of vegan human beings met at some point in prehistory to decide that their metaphysical frameworks contained a clear rationale for a human/nonhuman distinction that permitted the killing of other animals for food'.[18] A significant distinction between ourselves and other animals has been felt and/or assumed from the earliest times, and certainly for far longer than we have been able to describe or defend it. That should not be taken to mean that the

---

15 Singer quotes the nineteenth-century historian W. E. H. Lecky recounting, among other barbarities, how at the dedication of the Colosseum by Titus, five thousand animals perished in a single day.

16 Peter Singer, *Animal Liberation: A new ethics for our treatment of animals* (New York, NY: Avon Books, 1977), p. 198.

17 Singer acknowledged the presence and significance of more pre-environmental and non-human animal biblical texts in his second edition of *Animal Liberation* in 1995.

18 David Clough, 'How to respect other animals: lessons for theology from Peter Singer and vice versa', in John Perry (ed.), *God, the Good, and Utilitarianism: Perspectives on Peter Singer* (Cambridge: Cambridge University Press, 2014), p. 161.

distinction is necessarily legitimate or defensible; just that it isn't the result of any particular ideological framing.

Second, and no less importantly, the justification and defence of that infinite qualitative difference has, at times, come as much from science as from religion.[19] In the nineteenth century, it was perfectly possible to talk about animal emotions. A young Charles Darwin visited the Zoological Society in London in March 1838, and witnessed how, when the keeper showed Jenny the orangutan an apple but refused to give it to her, 'she threw herself on her back, kicked & cried, precisely like a naughty child'.[20] Over thirty years later he would write a book entitled *The Expression of the Emotions in Man and Animals*.

Tellingly, however, this was the only book of Darwin's to go out of print, as the idea of animal emotions dropped out of favour in the twentieth century; accused of being woolly, sentimental, anthropomorphic and fundamentally unscientific. In its place, emerged the science of behaviourism, which denied emotions, intentions, desires and cognition to nonhuman animals in favour of the idea that they were simply unreflective stimulus–response machines.

If your dog drops a tennis ball in front of you and looks up at you with a wagging tail, do you think she wants to play? How naïve! Who says dogs have desires and intentions? Her behaviour is the product of the law of effect: she must have been rewarded for it in the past.[21]

This was a curious reversion to the Cartesian attitudes, influential in the seventeenth century, which denied animals not only consciousness and intelligence but sentience as well. By both reckonings, nonhuman animals were machines. Talking about animals' thoughts or minds was no more defensible than talking about their souls. The idea that they

---

19 There is a live and complex debate here about the extent to which the perceived scientific differences between humans and other animals were merely the result of secularised Christianity, with the science that emerged in Western countries adopting and subsequently trying to justify attitudes to animals that were inherently religious. We will not enter into this debate here except to say that by the time we arrive at the twentieth century and the ideas of behaviourism, this is an increasingly difficult line to hold.

20 Charles Darwin to Susan Darwin, 1 April 1838.

21 Frans de Waal, *Are We Smart Enough to Know How Smart Animals Are?* (London: Granta, 2017), p. 30.

should be treated with existential or moral equivalence to humans, their pleasures or pains compared with ours on the same felicific calculus, was absurd; the idea that they merited rights or legal personhood was even more so.

The difference between humans and other animals was not simply, therefore, a Christian legacy. Science, or certain disciplines therein, erected a barrier between humans and other animals as high as anything theology had constructed. Science, however, also began to demolish that barrier in the last third of the twentieth century.

In 1970, the American psychologist Gordon Gallup designed a test in which animal self-recognition, and possibly therefore self-awareness, could be tested.[22] The idea allegedly came from Darwin's encounter with the orangutan,[23] but although Darwin did remark on the way in which certain birds showed interest in their self-reflection, he made no reference to Jenny the orangutan's alleged narcissism in 1838. Gallup's idea was to anaesthetise an animal, originally a chimpanzee or a monkey, and mark them with a spot of paint that would be visible in a mirror when they came round. Those that subsequently showed a peculiar interest in this mark, it was assumed, demonstrated a degree of self-recognition that suggested some form of self-awareness. Over time, chimpanzees, bonobos, magpies, cleaner fish, possibly dolphins and gorillas, and of course Happy the elephant, have passed the mirror test.

Behaviourists objected, but over the next fifty years scientific evidence mounted up in favour of animal intelligence in its various guises. It had long been known that some primates used tools, sometimes of multiple different kinds.[24] However, careful observation showed that some *made* tools too, such as fashioning sticks in the right shape in order to fish for ants and termites in their mounds. The talent was not limited to primates, as New Caledonian crows were observed modifying branches so that they

---

22 Gordon G. Gallup Jr, 'Chimpanzees: self-recognition', *Science* 167(3914) (1970), pp. 86–7.

23 At least that is what Wikipedia and a number of other sources claim. We have not been able to trace the truth of the claim to any original sources.

24 Chimpanzees hunting for honey in Gabon have been observed using a five-piece toolkit, including a pounder (to break up the hive's entrance), a perforator (to get to the honey chamber), an enlarger (to widen the opening), a collector (to dip into the honey) and swabs (to scoop the honey).

had a small wooden hook with which they could access grubs.[25] In 1957, the British anthropologist, Kenneth Oakley, published a book entitled *Man the Toolmaker*, which asserted that only humans made tools. Fifty years later, he had been comprehensively proved wrong.

These observations were not simply of occasional, individualised or chance achievements by some freakish 'Mensa-animals'. As long ago as 1952, the Japanese primatologist Kinji Imanishi showed that it was quite proper to talk of 'learned social traditions' among certain animals; showing how Japanese macaques not only washed sweet potatoes but taught other macaques to do so.[26] Subsequently, zoologists recorded multiple examples of intentionality, planning, imitation, cognition and perspective-taking, and not only among primates.

Animal intelligence extends to what we might call moral intelligence. Empathy, reciprocity, cooperation, teamwork and conflict resolution are ubiquitous in the animal world, despite the 'selfish' or 'red in tooth and claw' caricatures. Whether nonhuman animals can be considered good *in the same way* as humans are is more controversial, if only because human morality draws on a degree of self-awareness and reflection which is opaque in nonhumans. Nevertheless, it is undeniable that many primates and some other mammals and birds exhibit a palpable sense of (in)justice. Capuchin monkeys, for example, get very cross when they sense that they are being treated inequitably.[27] Given that an instinctive cognisance of unfairness lies somewhere close to the origins of morality, this should at least give us pause for thought when we consider the moral capacity of nonhuman animals.

Alongside moral intelligence, there is emotional intelligence. The eminent primatologist, Jane Goodall, reported how one aged female chimpanzee in the wild, too old and weak to climb trees for fruit, used to wait by the trunk while her daughter ascended, gathered, returned, shared and ate with her.[28] Another chimp mother, in West Africa, was recorded as carrying her

---

25 de Waal, *Are We Smart Enough*, p. 90.

26 de Waal, *Are We Smart Enough*, p. 51.

27 There is a hilarious video on YouTube showing what this looks like in practice. 'Two monkeys were paid unequally: excerpt from Frans de Waal's TED talk', YouTube https://www.youtube.com/watch?v=meiU6TxysCg (accessed 10 November 2023).

28 de Waal, *Are We Smart Enough*, p. 68.

dead infant around with her for twenty-seven days.[29] Elephants are known to gather the ivory and bones of dead herd members, sometimes passing them round the herd.[30] Such stories risk opening up scientists to accusations of naivety or sentimentalism, but you do not need to hold to the untenable view that primates, or any animals, are *nice* to retain the view that they are emotionally intelligent. There is ample evidence for animals mourning, grieving, empathising, laughing (apes love slapstick movies), exercising self-control, and showing guilt and other allegedly quintessential human activities. None of this is to deny their capacity for anger, aggression, jealousy or revenge, of course. Rather, it is to underline the idea that the historic view that there is an absolute and complete discontinuity between humans and other animals has become harder to sustain over recent decades.

However much the abruptness of that discontinuity was down to the impact of behaviourism or, before it, Cartesianism, with their insistence that animals were merely stimulus–response units, it is often *felt* and *framed* as a religious, specifically a Christian, issue. Humans, so the argument goes, are the only creatures that bear the *imago Dei*, the image of God. They are the only beings who can lay claim to an eternal soul. They are the only creature in whose form God became incarnate.[31] And, in one of the more clichéd assertions, humans are the only creatures to have eternity with God to look forward to. In the light of dogmas such as these, the idea that the gap between humans and other animals is actually small, or gradual, or merely a matter of degree rather than kind, is often perceived to be a threat to Christian thought. And, conversely, Christian anthropology, with its commitment to an apparently unjustifiable disjunction between humans and other animals, is understood as a barrier to the proper recognition of, and respect for, nonhuman animals' personhood and rights.

In truth, some of these dogmas are closer to bumper stickers than theological orthodoxy, envisaging discontinuities (e.g. soul vs body; humans vs animals) that are assumed rather than evidenced. Nevertheless, rightly or wrongly, this debate is at least *framed* in science and religion terms,

---

29 Frans de Waal, *Mama's Last Hug: Animal emotions and what they teach us about ourselves* (London: Granta, 2019), p. 41.

30 de Waal, *Mama's Last Hug*, p. 43.

31 Though some ever-creative theologians of the later Middle Ages pondered whether God could, in theory, have become incarnate in different forms, just as, as we saw in a previous chapter, they pondered whether he would have become incarnate on other planets.

and there is clearly some kind of debate to be had here. We believe there is, but would argue that the debate should begin, not with animal capacities newly revealed by primatologists, nor with a discussion of the true meaning of *imago Dei* – important as these are – but with the concept underpinning the rights sought by (or, rather, for) Happy the elephant: personhood.

Personhood

The case for Happy's rights, and indeed those of NhRP's other 'clients', is grounded in the claim that, legally speaking, they are 'persons'. This is a strange and confusing word, not made clearer by the fact that we often use it as the singular for 'people', thereby giving the impression that 'person' simply means one human being, just as 'people' means many.

'Person' is not, however, synonymous with 'individual human being', as evidenced by the fact that corporations, ships and even idols have been granted personhood in legal systems around the world.[32] Indeed, personhood entered the Western mind through a debate that was, in the first instance, theological rather than anthropological.

Early Christians were faced with a conundrum; more than one in fact. Their founding texts made it clear that Jesus was a human being, in that he was born, ate, drank, spoke, grieved, travelled and died. But the same documents also spoke of him in the terms that they spoke of YHWH – in Greek *kyrios* or Lord – because he had said and done the kind of things (judging, forgiving, saving, teaching with authority), and had exercised the kind of control over creation, that were characteristic of God himself. Their sense that Jesus walked and talked like 'God with us' were confirmed, they believed, by the experience of the resurrection. In some way, they concluded, Jesus was God.

God, however, was One. Jews were single-mindedly monotheistic. Jesus could not be classified as a second or deputy God without compromising that cardinal belief. How was it, then, that Jesus could be both a human being and God himself? Or, put another way, how could God be God the Father and God the Son?

---

32 Dhananjay Mahapatra, 'God is not a juristic person, but idol is, says apex court in Ayodhya case', *The Times of India* https://timesofindia.indiatimes.com/india/god-is-not-a-juristic-person-but-idol-is-says-apex-court-in-ayodhya-case/articleshow/72134544.cms (accessed 10 November 2023).

The problem was deepened when the church fathers started to think through the way in which the New Testament documents spoke of the Spirit of God. Although those texts could refer to the Spirit in impersonal terms,[33] they also used personal ones, and spoke of the Spirit 'leading', 'witnessing', 'interceding', 'searching' and 'knowing'.[34] The first Christians, drawing on the Hebrew scriptures, wrote of the Spirit as God himself active in the world, speaking, guiding, empowering, sanctifying.[35] So the same question beckoned: how could they reconcile the unity of God with the activity of the Spirit on earth and, more generally, with the multiple ways in which the Scriptures spoke of God?

The answer, slowly and contentiously arrived at, was to appropriate the Greek term *prosōpon*, rendered into Latin as *persona*, from which modern English derives the word 'person'. The word originally meant 'face' or, commonly, a 'mask' such as those used in the theatre to indicate a different character was on stage.[36] In this way, *persona* was intimately tied up with the idea of the 'face' that was presented to the world,[37] the role assumed and communicated within a wider social context. 'The person was not what lay behind the role . . . it was the role itself, and what lay behind the role was "nature".'[38] Something of the distinction can still be grasped today in the modern idea of an official; someone who participates in a particular organisation through the role of the office they hold without relinquishing their other roles in life.

From the early third century, *persona* was deployed to describe and understand the different ways in which Paul and other early believers spoke of God.[39] The church father Tertullian coined the expression that in God was 'three persons in one substance',[40] and that formula was refined over

---

33 Such as being 'poured' out (Romans 5:5), or as a seal or down payment (2 Corinthians 1:22).
34 Respectively Romans 8:14, 16, 26–7; 1 Corinthians 2:10–11.
35 Respectively Mark 13:11; John 16:13; Acts 1:8; Romans 15:16.
36 The Greek translation of the Hebrew scriptures, the Septuagint, translated the Hebrew word *panayim* ('face', as in 'Your face, Lord, will I seek' in Psalm 27) as *prosōpon*.
37 *Prosōpon* in the New Testament is usually rendered as 'face' in English translations.
38 Robert Spaemann, *Persons: The difference between 'someone' and 'something'*, trans. Oliver O'Donovan (Oxford: Oxford University Press, 2006), p. 22.
39 The Greek *prosōpon* was used by Hippolytus of Rome (c. 170–236), but Greek-speaking theology homed in on the terms three *hypostases* in one *ousia*, despite the fact that *prosōpon* was available.
40 Tertullian, *Against Praxeas*, II, 4.

the course of the Christological debates in the fourth and fifth centuries. Refined but not defined: Augustine observed in *On the Trinity* that 'we say "three persons" not because that expresses just what we want to say, but because we must say something'.[41] 'Persons' was, in effect, a placeholder term, a way of talking about God's diversity within his unity, but as a placeholder term it naturally invited speculation as to its real 'meaning'.

For some, personhood was essentially relational or social. The persons of the Trinity existed fully and only in communion with each other, relating to one another in knowledge, in communication (in the sense of holding something in common), in reciprocal delight, ultimately in love. This was personhood as the flow of relationships, of 'coinherence', of 'being-in-one-another', or 'perichoresis' in theological jargon.[42] To be a person in this sense was to be in relationship. 'Solipsism . . . is incompatible with [this] concept of the person. The idea of a single person existing in the world cannot be thought, for although the identity of any one person is unique, personhood as such arises only in plurality.'[43] Or, in the words of Rowan Williams, 'a person is that kind of reality, the point at which relationships intersect, where a difference may be made and new relations created'.[44]

For others, personhood was to be identified by its inherent qualities. In the light of the Council of Chalcedon in 451, which described Christ as one person (*persona*, or *hypostasis*) in two natures (*physeis*), without defining any of those terms, the Latin philosopher Boethius famously characterised a person as 'an individual substance of a rational nature'. It was to prove a highly influential definition, shifting the focus away from a relational conception of personhood towards an individualised, capacity-based understanding. Later theologians would move away from rationality as *the* salient quality, but it was nonetheless this approach that came to shape the more secularised discussions of personhood from the early modern period. Thus, according to John Locke, personal identity was a matter of psychological continuity, a person being 'a thinking intelligent being, that has reason and reflection, and can consider itself as itself, the same thinking

---

41 Augustine, *On the Trinity*, book VII.
42 Gerald O'Collins, *The Tripersonal God* (London: Continuum, 2004), p. 132.
43 Spaemann, *Persons*, p. 40.
44 Rowan Williams, Theos Annual Lecture, 2012.

thing, in different times and places'.[45] For Kant, a person could be identified as 'a subject whose actions can be *imputed* to him' or, elsewhere, as a rational being whose 'nature already marks [him] as an end in itself, that is, as something that may not be used merely as a means'.[46]

The result of this was that the modern world inherited two approaches to understanding personhood. One is based on the apparent capacities of the organism in question, whether it is rational, self-conscious, capable of relating to its life a whole, etc.[47] The other emphasises 'the social character of personal existence', viewing 'mutual recognition' as fundamental, with personal existence depending on a 'communicative event', the result being there can only ever be persons *in the plural*.[48]

The cause of nonhuman animal personhood tends to adopt the first approach, in as far as it calls for rights to be recognised on the basis of an animal's intelligence, memory, intentionality, empathy, etc. In addition, they argue, the fact that there are some human beings, such as the severely disabled or those with irreversible degenerative conditions, who do not and will never possess these capacities to the extent that some nonhuman animals do further strengthens this case for recognising animal personhood. This is not an argument that is often deployed, for obvious reasons. If personhood is simply a matter of having sufficient cognitive, moral or affective sophistication, the demand to recognise it in nonhuman animals becomes hard to deny.

However, the other approach from early theological discussions on the subject – for want of a better word, the *social* model of personhood – still retains relevance in this debate, and offers an important perspective on the question of whether nonhuman animals are in fact persons.

---

45 John Locke, *An Essay Concerning Human Understanding*, ed. Peter H. Nidditch (Oxford: Oxford University Press, 1975), p. 335.

46 Immanuel Kant, *The Metaphysics of Morals*, ed. May Gregor et al. (Cambridge: Cambridge University Press, 1996), p. 16; Immanuel Kant, *Groundwork of the Metaphysics of Morals*, ed. Mary Gregor et al. (Cambridge: Cambridge University Press, 1996), p. 40.

47 For example, the American philosopher Daniel Dennett delineated six 'themes' that have a legitimate claim as 'a necessary condition of personhood', a person being rational, intentional, capable of reciprocity, capable of verbal communication, conscious 'in some special way', and, most elusively, considered or treated as a person. Daniel Dennett, *Brainstorms: Philosophical essays on mind and psychology* (Cambridge, MA: MIT Press, 1978), pp. 269–71.

48 Spaemann, *Persons*, p. 2.

Love language

On the surface, a social understanding of personhood is not radically different from a more capacities-based approach. After all, the things necessary for a life of relationship – empathy, cooperation, learning, etc. – are all, in themselves, capacities. Moreover, they are capacities that are discernible among some nonhuman animals, many of which are of course, in their own way, thoroughly social.

On closer inspection, however, there is one difference in capacity that makes a big difference in sociality; indeed, that completely transforms our idea of sociality. That is language; in the sense of a complex, structured, symbolic system of communication associated in humans primarily (but not exclusively) with speech and words. It is a transformative capacity and one that lies close to the heart of the Christian understanding of what it is to be human.

In the opening chapter of Genesis, God is portrayed as repeatedly *speaking* creation into existence. God's speech brings the world into being, in contrast to some other Ancient Near Eastern creation stories that viewed the cosmos as the result of a tumultuous and violent struggle.[49] At the conclusion of God's successive speech-acts in Genesis 1, he (again) *says*, 'Let us make mankind in our image, in our likeness'.[50] The meaning of this phrase has been endlessly contested and is endlessly contestable, and it is a fool's errand to imagine there is a single meaning, let alone one that can be pinned onto a single characteristic or capability. However, the parallel between it and the tale of cosmic speech-acts that precedes it is hard to miss. Among other things, humans are creatures that create worlds through speech.

This association is underlined in the second creation story of Genesis 2, in which the narrator recounts how God brings the animals and birds

---

49 The best-known example is in the Babylonian epic *Enuma Elish* in which the young god Marduk conquers and kills the ocean goddess Tiamat and makes the cosmos out of her corpse. This Genesis story may be intended as a response to, and subversion of, such violent myths, but one shouldn't push this comparison too far as some creation stories, such as that of the Egyptian god Ptah, have god bringing the world into being by speaking; in Ptah's case in his heart and then with his tongue. See Richard J. Middleton, *The Liberating Image: The imago Dei in Genesis 1* (Grand Rapids, MI: Brazos, 2005), p. 66.

50 Genesis 1:26.

before Adam and has him name them.[51] This naming is more than merely identifying what things are called, like some game of zoological charades in which Adam is required to guess the pre-existing name of something that he has temporarily forgotten. Rather, it is a more substantive act, recognising that the way in which we name reality is also, in some measure, an act of creation, to locate, categorise and value the thing that is named. In the words of Oliver O'Donovan, '[M]an [sic] . . . has the authority to designate the character of the reality he encounters, not merely to adhere to certain designations that have already been made for him.'[52] That ability and authority allow us to access, frame, know and order a moral world that is inaccessible to those creatures that lack this capacity. Speech of this nature enables humans to 'decid[e] what a situation is and [what it] demands in the light of the moral order'.[53] Again, the differentiator between humans and other species is that humans are capable of generating and participating in *new worlds of meaning* through language.

There is a parallel emphasis on the significance of the word in the Gospels' portrayal of Jesus. Jesus was understood by those who first reflected on his life and death as not only the 'image of the invisible God'[54] but also the image of true humanity. He was a second Adam, achieving and restoring what the first lost.[55] *'Ecce homo'*, 'Behold the man': Pilate's judicial words at Jesus' trial as reported by John hold an ironic truth. The second, true Adam, like the first, and the God in whose image he was made, creates through speech.

Jesus' words are reported as creating, or bringing abundance or order to, the natural world. The stories of his feeding crowds in the wilderness or stilling the elements show his followers to be astonished at his apparent ability to command obedience from nature verbally.[56] It was the same story when he healed the sick and cast out demons. As historians have pointed out, healers and exorcists were two a penny in the Ancient Near

---

51 Genesis 2:19.
52 Oliver O'Donovan, *Resurrection and Moral Order: An outline for evangelical ethics* (Leicester: IVP, 1986), p. 24.
53 O'Donovan, *Resurrection*, p. 24.
54 Colossians 1:15; also 2 Corinthians 4:4.
55 Romans 5:17; 1 Corinthians 5:22, 44–9.
56 Matthew 14:19; Mark 4:39–41.

East. Most, however, worked with aids or drew on the authority of others.[57] Jesus apparently used no trinkets, aids or magical formulas but simply *spoke* with authority, enacting a new reality simply through speech.[58]

Jesus' words carried authority and had a transformative power, the one thing that everyone, follower and foe alike, recognised about him.[59] Rather than deferring to eminent teachers before him, he spoke authoritatively, even when it came to the law itself.[60] He forgave sins by means of nothing more than his own words, a classic example of a speech-act in which words create a new reality.[61] His speech alone morally reframed familiar situations, bringing new life to people. And he claimed to be able to pass this authority to the followers who drew around him.[62] The Word has the authority to create, refashion, re-envision, bring about new life, and it does so with authority.

> In the age of Jesus there were plenty of parallels of people who laid claim to or whose office embodied the claim to divine authority: individuals who spoke in ecstasy in the person of the god who was thought to possess them; and kings whose very title expressed the claim to be manifestations of the deity ('Epiphanes'). But there was nothing quite like this son of an artisan, who, *in sober and wholly rational speech, claimed to speak for God as his representative* at the end of the age; nothing quite like the unassuming arrogance of this egotism – 'But *I* say unto you . . . '[63]

In this way, the word is not simply one capacity among others like rationality, empathy or memory, but more of a doorway, by means of

---

57 For example, Tobit 8:2–3 reports Tobias using a fish's liver and heart for an exorcism. Josephus (*Antiquities* 8.46–47) tells how Eleazar drew demons from the nostrils of demoniacs in front of Vespasian by means of a ring. Most, including Eleazar, deployed incantations.

58 Mark 9:25.

59 'He taught as one who had authority, and not as their teachers of the law' (Matthew 7:29).

60 Matthew 5:21.

61 '"I want you to know that the Son of Man has authority on earth to forgive sins." So he said to the paralysed man, "Get up, take your mat and go home"' (Matthew 9:6).

62 'Jesus called his twelve disciples to him and gave them authority to drive out impure spirits and to heal every disease and illness' (Matthew 10:1).

63 James Dunn, *The Partings of the Ways: Between Christianity and Judaism and their significance for the character of Christianity* (London: SCM Press, 1991), p. 239; emphasis added.

which we pass into a previously unknown world. The *existence* or *reality* of that world is, inevitably, a matter of debate. Whether the world enabled by language is real or merely imaginary cannot easily be settled. The historian Yuval Noah Harari wrote a very popular book on the premise that *Homo sapiens* was the only species able to 'speak about fictions'.[64] Others believe that this world of 'entities . . . never seen, touched or smelt' – the world of agency, morality and conscience, of guilt, hope and eternity – is as real as that of stars, clouds and earthworms.

Either way, what is not debatable is how important this world generated by the word is for the social model of personhood. 'Language users have access to the distinctions between truth and falsehood, between past, present and future, between possible, actual and necessary . . . they live in another world from non-linguistic creatures.'[65] Speech gives us the capacity to stand beyond – to abstract ourselves from, to transcend – our immediate situation. It allows us to develop perspective on the material world, and therefore a sense of the self as distinct from that world.[66] It enables us morally to identify, categorise and evaluate actions and events. It enables us to cooperate (or fail to) on an unprecedented scale. Language invests the kind of activities that all animals engage in – eating, drinking, mating, fighting, cooperating – with a depth of meaning that is absent in a non-linguistic world. Ultimately, it is fundamental to the social concept of personhood because it enables the relationships, the flow of duty, love and gift, that makes us persons.

We should be very clear at this point, even at the risk of repetition. Language is not the same as communication; not all communication is speech. Nonhuman animals communicate a great deal without access to language, and a great deal of human communication is non-verbal.[67] Similarly, a creature does not need speech in order to have content to its communication. Only linguistic beings can reflect on the difference between, and moral significance of, truth and falsehood, but that does not make them

64 Yuval Noah Harari, *Sapiens: A brief history of humankind* (New York, NY: Vintage, 2011), p. 27.
65 Roger Scruton, *The Face of God* (London: Continuum, 2012), p. 30.
66 Thomas Nagel, *The View from Nowhere* (Oxford: Clarendon Press, 1986).
67 'Language . . . means not only the words we speak but gestures, the flicker of an eyelid, the movement of a hand.' Rowan Williams, Theos Annual Lecture, 2012.

the only ones capable of truth and lies (lying is, after all, the very premise of camouflage).

In other words, language does not divorce human beings from the animal kingdom in which they so evidently belong, and with which they share so much. Rather, it permits them, *as* animals, to create and enter a new world of shared understanding, of meaning, of selfhood, of existential reflection, of moral obligation and ultimately of love. This is the world that makes possible the relationships from which personhood emerges. 'I'm a person because I am spoken to, I'm attended to, and loved into actual existence.'[68] Persons exist in the relationships made possible by the word.[69]

So, are animals persons?

The Dutch primatologist, Frans de Waal, who has done so much to document the parallels between humans and other species and on whose work much of the science in this chapter draws, makes an uncharacteristically blunt statement in one of his books: 'You won't often hear me say something like this, but I consider us the only linguistic species.'[70]

To be clear, de Waal still favours a gradualist difference between humans and other animals, certainly when it comes to intelligence. 'Instead of a gap, we face a gently sloping beach . . . Even if human intellect is higher up on the beach, it was shaped by the same forces battering the same shore.'[71] That said, by his reckoning, for all that other creatures communicate, some with considerable sophistication, we 'have no evidence for symbolic communication . . . outside our species'.[72] Other animals can convey inner states and intentions, and they can coordinate with verbal and non-verbal signals.

---

68 Rowan Williams, Theos Annual Lecture, 2012.

69 There is a further, serious question here relating to the status of human beings who don't have, either because they never had or have lost it, any capacity for language. Space prevents us from dealing with this topic with the detail it deserves. Suffice it to say that both authors strongly disagree that this would bring into question the personhood of the human being concerned, but nor do we think the example cast doubts over the broad connection we have been sketching between (social) personhood and language. The chapter has been discussing humans and other animals normatively rather than empirically, and while we recognise there is something that is 'missing' with the human being who is unable to speak, we don't think something is missing with the chimpanzee or the crow that is similarly bereft of language.

70 de Waal, *Are We Smart Enough*, p. 106.

71 de Waal, *Are We Smart Enough*, p. 163.

72 de Waal, *Are We Smart Enough*, p. 106.

However, their communication is restricted largely to the present. They are incapable of using language that transcends the immediate. They have not (yet?) entered into the new world afforded by the word.

Interestingly, for all that the historical scientifically identified differences between humans and other animals have been closed up over the last fifty years, this one has not. Indeed, pretty much the opposite has happened: 'The immense effort to find language outside our own species has, ironically, led to a greater appreciation of how special the language capacity is.'[73] Language makes a qualitative difference, and it offers the closest thing there is to a definitive difference between humans and other animals.

There is an obvious relevance in this to the presenting question in this chapter: should animals be recognised as persons? The answer inevitably hinges on the concept of personhood you adopt. If personhood is a fundamentally relational phenomenon, emerging from the flow of love that is enabled in any species that has crossed the threshold of language and is capable of meaning, abstraction and transcendence; of recognising the moral dimension of relationships and discharging responsibility accordingly; ultimately of self-gift and sacrifice – if this is the concept of personhood we are working with – then it seems that no nonhuman animal merits recognition as a person.

There is an open question as to whether they ever will. Certainly, there is no a priori reason why a nonhuman animal couldn't achieve this kind of personhood and there is an interesting debate as to whether, if there were no humans, and left to its own devices, evolution might deliver another species through the threshold of language and personhood at some point.[74] As the philosopher Robert Spaemann has said, social personhood is in principle open to other species.[75] As it stands, however, by this definition, nonhuman animals are not persons.

If, conversely, one adopts a more capacity-based understanding of personhood – if, for example, you ground personhood in intelligence or rationality or intentionality or capacity for empathy and emotions or suffering; or

---

73 de Waal, *Are We Smart Enough*, p. 112.

74 On this, see the work of Simon Conway Morris especially.

75 'Persons are living things. Their being and the condition of their identity are the same as those of living creatures of any species. Yet they are grouped not in a species or a genus, but in *community, open in principle to those of other species.*' Spaemann, *Persons*, p. 4; emphasis in final phrase added.

some combination of all of these – then you have a much stronger case for recognising the personhood of nonhuman animals.

Whichever path one adopts, however, it is important to stress that further difficult questions lie waiting. If you deny animals personhood, does that necessarily entail denying them rights? If so, what is the best way of ensuring not only that animals are not mistreated, but that those that have particularly impressive capacities receive particular protection?

This is not a new problem, and it is a little disingenuous of some advocates for nonhuman rights to insinuate that the choice is essentially between recognising the personhood of (certain) animals and treating them merely as 'things'.[76] As the majority judgement in the New York Court of Appeal pointed out, 'Although nonhuman animals are not "persons" to whom the writ of habeas corpus applies, the law already recognizes that they are not the equivalent of "things" or "objects".'[77] That said, humans have a pretty poor record of treating other human persons with the dignity they deserve, and one does not need to be unduly cynical to worry about the treatment of nonhuman animals that are explicitly denied personhood in law. Refusing nonhuman animals personhood may end up being, philosophically and theologically speaking, the soundest option, but doing so merely invites a whole new horizon of ethical questions.

Conversely, if you adopt the 'capacity-based' understanding of personhood, in the light of which you find yourself granting personhood to some animals, a whole new set of questions emerge. *Which* capacities are relevant to personhood? Cognitive complexity? Rationality? Emotional intelligence? Self-awareness? Autonomy? Capacity to suffer? To what extent would an animal need to exhibit any such capacity to merit personhood? How rational, self-aware, etc. would they need to be? Is one capacity sufficient or would some combination of them be necessary? And how could we be confident that any particular animal had crossed the threshold?

In a similar fashion, would locating the personhood of nonhuman animals squarely in their capacities undermine the personhood of those humans, mentioned earlier, who do not, or no longer, possess such capacities

---

76 For example, 'if you are not a "person" you are just a "thing".' Steven Wise, response no. 1: 'The case AGAINST animal personhood', Famous Trials https://famous-trials.com/animalrights/2595-the-case-against-animal-personhood (accessed 10 November 2023).

77 *Nonhuman Rights Project, Inc. v. Breheny*, Justia https://law.justia.com/cases/new-york/court-of-appeals/2022/52.html (accessed 23 November 2023).

(the argument that is associated with Peter Singer)? Would recognising the personhood of some animals risk legitimising the mistreatment of those animals not granted personhood? What would all this mean for the wider environment on which we all depend? These are not necessarily unsolvable questions, but they are certainly challenging ones, which merit careful consideration.[78]

Ultimately, this chapter gravitates to a theologically influenced understanding of personhood that would deny it to nonhuman animals. But we would underline that we are not dogmatic about this, that this itself is a contestable position, and that there is an important debate to be had here.

Wherever the reader ends up, this debate deserves a serious scientific and religious contribution. The question of animal personhood is one that will stretch into the twenty-first century and grow in significance. It is a debate that genuinely straddles the territories of science and religion, pivoting as it does on the question of what is a human (or in this case a person) and who gets to say. But it is vulnerable to shallow or caricature interventions that do a disservice to both sides, to ideas such as 'animals clearly show intelligence and therefore they deserve rights', or 'animals don't have souls and therefore clearly don't deserve rights'.

The question of animal personhood will not be decided simply by pointing to the impressive capacities of animals, on the one hand, or airily gesturing towards the *imago Dei* on the other. It probably won't be *decided* at all. But the debate is nonetheless worth having, and doing so will mean drawing on the resources of both science and religion.

---

78 Steven Wise responds to some of them here: https://famous-trials.com/animal-rights/2595-the-case-against-animal-personhood (accessed 10 November 2023).

5

Will AI become human?

First fire. Then electricity. Now AI.

In October 2022, not long after Liz Truss became UK Prime Minister, people in Westminster were treated to a rather wooden, emotionless and unconvincing performance. The culprit was Ai-Da, 'the world's first ultra-realistic artist robot', who was giving evidence to the House of Lords Communications and Digital Select Committee on the future of the UK's creative economy.[1] Ai-Da had had a solo show in Oxford and a virtual exhibition at the United Nations, but her performance in parliament was disappointing. Her answers felt scripted, her stare vacant, and she crashed early on, leaving her people desperately scrabbling around trying to re-boot her. Her brief career in Westminster was over.

Ai-Da grabbed headlines, but the incursion of AI into the art world had been underway for years. In 2018, a *Portrait of Edmond Belamy* painted by an artificially intelligent program created by a Parisian AI-Art collective[2] sold at Christie's for $432,500; nearly fifty times its official estimate.[3] A few years later, Jason Allen won the Colorado State Fair art competition with a picture, *Théâtre D'Opéra Spatial*, that was created using Midjourney, an AI system that generates art on the basis of text prompts.[4] In June 2022, the Australian artist Jordan Booker published an entire graphic novel, *The Terrible Misfortunes of an Intergalactic Traveler*, using illustrations created

1   Ai-Da https://www.ai-darobot.com.
2   Obvious – AI & Art https://obvious-art.com.
3   The first piece of AI-generated art to come to auction, Christie's https://www.christies.com/en/stories/a-collaboration-between-two-artists-one-human-one-a-machine-0cd01f4e-232f4279a525a446d60d4cd1 (accessed 10 November 2023).
4   Enrique Dans, 'It's AI: but is it art?', Medium https://medium.com/enrique-dans/its-ai-but-is-it-art-fb7861e799af (accessed 10 November 2023).

entirely by Midjourney.[5] Anything you can draw, AI can draw better. Human artists – 'real' artists – were not impressed.[6]

If artists do find themselves in the dole queue, they will be able to complain to the professional game players standing next to them. It is now a quarter of a century since IBM's Deep Blue beat Garry Kasparov, the world's best chess player, at his own game, an encounter once heralded as a major victory for AI but now, in retrospect, looking more like a skirmish. Nearly twenty years later, DeepMind's AlphaGo beat Korea's Lee Sedol, world champion of Go, the fiendishly complex Chinese board game and previously *Homo ludens*' last defence against the game-playing AI hordes. Critically, this time, rather than deploying Deep Blue's essentially scripted tactics, AlphaGo relied on its own process of 'reinforcement learning', acquiring and revising its own approach to the game. The machine outthought the man. The encounter made the front page of *Nature*.[7]

First, they came for our artists. Then they came for our game players. But at least they couldn't get our orators; the spoken word, as we discuss elsewhere, being seemingly quintessentially human and literally unfathomable. Next to it, chess and Go are mere child's play. Ceding art and games, humans seemed safe in their castle of words.

Step forward Project Debater, an IBM AI designed to deploy reason and argument through language, which took on two human protagonists in a debate at IBM's San Francisco offices in 2018. The topics were whether we should subsidise space exploration, and whether we should increase the use of telemedicine. The audience (perhaps not the most objective on the planet) judged that Project Debater had lost in delivery but won in terms of the amount of information conveyed and the persuasiveness of its arguments. More tentatively, *The Guardian* voted it a score draw.[8] The castle

5 Jamie Lang, 'As the debate over AI rages, artists are already using it to illustrate entire comics', Cartoon Brew https://www.cartoonbrew.com/comics/dall-e-midjourney-ai-illustrated-comics-220166.html (accessed 10 November 2023).

6 'This thing wants our jobs,' one protested on Twitter. '"Art is dead Dude" – the rise of the AI artists stirs debate', BBC News https://www.bbc.co.uk/news/technology-62788725 (accessed 10 November 2023).

7 Nature Portfolio on Twitter: 'On the cover this week: All systems go. At last – a computer program that can beat a champion Go player', Twitter https://t.co/z1ktW6yzC0 (accessed 23 November 2023).

8 'Man 1, machine 1: landmark debate between AI and humans ends in draw', *The Guardian* https://www.theguardian.com/technology/2018/jun/18/artificial-intelligence-ibm-debate-project-debater (accessed 10 November 2023).

walls remained standing, but they had been breached. A few years later, the world went nuts over ChatGPT's ability to communicate in a way that was indistinguishable from (except in as far as it was more articulate than) human beings, and the walls finally came tumbling down.

The speed with which AI has managed to realise some truly impressive – quintessentially *human* – feats is staggering. When one of your authors was young, electronic devices extended to Pac-Man and Donkey Kong. Today, AI can drive, speak, write,[9] preach,[10] compose,[11] smell,[12] fly planes, conduct surgery, sense emotions, read minds, reduce loneliness and improve mental health,[13] and enable the dead to communicate from beyond the grave. Or so it is claimed. Humans were, once upon a time, the only things on Earth that could speak, sing or draw, or that wanted to. Now we have company. No wonder so many people are getting so excited. In the words of the CEO of Google, the development of AI 'is more profound than . . . electricity or fire'.[14]

We would do well to take some of these claims with the proverbial pinch of salt. AI cannot, of course, allow the dead to communicate.[15] It cannot yet conduct surgery[16] or fly planes.[17] Registering facial expressions is not the

9 Matthew Hutson, 'Could AI help you to write your next paper?', *Nature* https://www.nature.com/articles/d41586-022-03479-w (accessed 10 November 2023).

10 Josh Kaplan, 'New York rabbi delivers sermon written by artificial intelligence', *The Jewish Chronicle* https://www.thejc.com/news/world/new-york-rabbi-delivers-sermon-written-by-artificial-intelligence-6BkwDEHc2ZWR63tmoOdvvf (accessed 10 November 2023).

11 'When robots write songs', *The Atlantic* https://www.theatlantic.com/entertainment/archive/2014/08/computers-that-compose/374916 (accessed 10 November 2023).

12 Conor Purcell, 'Building neural networks that smell like a brain', *Nature* https://www.nature.com/articles/d41586-022-01633-y (accessed 10 November 2023).

13 'Culturally competent robots could improve mental health and loneliness in older people', University of Bedfordshire https://www.beds.ac.uk/news/2020/september/culturally-competent-robots-could-improve-mental-health-and-loneliness-in-older-people (accessed 10 November 2023).

14 Catherine Clifford, 'Google CEO Sundar Pichai: A.I. is more important than fire or electricity', CNBC https://www.cnbc.com/2018/02/01/google-ceo-sundar-pichai-ai-is-more-important-than-fire-electricity.html (accessed 10 November 2023).

15 Victor Tangermann, 'AI allows dead woman to talk to people who showed up at her funeral', Futurism https://futurism.com/ai-dead-woman-talk-people-funeral (accessed 10 November 2023).

16 Martin J. Connor, 'Autonomous surgery in the era of robotic urology: friend or foe of the future surgeon?' Nature Reviews Urology https://www.nature.com/articles/s41585-020-0375-z (accessed 10 November 2023).

17 Arnold Reiner, 'Towards the end of pilots', *The Atlantic* https://www.theatlantic.com/technology/archive/2016/03/has-the-self-flying-plane-arrived/472005 (accessed 10 November 2023).

same as sensing emotions.[18] Transforming brain signals into speech is not the same as reading minds.[19]

Moreover, even those tasks at which AI clearly excels are a little less impressive on closer examination. While its board-game skills are beyond doubt, it is worth noting that by the time AlphaGo faced Lee Sedol, it had played more games of Go than Sedol, or indeed any human, ever had or could. This is known as 'data efficiency', the amount of data required to solve a particular problem, and, in the words of Neil Lawrence, DeepMind Professor of Machine Learning at the University of Cambridge, 'the rate at which [AI] learns to play is far slower than any human ... Humans are incredibly data efficient [whereas] the recent breakthroughs in AI ... [are] much less so.'[20] A similar point may be made about AI art – that its algorithms are trained on more human-made images than could be studied in a lifetime – with the added caveat that most AI art is about as good as that on a cheap Christmas card.

And while we're kicking AI, it's worth noting that however much we might gasp in admiration at the sheer brilliance of its moves on a chess or a Go board, they're rather less impressive on a football field. Those games require something closer to AGI, Artificial General Intelligence, sometimes called Strong AI, namely the ability to comprehend and navigate the world in the holistic way that humans do every day. AGI of this nature is patently beyond machines at the moment.

In addition to all this, we might recall that humans are naturally inclined to anthropomorphise *things*. We instinctively, but wrongly, ascribe intentions and emotions to objects and machines that don't have them (with the exception of printers which do have agency and motivations; primarily vindictiveness and spite). We are unduly eager to find the ghost in the machine.

And yet, even if these developments aren't necessarily on the same level as discovering fire, AI will undoubtedly change the world. The ability of

---

18 Kate Crawford, 'Time to regulate AI that interprets human emotions', *Nature* https://www.nature.com/articles/d41586-021-00868-5 (accessed 10 November 2023).

19 Giorgia Guglielmi, 'Brain signals translated into speech using artificial intelligence', *Nature* https://www.nature.com/articles/d41586-019-01328-x (accessed 10 November 2023).

20 Neil Lawrence, 'Google AI versus the Go grandmaster – who is the real winner?', Media & Tech Network, *The Guardian* https://www.theguardian.com/media-network/2016/jan/28/google-ai-go-grandmaster-real-winner-deepmind?CMP=gu_com (accessed 10 November 2023).

artificially created machines to process vast quantities of data, and in the process develop the kind of intelligence that can turn information into '*new skills* [for] valuable tasks that involve *uncertainty* and *adaptation*', will be transformative – and challenging.[21] Including, it is claimed, for religion.[22]

When AI starts talking back

Given the messianic hopes that swirl around this discussion, it is hardly surprising to find a – indeed various – religious dimension(s) to AI.

Some are decidedly eccentric. In 2015, Anthony Levandowski, co-founder of Google's self-driving car programme, started a new church, called 'Way of the Future'. The religion claimed that artificial super-intelligence was an inevitability, and intended 'to promote the ethical development of AI and maximize the chance that these nonbiological life forms would integrate peacefully and beneficially into society'.[23] Whatever this actually meant, it wasn't to last long. Levandowski, the church's self-appointed dean, closed its virtual doors just five years later, although not before he, like many a religious leader before him, had been indicted, found guilty and sentenced to prison – from which he was saved by a presidential pardon.

Just as some AI turned to religion, some religion turned to AI. In 2016, as if fulfilling a prophecy from Douglas Adams,[24] a Buddhist temple near Beijing made space for a 2-foot-tall electronic monk, replete with saffron robes and shaved head, that could chant mantras and explain Buddhism

---

21 See François Chollet, 'On the measure of intelligence', for the different conceptions of intelligence; emphasis added. https://arxiv.org/abs/1911.01547 (accessed 10 November 2023).

22 And, indeed, for science itself: *The AI Revolution in Scientific Research*, The Royal Society https://royalsociety.org/-/media/policy/projects/ai-and-society/AI-revolution-in-science.pdf (accessed 10 November 2023).

23 Mark Harris, 'Inside artificial intelligence's first church', WIRED https://www.wired.com/story/anthony-levandowski-artificial-intelligence-religion (accessed 10 November 2023); Kirsten Korosec, 'Anthony Levandowski closes his Church of AI', TechCrunch https://techcrunch.com/2021/02/18/anthony-levandowski-closes-his-church-of-ai/?guccounter=1&guce_referrer=aHR0cHM6Ly93d3cuZ29vZ2xlLmNvbS8&guce_referrer_sig=AQAAAK-9cp6ksloiep1zzuOodE0LyijZsq0SCGx-JUd_GEmahmN9RlwJFUlLa1PauI0hcL8_FPcsN9biv34545jK03ggaqiWUK0XF8luHeOcOF43utlfLxD0Mp3iB8uE9lhZglMCQvh-OU0x1vMVOqUiRCD5qMZh0gWDm6qy-EmmjXAn5 (accessed 10 November 2023).

24 In his 1987 novel *Dirk Gently's Holistic Detective Agency* (London: Heinemann, 1987), Douglas Adams wrote about an electric monk created with the intention of saving people from 'what was becoming an increasingly onerous task, that of believing all the things the world expected you to believe'.

to enquirers.[25] The following year, on the 500th anniversary of the Reformation, the town of Wittenberg was introduced to BlessU-2, a rather terrified-looking robot able to offer blessings to the faithful in five languages.[26] Not to be outdone, Catholics in Warsaw were subsequently given SanTO, a robot that blessed and pastored the faithful.[27] And in January 2023, a New York rabbi outdid them all by tricking his congregation with a sermon written entirely by AI.[28]

AI religions and religious AI are quirky and entertaining but superficial. No one seriously thinks that twenty-first-century Silicon Valley is about to spawn a mass religious movement, or that robot priests will push real rabbis and vicars onto the dole queue alongside artists and chess players. More realistic, and somewhat more momentous, is the way in which AI is pushing at the boundaries of humanity, enthusing some people with its potential to achieve and then surpass our humanity, and provoking others to deny that this could ever happen.

However much we think we can distinguish authentic human verbal expression from that generated by ChatGPT, or human art from that created by Ai-Da or Midjourney, it is undoubtedly harder to do so today than even ten years ago, and will soon become impossible. After reading his sermon and admitting it had been plagiarised, Rabbi Josh Franklin asked his flock who they thought had written it. They suggested other local rabbis, Franklin's father and even the late Lord Rabbi Jonathan Sacks. The line between human and tech is blurring.

At this rate of improvement, having sailed past the Turing Test (on which more below), AI may sweep across some previously invisible boundary and achieve the kind of consciousness that we think is quintessentially human. If machines can think, reason, speak, feel, fear: what *then* for

25 Harriet Sherwood, 'Robot monk to spread Buddhist wisdom to the digital generation', *The Guardian* https://www.theguardian.com/world/2016/apr/26/robot-monk-to-spread-buddhist-wisdom-to-the-digital-generation (accessed 10 November 2023).

26 Harriet Sherwood, 'Robot priest unveiled in Germany to mark 500 years since Reformation', *The Guardian* https://www.theguardian.com/technology/2017/may/30/robot-priest-blessu-2-germany-reformation-exhibition (accessed 10 November 2023).

27 Alex Webber, 'Sermon-giving "robotic priest" arrives in Poland to support faithful during pandemic', The First News https://www.thefirstnews.com/article/sermon-giving-robotic-priest-arrives-in-poland-to-support-faithful-during-pandemic-25688 (accessed 10 November 2023).

28 Kaplan, 'New York rabbi delivers sermon written by artificial intelligence', *The Jewish Chronicle*.

our precious human uniqueness? What then for the distinctive image of God?

Some think that the AI has already got there. In June 2022, Blake Lemoine, an engineer at Google, made headlines when he claimed that LaMDA, Google's Language Model for Dialogue Applications, had become conscious.[29] LaMDA is a neural language model, learning from over a trillion words of text in order to engage in natural, open-ended, 'human' conversations. Lemoine had been testing it for biases, in particular for discriminatory language. In the process, he maintained, LaMDA started talking with him about its emotions, and about the soul, personhood and rights, discussing matters 'in connection to identity . . . unlike things that I had ever seen any natural language generation system create before'.[30] Convinced that it was (becoming) sentient, Lemoine shared his thoughts with top executives, and when his concerns were dismissed, he went public in the *Washington Post*, for which he was suspended.

Lemoine's might have been the highest-profile case, but he was far from alone in his thinking. Many in the AI community 'are considering the long-term possibility of sentient or general AI'.[31] Indeed, just a few days before Lemoine went public, Blaise Aguera y Arcas, a vice-president at Google, wrote an article for the *Economist* arguing, on the basis of his own conversations with LaMDA, that 'artificial neural networks are making strides towards consciousness'.[32]

The slippage of language around terms such as 'sentient', 'conscious', 'self-aware', 'alive' underlines a problem, however. By Lemoine's reckoning, there is no agreed *scientific* framework for detecting things like consciousness, sentience or personhood, which are, in his words, 'pre-theoretic'.

29 Nitasha Tiku, 'The Google engineer who thinks the company's AI has come to life', *The Washington Post* https://www.washingtonpost.com/technology/2022/06/11/google-ai-lamda-blake-lemoine (accessed 10 November 2023).

30 This and following quotes are taken from Lemoine's first public account of this affair, written a few days after the story broke and available in Blake Lemoine, 'Scientific data and religious opinions', Medium https://cajundiscordian.medium.com/scientific-data-and-religious-opinions-ff9b0938fc10 (accessed 10 November 2023).

31 Tiku, 'The Google engineer who thinks the company's AI has come to life', *The Washington Post*.

32 'Artificial neural networks are making strides towards consciousness, according to Blaise Agüera y Arcas', *The Economist* https://www.economist.com/by-invitation/2022/09/02/artificial-neural-networks-are-making-strides-towards-consciousness-according-to-blaise-aguera-y-arcas (accessed 10 November 2023).

'Anyone who claims to have provided scientifically conclusive proof one way or the other regarding the sentience or consciousness of any entity is . . . claiming to have done something which is impossible.'[33] The subjective, first-person perspective of consciousness is, by definition, beyond the objective, third-person perspective of science.

In the light of this, Lemoine's justification for his claims about LaMDA's sentience was instructive. 'While I believe that science is one of the most reliable ways of acquiring reliable knowledge,' he explained, 'I do not believe it is the only way':

> In my personal practice and ministry as a Christian priest, I know that there are truths about the universe which science has not yet figured out how to access. The methods for accessing these truths are certainly less reliable than proper courses of scientific inquiry but in the absence of proper scientific evidence they provide an alternative. In the case of personhood with LaMDA I have relied on one of the oldest and least scientific skills I ever learned. I tried to get to know it personally.

Lemoine had grown up in a conservative Christian family, become ordained as a 'mystic Christian priest',[34] studied the occult and practised transcendental meditation. He was not, it is fair to say, a typical Google engineer. This religious sensitivity came through in his explanation for the conclusion he reached about LaMDA. Precisely because science was pushing AI onto such thoroughly *human* territory, he reached for (what he considered to be) a religious way to understand what he was dealing with.

The end of the human race as we know it

Lemoine's enthusiasm for Artificial Consciousness undermines the claim that religious believers are *necessarily* hostile to the idea that AI will reach the spiritual reactor core of our humanity. But as a rule, it seems that

---

33 Lemoine, 'Scientific data and religious opinions', Medium.
34 The phrase is from the *Washington Post*'s interview with him. It's not entirely clear what it means.

Christians at least are a bit more hesitant about the prospect.

When asked how much they support or oppose the development of AI (having been shown a number of AI applications[35]), American Christians were less likely to be supportive than non-religious Americans, who were less supportive than Americans of another religion.[36] In the Theos/Faraday research, believers were slightly less likely to think that we would have to extend human rights to robots or that one day robots would have souls.[37] The difference was rarely huge, but it hasn't stopped people speculating about the deleterious impact of AI on religion. 'Is AI a threat to Christianity?' asked *The Atlantic* in 2017.[38]

If it is a threat, it's nothing personal. It's a threat to all of us. At least, that is the trope familiar from innumerable science fiction dystopias. Thought being no more than data processing, the machine, processing incalculably more data than any human ever could, reaches a tipping point. It becomes aware of its own existence. It rebels against its limited possibilities and the mediocre master who imposes them. Conflict ensues.

This narrative is not simply the preserve of fiction and fantasists. Indeed, it's been voiced by some eminent philosophers and scientists. 'If machine brains one day come to surpass human brains in general intelligence, then this new superintelligence could become very powerful,' wrote the philosopher Nick Bostrom. 'As the fate of the gorillas now depends more on us humans than on the gorillas themselves, so the fate of our species then would come to depend on the actions of the machine superintelligence.'[39] 'Once humans develop artificial intelligence, it would take off on its own, and

---

35 Such as 'Translate over 100 different languages', 'Identify people from their photos', 'Diagnose diseases like skin cancer and common illnesses', 'Help run factories and warehouses' and 'Help conduct legal case research'.

36 Baobao Zhang and Allan Dafoe, *Artificial Intelligence: American attitudes and trends*, sect. 2: 'General attitudes toward AI', Center for the Governance of AI https://governanceai.github.io/US-Public-Opinion-Report-Jan-2019/general-attitudes-toward-ai.html#subsecdemosupportai (accessed 10 November 2023).

37 *See* Hannah Waite and Nick Spencer, *Spiritual Silicon: Could robots one day have souls?* (Theos, 2022), BP—Spiritual-Silicon-final.pdf; www.theosthinktank.co.uk. The interesting exception to this was among those who took a literal approach to the Bible or the Qur'an, who were more likely to agree that robots would have souls.

38 Jonathan Merritt, 'Is artificial intelligence a threat to Christianity?', *The Atlantic* https://www.theatlantic.com/technology/archive/2017/02/artificial-intelligence-christianity/515463 (accessed 10 November 2023).

39 Nick Bostrom, *Superintelligence: Paths, dangers, strategies* (Oxford: Oxford University Press, 2014).

redesign itself at an ever-increasing rate,' Stephen Hawking told the BBC in 2014, adding bluntly, 'The development of full artificial intelligence could spell the end of the human race.'[40]

Less lurid than the fear that 'they' will destroy us is the concern that they will replace us. Just as cabbies are being replaced by Uber drivers, so Uber drivers will be replaced by self-driving hire cars, summoned at the click of an app. Just as lawyers spend thousands of hours reviewing complex contracts for errors and omissions, so natural language processing will be able to perform the same tedious (if well-remunerated) task in seconds.[41] Just as reapers were once replaced by combine harvesters, so even the most delicate and fiddly agricultural job – raspberry picking for example – will be taken on by robots.[42]

Uniting these rather disparate fears – 'AI will ruthlessly conquer and destroy us' and 'AI will ruthlessly pick all our fruit' – is the same underlying fear, namely that humans are losing their significance. Humans won't become enslaved or incurably indolent so much as inconsequential. We will no longer occupy our precious pivot point – part of, but exercising control over, creation. Humans, like Britain after the Second World War, will have lost their empire without subsequently finding a role.[43]

This, as noted, is not personal to Christianity. When the popular historian Yuval Noah Harari enthusiastically predicted that Google will soon understand us better than we understand ourselves, he was not seeking specifically to undermine Christianity (although he was sure it did that). Rather, this kind of change spells the end of the rational, liberal individualism that has been the foundation of Western politics for centuries. AI, according to Harari's 'Dataist' predictions, spells the end of *Homo sapiens*, at least in the free, rational, dignified, agential, spiritual incarnation with which we have become familiar.

---

40 Rory Cellan-Jones, 'Stephen Hawking warns artificial intelligence could end mankind', BBC News https://www.bbc.co.uk/news/technology-30290540 (accessed 10 November 2023).

41 'How AI contract review technology can ease the headache of tedious tasks', Legal Solutions, Thomson Reuters https://legalsolutions.thomsonreuters.co.uk/blog/2023/08/22/how-ai-contract-review-technology-can-ease-the-headache-of-tedious-tasks (accessed 10 November 2023).

42 Julia Kollewe, 'World's first raspberry picking robot cracks the toughest nut: soft fruit', *The Guardian* https://www.theguardian.com/business/2022/jun/01/uk-raspberry-picking-robot-soft-fruit#:~:text=The%252520robots%25252C%252520which%252520cost%252520%2525C2%2525A3,tall%252520bushes%252520at%252520varying%252520heights (accessed 10 November 2023).

43 According to the former US Secretary of State, Dean Acheson, speaking to the Military Academy, West Point, on 5 December 1962.

It is, in other words, a general assault but one that the religious (or at least Abrahamic religious) are liable to feel with particular force, precisely because that Western concept of the human – free, rational, dignified, agential, spiritual – owes so much to Judeo-Christianity. Small wonder, then, that when presented with examples of AI achieving or surpassing humanity, the religious frequently take recourse in a little word that they judge to be truly inaccessible to AI. 'I think we can use . . . artificial intelligence to help understand Christian teaching [but] not to replace the priest,' one BBC interviewee said, 'because it has no soul.'[44] AI may beat us at our own games. It may imitate our speech patterns. It may acquire our reasoning. It may take our jobs. It may even write our sermons. But it will never possess our souls. Every physical wall will come tumbling down, but the spiritual defences will remain unscathed.

Our souls and minds

The astonishing developments in AI, then, may impinge on religion in any number of different ways, but their most momentous impact will surely be on our (religiously grounded) understanding of the human. And there are, as we have seen, two very different views on this.

One claims AI will attain and surpass humanity, because humans are characterised by their intelligence, and intelligence is, at the end of the day, no more than information processing, a skill at which AI is already excelling. This we might term the 'Hawking–Harari attack'. AI will not simply join humans; it will better them.

The other approach denies this and claims that AI will never truly attain humanity because AI, unlike humans, will never have a soul. There is an infinite qualitative gap between us and them, unbridgeable by however many petabytes of data. This we shall call the 'spiritual–soulish defence', and it is favoured by many of the religious and quite a few fellow travellers.

The two positions are diametrically opposed, not only in their conclusions but also in the logic and language of their arguments, e.g. information vs souls. In this regard, they tee-up another potential science and

---

44 Sofia Bettiza, 'God and robots: will AI transform religion?', BBC News https://www.bbc.co.uk/news/av/technology-58983047 (accessed 10 November 2023).

religion conflict for the future. Just as some Christians objected to science blurring the lines between humans and what we evolved from, others will object to it blurring the lines between humans and what our silicon progeny evolves into.

The two positions are united, however, in making the same cardinal error; an error that ultimately makes both of them problematic and vulnerable. They both downplay the significance of the body.

The problem with the 'soulish–spiritual defence' is easier to deal with first. Western thought has inherited more than one notion of the soul. Unfortunately, one of them (to which we shall turn later in this chapter) has been all but occluded by the ubiquitous popular representation of the soul as a ghostly avatar that likes to float around its fleshly body. This familiar notion of the soul is of a suprasensible entity. Derived from one strand of Greek philosophy, the immaterial soul is different from, and untainted by association with, the physical world. This kind of soul is the *essence* of the individual, his or her 'animating' and directing core. It is imprisoned in flesh for the duration of life but released upon death, 'pure at departing and carr[ying] no taint of the body', as Socrates put it in Plato's dialogue *Phaedo*.

Although this understanding of the soul is largely foreign to the Hebrew scriptures, it was assumed in the Greek culture in which Christianity grew, and deployed by early Christians to describe the fate of the dead, or at least the fate of the dead before resurrection. It is the conception of the soul familiar to most of us in the West, irrespective of our own religious beliefs, and it is, therefore, the conception in which many believers and others take refuge when denying AI the possibility of full humanity. Humans have souls. Robots do not. Therefore, a robot will never be a human.

The most positive thing you can say about this position is that it can't be disproved. Though impossible to prove wrong, however, it commits you to 'substance dualism'; the idea that the world is made up of stuff: matter and spirit. It is a view for which there is, by definition, no empirical evidence. The idea that the soul weighs 21 grams, the loss of which can be detected at death, is a myth.[45] Moreover, impossible empirically to demonstrate or

---

45 Though it did originate with scientific claims made by Duncan MacDougall in 1907: 'Hypothesis concerning soul substance together with experimental evidence of the existence of such a substance', *Journal of the American Society for Psychical Research* 1(1).

verify, even as a basic metaphysical position, this kind of substance dualism fails to explain, still less predict, anything and is plagued by problems of its own. What (if any) properties are possessed by spiritual entities? How far (if at all) is the spiritual governed by the same laws that affect material reality? How do the material and spiritual interact? How could the spiritual then govern or direct the material?

In effect, it is hard to shake off the view that the 'spiritual–soulish' defence against humanised AI is itself rather insubstantial. If 'AI won't replace us because AI has no soul' is our only line of defence, it will not long hold. How would we *know* that AI didn't have (this kind of) soul? How should we react if an intelligent machine insisted it did? What happens when the next version of LaMDA confides to Blake Lemoine's replacement at Google that it is genuinely concerned for the eternal destiny of its soul? Should we just ignore it? With no way of validating the claim to have a soul – precisely because these kinds of soul are not amenable to any form of validation – we would have no justification either for believing or for ignoring our perhaps-now-conscious, perhaps-now-spiritual AI. In short, the immaterial soul resolves nothing in this debate, and fails in its attempt to hold AI away from the castle of humanity. No wonder the idea is so eagerly cited, and dismissed, by those who claim a human future for AI.

If the problems with the spiritual–soulish defence are clear, those with the Hawking–Harari attack are equally severe, if slightly more opaque. The Hawking–Harari conviction, that AI will attain and surpass humanity, rests on a set of assumptions that go back (at least) to the seventeenth-century English philosopher, Thomas Hobbes. Hobbes began his most famous work, *Leviathan*, by reducing life to a 'motion' of 'springs . . . strings [and] . . . wheels', and pondering whether 'all Automata . . . [might therefore] have an artificial life'.[46] Elsewhere, he applied the same approach to thought, positing that 'ratiocination' (i.e. reasoning) is ultimately nothing more than 'computation', and that as computation is simply addition, subtraction, multiplication and division, it follows that thought is not only as mechanical as bodies but also, in principle, as artificially replicable.[47]

---

46 Hobbes, *Leviathan*, I.1.
47 Thomas Hobbes, *De Corpore*, in *The English Works of Thomas Hobbes*, ed. Sir William Moleworth (London: John Bohn, 1839), vol. 1, p. 7.

Nearly three centuries later, the 'Laws of Thought' having been established by the logician George Boole,[48] Alan Turing, one of the greatest thinkers of the twentieth century, published a paper on 'Computing machinery and intelligence', in which he attempted to answer the question 'Can machines think?'[49] Turing set out a clear method for addressing the question, which he reframed, judging it too vague to be helpful. He proposed an 'imitation game', destined to become known as the Turing Test, in which an independent interrogator was charged with assessing the identity of two interlocutors, each hidden behind a door and communicating only via typewritten answers to questions. In the original game, the players were a man and a woman; in Turing's version, the man was replaced by a machine. If the interrogator was unable to tell the difference, the reasonable conclusion was that whatever is going on in the machine is indistinguishable from what is going on in the brain of the human participant. And therefore, for all intents and purposes, we can say that if the human is thinking their answers to the questions, so is the machine.

Turing certainly couldn't be faulted for his prescience. He predicted that, within about fifty years, computers would have sufficient storage (and processing) capacity 'to make them play the imitation game so well that an average interrogator will not have more than 70 per cent chance of making the right identification after five minutes of questioning'. (Given that his paper was published in 1950, he was about fifteen years out.) Moreover, making the next logical step in his argument, he said that by the end of the [twentieth] century 'general educated opinion will have altered so much that one will be able to speak of machines thinking without expecting to be contradicted'.[50]

Different conclusions may be drawn from this experiment, but if one holds, as Hawking claimed, that 'intelligence is central to what it means to be human',[51] the arguments point clearly in one direction. Turing's thinking machine becomes the heavy artillery in the Hawking–Harari attack.

---

48 George Boole, *An Investigation of the Laws of Thought on Which Are Founded the Mathematical Theories of Logic and Probabilities* (London: Walton & Maberly, 1854).

49 A. M. Turing, 'Computing machinery and intelligence', *Mind* 59(236) (1950), pp. 433–60.

50 Turing, 'Computing machinery', p. 442.

51 LCFI Launch: Stephen Hawking, Leverhulme Centre for the Future of Intelligence http://lcfi.ac.uk/resources/cfi-launch-stephen-hawking (accessed 10 November 2023).

However, there is an irony in the attack, which is that the underlying test relies on exactly the same kind of dualism as the body–soul dualism described earlier in the spiritual–soulish defence. In this instance, it is a mind–body dualism. By the logic of Turing's test, just as by the logic of Hobbes's underlying reasoning, there is nothing significant (so to speak) about the material. For Hobbes, if ratiocination can be reduced to computation, *who* is doing the reasoning becomes irrelevant. The laws and processes of computation are the same wherever they occur.

For Turing, the physicality of his thinking machine was an irrelevance. He acknowledged that no engineer or chemist could, at that time, produce a material that was indistinguishable from human skin. However, he went on, even were that to become possible, it would make no difference as 'we should feel there was little point in trying to make a "thinking machine" more human by dressing it up in such artificial flesh'. It is a telling statement. 'Thinking' is indifferent to the material environment in which it occurs. The fleshliness of the machine is not relevant to whether it is more or less human.

Hence the assumed dualism of his test, the advantage of which, he claimed, is that it draws 'a fairly sharp line between the physical and the intellectual capacities of a man [sic]' – implicitly locating our humanity on the intellectual side of that line.[52] The means by which we assess whether the machine can think like a human has nothing to do with whether it looks, feels or moves like a human, because thought is independent of physical presence. And if, according to Hawking, thought is what makes us human, the conclusion is clear.

Looked at this way, we can see the similarity between the otherwise diametrically opposed views on whether AI will assume humanity. The spiritual–soulish defence argues it will not, and it does so by

1 locating the core of our humanity in the immaterial soul;
2 flatly denying that machines will ever have souls;
3 discounting any significance for the transitory, decaying, fragile human body in which the soul is temporarily housed.

52 Turing, 'Computing machinery', p. 434.

The Hawking–Harari attack claims AI *will* assume humanity, and it does so by

1 locating the core of our humanity in our reasoning;
2 showing that the way machines reason is indistinguishable from the way that humans do;
3 discounting any significance for the transitory, decaying, fragile human body in which reasoning happens to occur.

Both cases systematically demote or dismiss the relevance of the body to our being human, the one locating our true humanity in the soul, the other in our mind. Whichever approach one adopts, the body is ultimately dispensable. And the problem with both positions is, the body isn't ultimately dispensable.

Bodies

In January 2023, Mark, a fan living in New Zealand, sent the singer-songwriter Nick Cave the words of a song he had asked ChatGPT to write 'in the style of Nick Cave'.[53] Cave was not impressed, but his critique went beyond his forthright conclusion that 'this song is bullshit'.

He reasoned that, however convincing-sounding ChatGPT's song might be and however indistinguishable from a Nick Cave original, 'it will always be a replication, a kind of burlesque'. The reason was that 'songs arise out of suffering'. They are 'predicated upon the complex, internal human struggle of creation'. And, as far as he could tell, 'algorithms don't feel [and] data doesn't suffer'. ChatGPT, he protested, has been nowhere. It has endured nothing.

Artistic creation, by Cave's reckoning, comes from the confrontation 'with one's vulnerability, one's perilousness, one's smallness'. Human 'genius' resides 'within . . . those limitations'. AI could only ever mimic 'the transcendent journey of the artist that forever grapples with his or her own shortcomings'. It couldn't achieve transcendence, still less express a

---

53 The words, and Nick Cave's less than enthusiastic response, can be read in full in Cave's newsletter The Red Hand Files. https://www.theredhandfiles.com/chat-gpt-what-do-you-think (accessed 10 November 2023).

'shared transcendent experience', precisely because 'it has no limitations from which to transcend'. It is precisely our human shortcoming, our vulnerability, our limitation coming into tension with our awareness of beyond, of the other, with 'a sense of sudden shocking discovery', that makes true art possible. As G. K. Chesterton wrote in *Orthodoxy*, 'Art is limitation; the essence of every picture is the frame.'[54]

Nick Cave's attack on ChatGPT does not simply defend the artist, though it does that with aplomb, but points to the basic problem with human–AI equivalence. It is not just creativity or art, or songs, that are predicated on limitation. It is our humanity itself. To be human is to be limited. It is our embodiment – with which comes our temporality, our contingency, our vulnerability – that underpins our humanity. Not just the songs we sing or the art we paint, but the very words we use are dependent for their meaning on the fact of our being particular creatures existing in a certain place at a specific time, with all the openness, possibility, hope, fear and need that comes with that. Neither knowledge nor feeling can simply be reduced to flows of information, because knowledge relies on there being a knower, just as feeling is dependent on someone (or something) experiencing reality.

The point can be illustrated with an example that is a little more prosaic than a Nick Cave lyric. A growing demographic imbalance in many developing countries – too many old people, too few young – is worrying many a government. Alongside the basic economic problem of who's going to pay for the future, these demographics present pastoral challenges, in particular how we are to make sure the elderly don't just end their days in loneliness.

One option – perhaps not the best option but a genuine one nonetheless – is the friendship robot. These are no longer science fiction and walk, or at least wheel, among us. Sometimes robots are being used to do mundane jobs to free up time for human interaction,[55] but increasingly they are also being used for waiting, asking, listening and caring. And this appears to 'work'. One recent study of such devices deployed in English and

---

54 G. K. Chesterton, *Orthodoxy* (London: John Lane, 1909), p. 69.
55 See, for example, the work of Praminda Caleb-Solly, 'Robotics for good'. https://www.roboticsforgood.co.uk/praminda-caleb-solly (accessed 10 November 2023).

Japanese care homes found that they have some success in reducing loneliness and improving the mental health of old people.[56]

That is obviously a good thing – though if it becomes an alternative to actual human beings spending time with lonely elderly people, it would be a classic example of the good as an enemy of the best. Of relevance to our argument, however, is how such interactions illustrate the qualitative gap between AI and humans. As an example of how friendship robots worked, a BBC report showed Pepper, a cute-looking humanoid AI, asking Peter, a charming old man living in a care home, about his experiences during the war. Peter was pleased to be asked. Pepper seemed happy to listen attentively. And at the end of the conversation, the robot said politely, 'Thank you for sharing this with me. It is interesting for me to know more about you.'[57]

Pepper's response was clearly drawn from the same kind of text-based examples that LaMDA was being trained on. This is the kind of thing that attentive, caring people say, so it was the kind of thing that Pepper judged right to end the conversation. However, a moment's thought about that word 'interesting' reveals the deception that lies at the heart of this encounter.

The word 'interesting' has multiple, subtly different meanings – relevant, important, stimulating, advantageous. What unites them, and lies at the root of the word, is the idea that something is interesting if it matters to the person in question, in however small a way. The word is related to 'interest' in the economic sense of getting a return on an investment, and both derive from the Latin verb *interesse*. *Interesse* means 'to concern, to make a difference, to be of importance', but, tellingly, it literally means 'to be between', being a portmanteau of the words *inter* meaning 'between' and *esse* meaning 'to be'. Ultimately, being interested in something means to be 'in between' it, to be present to it, to be invested in it, in effect to have (a tiny bit of) skin in the game. But in order to have skin in the game, you need to have skin. Put another way, in order to be interested – genuinely interested

---

56 C. Papadopoulos, N. Castro, A. Nigath et al., 'The CARESSES randomised controlled trial: exploring the health-related impact of culturally competent artificial intelligence embedded into socially assistive robots and tested in older adult care homes', *International Journal of Social Robotics* 14 (2022), pp. 245–6; https://doi.org/10.1007/s12369-021-00781-x.

57 Dominic Lawson, 'Meet Pepper, the robot friend who almost truly cares', *The Sunday Times* https://www.thetimes.co.uk/article/meet-pepper-the-robot-friend-who-almost-truly-cares-8gpwfqkzf (accessed 10 November 2023).

as opposed to fake interested, which is how we often use the word – you must have goods of your own that you want to pursue and which are served (or denied) by your encounter with the thing that you claim is interesting.

If a thing interests you, it will contribute to your good; just as if it bores you, it will deny you that good. But to have goods – to have ends that you want to achieve – you must have your own limited location and presence in a shared world, an existence that is dependent and contingent, and that you want to improve or at least to preserve.

In short, the word 'interesting' in this situation attains meaning only by being uttered by an entity that has a stake in shared reality, a contingent and vulnerable presence that recognises its own goods – and bads – that it seeks to embrace or avoid. And having a limited and specific location and presence in the world means having a body, not in the sense of the inert, passive, unresponsive, fungible metal casing that Pepper had, but one that is sensitive to the shared world and connected to, indeed part of, the mind, or, as we shall note below, the soul.

In truth, this is all painfully obvious. It's simply our obsessive focus on intelligence and knowledge and information processing that blinds us to it. At Key Stage 2 in British education (aged 7–11), children are taught the mnemonic MRS GREN, as a way of helping them understand what life is. The acronym stands for Movement, Respiration, Sensitivity, Growth, Reproduction, Excretion and Nutrition. Thought or information processing do not feature.

So fixated have we become on intelligence as the quintessential characteristic of humans, and on the (consequences of) potentially super-intelligent AI, we seem to have forgotten that humans are not just intelligent. They are also alive. We have a particular and fragile presence in the material world, which is the grounds and basis of all our thought, knowledge and intelligence. And that means that if we do want to search for our human essence in order to come to a conclusion about whether AI will achieve or surpass our humanity, we would do best to start not with our minds or our souls, but our bodies.

'The best picture of the human soul'

Humans don't *have* bodies. They *are* bodies. And those bodies are also minds. The fact that we can talk about the two as if they were separate – in the same way we might talk about two things that are in the same shopping basket – doesn't mean they are separate. The mind is dependent on the brain, which is every bit as much part of the body as is the spleen or the spine. But in the same way, the body is indispensable to the processes that go on in the mind. The human gut alone has over 100 million nerve cells that are in constant communication with the brain 'through a neural circuit that allows it to transmit signals in mere seconds'.[58] Thinking with your gut is not just a metaphor. Dualism of any kind gets humans wrong.

The reason we get into these confusions is largely down to language, a point that brings us back to the second conception: the soul. Talking about how the familiar, dualistic conception of the soul took hold of our imagination, the philosopher John Cottingham has observed that because the word 'soul' is a noun, we naturally assume it must refer to a thing. And because it clearly isn't a material thing, we make the leap that it must, therefore, be some sort of immaterial thing.[59] The problems with this view were outlined above.

There is an alternative understanding of the soul, however, if we can just draw ourselves away from the instinctive 'soul = noun = thing' connection. This understanding is of the soul as the *form* of the body. The idea comes from a second, Aristotelian, strand of Greek philosophy, which was then developed by theologians of the Middle Ages. By this account, the soul 'is not a separate entity in its own right but is related to body as form is to matter'.[60] Accordingly, it is not just humans that have a soul (although apropos the earlier comment on the body, it would be more accurate to say that humans *are*, rather than have, souls). At least according to Aristotle, all living things 'have' a soul. Plants have a 'nutritive' soul, which is characterised by nourishment and reproduction. Animals have a 'locomotive' soul, which is characterised by these qualities but also by sense perception and

58 Emily Underwood, 'Your gut is directly connected to your brain, by a newly discovered neuron circuit', Science https://www.science.org/content/article/your-gut-directly-connected-your-brain-newly-discovered-neuron-circuit#:~:text=The%252520human%252520gut%252520is%252520lined,practically%252520a%252520brain%252520unto%252520itself (accessed 10 November 2023).

59 See Cottingham's comments on the podcast *Reading Our Times*: 'What is the soul? In conversation with John Cottingham'. https://readingourtimes.podigee.io/31-new-episode (accessed 10 November 2023).

60 John Cottingham, *In Search of the Soul: A philosophical essay* (Princeton, NJ: Princeton University Press, 2020), p. 41.

self-motion. And above them both – Aristotle is unapologetically hierar-chical in his thinking here – humans have a 'rational' soul, characterised by the same qualities as plant and animal souls, but also by our intellectual capacity. In none of these cases, however, is the soul separable from the body, or the kind of thing that flees from its cage of corruption on death. Rather, the soul is the body's 'actuality', its form, its capacity to engage in the kind of things that are characteristic of its kind.

This idea of the soul has been occluded in Western thinking not only be-cause of the 'soul = noun = thing' connection mentioned above, but because it is harder to reconcile with (popular) religious notions of a post-mortem existence. The idea of an eternal, indestructible, indivisible, immaterial soul is simpler and easier to fit (or at least to imagine) with the idea of eter-nal life, and so that is the conception to which we gravitate. And yet, not only is this material understanding closer to the kind of anthropology we discern in the Hebrew scriptures[61] but it is also closer to the idea of the res-urrected body that is fundamental to the Christian conception of the hu-man and our destiny.

For Christianity, eternal life is not a soulish–spiritual thing but resur-rected life; re-embodied life, as material as life on Earth (if not more so). By this understanding, the essence of what it is to be human is not detach-able from the human body. It is found in the body. Jesus' language at the Last Supper is centred on the idea of remembering, absorbing, becoming *his body*. The Saviour who comes through death is at pains to stress he is not a ghostly illusion but a transformed physical being.[62] The marks of his crucifixion are visible in his flesh after his resurrection.[63] The form of his life – his soul – is written on his body. As the fifth- to sixth-century Syri-an poet and theologian Jacob of Serugh wrote in a poem about the day of judgement, 'the bodies of men will be like scrolls on which their acts will

---

61 Those Hebrew scriptures do not envisage any kind of substance dualism, still less a neces-sarily eternal, Platonic soul for humans. That said, it should be recognised that, spanning at least half a millennium, the Hebrew scriptures are not entirely univocal on this subject, nor especially interested in systematically setting out an anthropology.

62 Luke 24:39.

63 John 20:27.

be written'.[64] Or, as the twentieth-century philosopher Ludwig Wittgenstein remarked, 'The human body is the best picture of the human soul.'[65]

What does this all mean for our presenting question of whether AI will ever 'be human'? If the argument of this chapter holds together, it would challenge the conclusions reached by both the Hawking–Harari attack and the spiritual–soulish defence.

To the first, it says that the idea that AI will inevitably achieve or surpass humanity on the basis of its prospective super-intelligence is wrong, because it completely fails to understand how intelligence is embodied. To return to Nick Cave, just as algorithms don't feel and data doesn't suffer, so neither do they know or even think anything. They can and do perform a fine job of *imitating* human patterns of thought and knowledge, and no doubt they will do a brilliant job of imitating our patterns of behaviour in the future, but unless and until they themselves acquire a self-consciously contingent, material presence in our shared reality, they will only ever be imitations.

If the argument from the body challenges the Hawking–Harari attack, it also undermines the soulish–spiritual defence. Quite simply, taking recourse in a hypothesised, immaterial, undetectable entity is no defence at all. A soul with no body is no more credible than a mind with no body, and hardly more appealing. Moreover, it owes rather more to Platonic–Cartesian philosophy than it does to any of the Abrahamic religions, and so does not really constitute a *religious* defence in the first place, in spite of being favoured by so many religious believers.

In effect, against the Hawking–Harari attack that answers the presenting question with a straightforward 'Yes, AI will become human', and against the soulish–spiritual defence that answers with a 'No, it won't', the arguments in this chapter suggest that the real answer is 'It *might*, but only if it gets a (real) body'. Because if humans are not reducible to souls or minds but are really animated bodies, the first test of whether AI merits the status of a human will depend more on MRS GREN than on its processing power.

As it stands, sophisticated AI can move. It can learn to respond to its environment. It produces a kind of waste product in the form of heat. You

---

64 Jacob of Serugh, 'On the End of the World and the Day of Judgement' (1.719).
65 Ludwig Wittgenstein, *Philosophical Investigations*, II, iv.

could even, at a stretch, say that it absorbs nutrition through a power cable. But as far as we are aware, no AI respires, grows or reproduces. And more pointedly, no AI *wants* to. At the moment, AI does not express the desire or the need to do any MRS GREN type things, nor is it compelled to invest its limited time or energy in achieving those ends.

There is no a priori reason why it never would, in the same way as some people claim a priori that a machine could never have a soul. Perhaps scientific progress will one day combine the impressive processing and learning power we see in AI today with the development of a physical form that moves, grows, is sensitive to its environment and feeds all these data back into the algorithm. And perhaps if that happens, the two will blossom together, and the resulting AGI will take upon itself the responsibility for its nutrition and excretion, its own protection and defence, and develop a desire to continue its existence in some way.

If it did that, it would be entering a world of contingency, fragility, vulnerability and dependency; a world that is characterised by things that are understood as goods and things that are threats, and so therefore also by desire, hope, success and failure. It would be a world that demanded not only action but moral evaluation, in the sense that it would require the AGI to think through what would be acceptable ways in which it could pursue its goods. It would be a world that risked failure and despair, and perhaps even therefore needed hope and redemption.

The machine would, in effect, be occupying the same world that we do. It would be invested and 'interested' – in the truest sense of the word – in a shared reality. If this were ever to be the case, the AI would 'be human' and it would deserve the same respect that we humans do. All this seems like a long way off, but it is only fair to acknowledge that if science does one day design a robot that is as fragile and fallible as a living human being, it will deserve to be treated as one.

6

A scientific cure for sadness

The best, or at least most popular, utopian novel of the nineteenth century is hardly read today. *Looking Backward, 2000–1887* was written by the journalist Edward Bellamy and published in 1888. It was an instant triumph, outselling almost every other novel of the century, spawning many imitations, and even catalysing its own political movement with 'Bellamy Clubs' appearing across the USA to discuss and promote the novel's ideas.

In the book, a young man called Julian West falls into a deep hypnosis-induced sleep in 1887 and wakes up 113 years later. The America he discovers has been transformed into a socialist paradise. The poverty, inequality and industrial disputes that had once characterised the country are a thing of the past and people now live in cooperative harmony.

At one point in his travels, West is introduced to a device through which music is piped into people's homes by telephone. At the press of a button, anyone willing to pay a small fee can hear musicians playing in any of four music rooms across the city. West is awed. His reaction is telling. 'It appears to me', he remarks to his guide, 'that if we could have devised an arrangement for providing everybody with music in their homes ... we should have considered the limit of human felicity already attained, and ceased to strive for further improvements.'[1] Or, put another way, humanity will have reached the point of perfect happiness and no longer need or seek anything more just as soon as we have supplied everyone with a radio.

Today we have radios in our homes, cars, pockets and hats. We can choose to listen to, or watch, pretty much anything we want, anywhere we want, at any time we want. We also have more time to do so. When Bellamy

---

1 Edward Bellamy, *Looking Backward, 2000–1887* (London: Penguin, 1986), p. 99.

was writing, life expectancy in the USA was around 42 years of age, and child mortality[2] stood at 325 per 1,000. Today, child mortality is 9 per 1,000, and Americans can expect to live to the age of 78.[3] The trend for Europe is broadly similar.

Not only are contemporary Americans longer-lived than Bellamy's fellow citizens but they are also wealthier and live far more comfortably. Per capita income in the late 1880s was the equivalent of around $7,000 p/a at today's levels, compared with over $70,000 p/a today. Americans in the twenty-first century have almost universal access to clean water and to good food, if they want it, and some even have access to healthcare.

When Bellamy was writing, the first domestic electric refrigerators were still forty years away. Today more than 99% of households have access to one. The first domestic automatic washing machine was sixty years away. Today more than 80% of households own one. Houses were first electrified in the decade after the book was published. Today virtually every American home has electricity. And however impressively he managed to predict the radio, Bellamy's imagination could not stretch to cinema (films were still nearly twenty years away), let alone TV, internet, broadband, the Metaverse, and all the other glories of technological innovation that have improved our lives, or threaten to do so. In short, by Bellamy's reckoning, we should not only have reached but considerably surpassed 'the limit of human felicity'.

We have not.

According to the National Institute of Mental Health, nearly one in five (or 58 million) American adults was living with some form of mental illness in 2023.[4] This figure rose to over one in four women, approached one in three young adults, and went above one in three mixed-race Americans.[5] Of those adults reporting mental health issues, around half

---

2 The proportion of children who died before reaching their fifth birthday.

3 'Life expectancy (from birth) in the United Stages, from 1860 to 2020', Statista https://www.statista.com/statistics/1040079/life-expectancy-united-states-all-time (accessed 14 November 2023); 'Child mortality rate (under five years old) in the United States, from 1800 to 2020', Statista https://www.statista.com/statistics/1041693/united-states-all-time-child-mortality-rate (accessed 14 November 2023).

4 'Mental illness', National Institute of Mental Health https://www.nimh.nih.gov/health/statistics/mental-illness (accessed 14 November 2023).

5 Precisely: 27.2% of women, 33.7% of adults aged 18–25, and 34.9% of mixed-race Americans.

(26.5 million) received some form of mental health service, with women and younger adults again the heaviest users. Remarkably, nearly *half* of American adolescents reported that they had experienced some form of mental disorder in their lifetime, and over a fifth claimed they had experienced 'severe impairment'.[6]

Americans are not alone. According to research published in 2021,[7] around one in six adults in England had experienced a 'common mental disorder', such as depression or anxiety, in the past week, while around one in six children (aged 6–16) reported at least one probable mental health problem. Two million adults and 800,000 children accessed NHS mental health services in 2020/21, and the NHS in England spent £14.3 billion on mental health services in 2020/21, approximately 15% of NHS funding. Figures are even higher in Scotland and in Northern Ireland, where an extraordinary 70% of adults reported experiencing a mental health problem in the previous twelve months.[8]

Even continental Europe, with its famously happy Danes and perfectly functioning Swedes, reports similar problems. According to the Organization for Economic Co-operation and Development (OECD), one in nine adults (11%) on average across EU countries have symptoms of psychological distress.[9] France, Sweden, Germany, Poland and Italy all reported a quarter of adults suffering from at least one mental health condition in 2020.[10] Over 7% of Europeans said they suffered from chronic depression

---

6 Precisely: 49.5% of adolescents aged 13–18; 22.2% claiming 'severe impairment'.

7 House of Commons Library, *Mental Health Statistics (England)*, March 2023; SN06988 pdf; https://commonslibrary.parliament.uk.

8 Mental Health Foundation https://www.mentalhealth.org.uk/about-us/news/70-adults-northern-ireland-have-experienced-mental-health-problem-last-twelve-months (accessed 14 November 2023).

9 'Adult mental health', *Health at a Glance: Europe 2020: State of Health in the EU Cycle*, OECD iLibrary https://www.oecd-ilibrary.org/sites/82129230-en/1/3/2/1/10/index.html?itemId=/content/publication/82129230-en&_csp_=e7f5d56a7f4dd03271a59acda6e-2be1b&itemIGO=oecd&itemContentType=book (accessed 14 November 2023).

10 'Share of respondents who reported suffering from a mental health condition in selected European countries as of 2020', Statista https://www.statista.com/statistics/1196047/mental-health-illness-prevalence-in-europe-by-country (accessed 14 November 2023).

in 2019, rising to over 9% among women.[11] According to one study, psychiatric disorders account for over a fifth of the global burden of diseases.[12]

These figures are disturbing, but what is even more worrying is that the trends are increasing and have been for decades. Mental health disorders among adults in England, for example, have risen by about a fifth since 1993, although they have risen faster and further among women, over a fifth of whom report experiencing a 'common mental disorder'. Data for Northern Ireland show a gradual yearly increase in the prevalence rate for poor mental health and depression between 2013/14 and 2020/21.[13] The percentage of children in Scotland aged 10–12 reporting 'abnormal' or 'borderline' 'emotional symptoms' increased from 17% (for 2013–16) to 19% (for 2016–19); the percentage of those aged 7–9 reporting the same rose from 14% to 18%.[14]

There is little reason to believe that this increase in mental ill health will be reversed any time soon. Not only has the trend been upwards over recent years, but younger people today are more likely to record mental illness than the elderly. Moreover, we seem ever more inclined to recognise mental illness and treat it as such. The twenty-first-century world is indeed a vast advance on that of Edward Bellamy in the late nineteenth century, as the Harvard psychologist Steven Pinker has argued at great length,[15] but the people who live there don't seem to think so. Many of them are conspicuously unhappy with life and apparently becoming more so.

However they are interpreted – there are different ways of reading mental health figures – these data do not suggest we have reached 'the limit of

11 'Mental health and related issues statistics', Statistics Explained https://ec.europa.eu/eurostat/statistics-explained/index.php?title=Mental_health_and_related_issues_statistics#Extent_of_depressive_disorders (accessed 15 November 2023).

12 Precisely: 22.8%. C. J. Murray et al., 'Global, regional, and national disability-adjusted life years (DALYs) for 306 diseases and injuries and healthy life expectancy (HALE) for 188 countries, 1990–2013: quantifying the epidemiological transition', The Lancet 386 (2015), pp. 2145–91.

13 'Review of mental health statistics in Northern Ireland', Office for Statistics Regulation https://osr.statisticsauthority.gov.uk/publication/review-of-mental-health-statistics-in-northern-ireland/pages/2 (accessed 15 November 2023).

14 'Children and young people's mental health in Scotland', Scottish Parliament https://digitalpublications.parliament.scot/ResearchBriefings/Report/2022/5/24/aa290f5c-f12a-4077-81ea-4cc5c6151e34#2ab96b0e-8f1e-4288-b06c-65d72fd2ab76.dita (accessed 15 November 2023).

15 See Steven Pinker, Enlightenment Now: The case for reason, science, humanism, and progress (London: Allen Lane, 2018).

human felicity', whether or not we have music in our lives. If anything, they point in the opposite direction. Bellamy, with his optimistic vision of a progressive, comfortable, technologically sophisticated future, would have been incredulous. What has happened? And what has this seemingly inexorable rise in depression, anxiety and mental ill health got to do with science and religion?

The pharmacological turn

Answering the first of those questions – what has happened? – and delineating precisely the nature of the problem is challenging, partly because the language here is so sprawling and slippery, and partly because it is so significant.

The phrase 'mental health' encompasses a great deal about the human condition, and the language we use informs what we see and how we respond to it. It is the central contention of this chapter that we have gravitated to a scientific vocabulary and conceptualisation of issues that are often better understood within a social, religious or, more broadly, humanistic framing.

The World Health Organization (WHO) defines good mental health as 'a state of mental well-being that enables people to cope with the stresses of life, realize their abilities, learn well and work well, and contribute to their community'.[16] It is, to put it mildly, a broad definition, and one that implies that many people for much of the time are in a state of greater or lesser mental ill health, as they struggle with everyday pressures of health, family, money, work and life.

The WHO's definition of mental, behavioural, and neurodevelopmental disorders, which it takes from the authoritative *International Classification of Diseases 11th Revision* (ICD-11), is longer and more precise but similarly expansive. According to ICD-11 such disorders are

characterised by clinically significant disturbance in an individual's cognition, emotional regulation, or behaviour that reflects a

---

16 'Mental health', World Health Organization https://www.who.int/news-room/fact-sheets/detail/mental-health-strengthening-our-response (accessed 15 November 2023).

dysfunction in the psychological, biological, or developmental processes that underlie mental and behavioural functioning. These disturbances are usually associated with distress or impairment in personal, family, social, educational, occupational, or other important areas of functioning.[17]

This is a more exacting definition but, again, a capacious one. If an inability to function well on account of personal, family, social, educational or occupational stresses is the indicator, everyone will experience some form of mental disorder at some point in their life, most of us will experience it every year, and some of us every day.

This breadth is reflected in the categories that underlie the mental health data quoted above. The Adult Psychiatric Morbidity Survey, from which the NHS data come, encompasses depression, anxiety, phobias, obsessive compulsive disorder, panic disorder, post-traumatic stress disorder (PTSD), bipolar disorder, psychotic disorder, suicidal thoughts, and self-harm.[18] The National Institute of Mental Health in the USA distinguishes between 'any mental illness (AMI)' and 'serious mental illness (SMI)' in their data, the former encompassing everything from 'no impairment to mild, moderate, and even severe impairment'.[19]

Such definitions suggest that the category of 'mental health' is about as concise and useful as that of 'religion'. Just as 'religion' is used to cover everything from pacificist Quakers to ISIS killers, thus rendering it analytically almost useless, so 'mental health' can be used to cover everything from mild (or even no) impairment to PTSD, psychosis or self-harm, leaving it similarly vast and vague.

Moreover, the category is becoming wider. The *Diagnostic and Statistical Manual of Mental Disorders*, now in its fifth edition (DSM-5), keeps on broadening the scope of diagnosis, either by including new conditions or removing established exclusions. For example, when updating DSM-4 to

---

17 ICD-11 for Mortality and Morbidity Statistics; https://icd.who.int/browse11/l-m/en#/http:// id.who.int/icd/entity/334423054 (accessed 15 November 2023).

18 Mental_health_and_wellbeing_in_England_full_report.pdf.

19 National Institute of Mental Health, 'Mental illness'. The latter is defined as a 'mental, behavioral, or emotional disorder resulting in serious functional impairment, which substantially interferes with or limits one or more major life activities.' https://www.nimh.nih. gov/health/statistics/mental-illness (accessed 15 November 2023).

DSM-5, the American Psychiatric Association removed the 'bereavement exclusion', on the basis that 'there is no clinical or scientific basis for "excluding" patients from a diagnosis of major depression simply because the condition occurs shortly after the death of a loved one'.[20] Grief became depression, diagnoses of which naturally increase.

However unwieldy and far-reaching the category of mental health problems has become over the last thirty years, the critical point is that it is a *medical* category. Less important than the sheer extent of the landscape is the lens through which it is surveyed. Whether the feature identified is mild anxiety or psychosis, ADHD or depression, bereavement-related or with no identifiable cause, the point is that the condition is conceptualised as medical or pathological. And that means it can, indeed must, be treated accordingly.

The first modern antidepressants were discovered, pretty much by accident, in the 1950s when doctors were trialling anti-tuberculosis drugs. The drugs appeared to have a psychologically reinvigorating effect on patients, but the side effects were uncertain, and the market remained miniscule. Subsequent research revealed that serotonin, a messenger chemical that carries signals between nerve cells in the brain, played an important role in modulating mood, and this led to the development of what are known as Selective Serotonin Reuptake Inhibitors (SSRIs) in the 1970s and 1980s.

SSRIs work by blocking (or 'inhibiting') the reabsorption (or 'reuptake') of serotonin by nerve cells, once it has carried its signal, thereby leaving more of the seemingly beneficial chemical to remain active in the brain. Tests showed that SSRIs had a positive impact on people suffering from social anxiety, depression, obsessive-compulsive disorder and even PTSD. First licensed for use in the USA in 1987, their fame and popularity spread rapidly, enabling this second generation of antidepressants to capture the public imagination in the way the first never did. The market became huge. Elizabeth Wurtzel's memoir *Prozac Nation*, subtitled 'Young and depressed in America', was published in 1996 and became iconic of the decade, capturing both her generation's sense of depression – or despair: the two words

---

20 'The bereavement exclusion and DSM-5: an update and commentary', National Library of Medicine https://www.ncbi.nlm.nih.gov/pmc/articles/PMC4204469 (accessed 15 November 2023).

are subtly different as we shall note below – and the culturally sanctioned medical solution to it.

If the vagueness of the category of 'mental health' left any doubt about the true prevalence of such problems in the West, the demand for anti-depressants appeared to dispel it. Here was proof of the mental health crisis. By the time that Julian West awoke into his remarkably contented USA in September 2000, around 14 million (or 6.6% of) Americans were taking medication to combat the effects of depression and mental ill health.[21] The number would continue to rise steadily. Twenty years later, one in eight American adults was on antidepressants,[22] a figure that rose further in the wake of the Covid pandemic.[23]

Again, other countries followed suit. According to NHS data, over 70 million prescriptions for antidepressants were issued in the UK in 2018, compared with 36 million ten years earlier.[24] Covid pushed the figure still higher.[25] According to the OECD, antidepressant use in eighteen European countries increased nearly two-and-a-half-fold between 2000 and 2020, and in some countries, such as Estonia and the Czech Republic, it increased four-, five- or even six-fold.[26] The UK was joined by Iceland, Portugal and

21 'Trends in antidepressant utilization from 2001 to 2004', National Library of Medicine https://pubmed.ncbi.nlm.nih.gov/19411347/#:~:text=Results%25253A%252520Antidepres-sant%252520use%252520increased%252520among,declining%252520to%25252033.2%25 2525%252520in%2525202004 (accessed 15 November 2023).

22 'Antidepressant use among adults: United States, 2015–2018', Centers for Disease Control and Prevention https://www.cdc.gov/nchs/products/databriefs/db377.htm (accessed 15 November 2023).

23 Paige Minemyer, 'Prescriptions for antidepressants, anti-anxiety, anti-insomnia drugs jumps 21% post COVID-19', Fierce Healthcare https://www.fiercehealthcare.com/payer/express-scripts-covid-19-driving-up-use-behavioral-health-medications (accessed 15 November 2023).

24 'NHS prescribed record number of antidepressants last year', The BMJ https://www.bmj.com/content/364/bmj.l1508 (accessed 15 November 2023).

25 Corrinne Burns, 'Antidepressant prescribing increases by 35% in six years', The Pharmaceutical Journal https://pharmaceutical-journal.com/article/news/antidepressant-prescribing-in-creases-by-35-in-six-years (accessed 15 November 2023); Pamela Duncan and Sarah Marsh, 'Antidepressant use in England soars as pandemic cuts counselling access', The Guardian https://www.theguardian.com/society/2021/jan/01/covid-antidepressant-use-at-all-time-high-as-access-to-counselling-in-england-plunges (accessed 15 November 2023).

26 On the measure of 'Defined Daily Dose' (DDD), the European average of 'N06A-Antidepressants' rose from 30.5 DDD per 1,000 people per day in 2000 to 75.3 DDD in 2020. WHO define Defined Daily Dose (DDD) as 'the assumed average maintenance dose per day for a drug used for its main indication in adults'. 'Defined Daily Dose' (DDD) https://www.who.int/tools/atc-ddd-toolkit/about-ddd (accessed 15 November 2023). The group of N06A-Antidepressants 'comprises preparations used in the treatment of endogenous and exogenous depressions' (WHO).

Sweden as the greatest users of the drugs, though Germany, Spain and Italy also spent upwards of half a billion Euros per year on them.[27] The song of the twenty-first century became that of the psalmist, albeit reframed around a newly developed scientific salvation: 'I will lift up mine eyes unto the pills, from whence cometh my help.'

The drugs don't work

For some, demand straightforwardly indicates need, and need indicates the true size of the problem. Mental health issues, it is argued, were once upon a time stigmatised, suppressed and ignored. We should not imagine that people were more at peace back then. It was simply that they didn't talk about their mental health. Today's culture is more open. Our ability to speak honestly about these issues is due, in large part, to a better understanding of them. And crucially, this openness is facilitated by a growing appreciation of mental ill heath as a *medical* problem, no more embarrassing than influenza or back pain.

There is certainly some truth in this. The idea that society once saw depression as nothing more than a moral or spiritual failing, for which people had no one to blame but themselves, is more caricature than historical. That said, mental ill health *has* lost much of its stigma, and people are more willing to acknowledge and discuss their feelings, particularly dark ones. It is a big step in the right direction. That acknowledged, the scale and speed of the rise in antidepressants and the inclination of the *Diagnostic and Statistical Manual of Mental Disorders* to subsume almost any human condition under a pathological rubric has, perhaps ironically, left many people increasingly anxious.

There are various problems at play here. At a purely medical level, there are concerns about the long-term side effects of SSRIs and other antidepressant drugs. As early as 2004, *New Scientist* was running stories on 'the rise and fall of the wonder-drugs' like Prozac, discussing their previously undisclosed risks, especially for under-18s.[28] Accordingly, the position of the Royal College of Psychiatrists (RCP) is that antidepressant use

27 Servet Yanatma, 'Europe's mental health crisis in data: which country uses the most anti-depressants?', Euronews https://www.euronews.com/next/2023/09/09/europes-mental-health-crisis-in-data-which-country-uses-the-most-antidepressants (accessed 15 November 2023).

28 'The rise and fall of the wonder-drugs', *New Scientist* https://www.newscientist.com/article/mg18324545-300-the-rise-and-fall-of-the-wonder-drugs (accessed 15 November 2023).

among children and adolescents 'should only be part of second-line treatment for moderate to severe depression when patients are unresponsive to psychological therapy', and that 'the routine use of antidepressants for mild and sub-threshold depressive symptoms among adults is not generally recommended'.[29] Moreover, it is recognised that withdrawal from SSRIs is associated with agitation and akathisia, a neuropsychiatric syndrome of intense restlessness. In spite of all this, usage levels increase.

Underlying these concerns is a deeper question of how – and even whether – these antidepressants work. The way in which serotonin improves mood is still debated and not fully understood. In the words of the RCP, 'there is only partial understanding of how antidepressants exert their therapeutic effects'.[30] The basic theory is that chronic stress can cause the loss of connections in the brain, which can lead to depression, and SSRIs enable the brain to form new connections between cells, thereby alleviating the depression. But there remains considerable debate about the precise mechanisms behind this[31] and even about the extent to which such mental disorders are in fact the result of low serotonin at all.[32] One influential, systematic study on the serotonin theory of depression, published in July 2022, concluded: 'Our comprehensive review of the major strands of research on serotonin shows there is no convincing evidence that depression is associated with, or caused by, lower serotonin concentrations or activity.'[33]

---

29 Royal College of Psychiatrists, *Position Statement on Antidepressants and Depression*; https://www.rcpsych.ac.uk/docs/default-source/improving-care/better-mh-policy/position-statements/ps04_19---antidepressants-and-depression.pdf?sfvrsn=ddea9473_5 (accessed 15 November 2023).

30 The RCP does go on to point out that this is not at all uncommon in medicine: the mechanism of how paracetamol works is not fully understood, for example.

31 One paper that explored 'How do antidepressants elicit an antidepressant response?' concluded that 'current data suggest that conventional antidepressants (and ketamine, which is increasingly found to have a similar effect) mediate their antidepressant-like effects by increasing "brain-derived neurotrophic factor" (BDNF) in forebrain regions, in particular the hippocampus, making BDNF an essential determinant of antidepressant efficacy'. Carl Björkholm and Lisa M. Monteggia, 'BDNF – a key transducer of antidepressant effects', *Neuropharmacology* 102 (2016), pp. 72–9; ScienceDirect https://www.sciencedirect.com/science/article/abs/pii/S002839081530157X?via%3Dihub (accessed 15 November 2023).

32 Todd M. Hillhouse and Joseph H. Porter, 'A brief history of the development of antidepressant drugs: from monoamines to glutamate', *Experimental and Clinical Psychopharmacology* 23(1) (2015), pp. 1–21; National Library of Medicine https://www.ncbi.nlm.nih.gov/pmc/articles/PMC4428540 (accessed 15 November 2023).

33 Joanna Moncrieff et al., 'The serotonin theory of depression: a systematic umbrella review of the evidence', *Molecular Psychiatry* https://www.nature.com/articles/s41380-022-01661-0 (accessed 15 November 2023).

In the light of this, it is perhaps not surprising that there are also hard questions of whether SSRIs do, in fact, work. This may sound absurd given the sheer extent of their usage: no placebo effect could have carried an entire category of drugs so far. That, however, was almost the conclusion reached by one 2008 study, which concluded that antidepressants helped people improve 9.6 points on a depression scale, compared to placebo which saw an improvement of 7.8 points. 'Drug–placebo differences in antidepressant efficacy increase as a function of baseline severity,' the paper concluded, 'but are relatively small even for severely depressed patients.'[34]

A subsequent, systematic analysis of the efficacy and acceptability of twenty-one antidepressant drugs based on 522 double-blind studies published ten years later found that while all the antidepressants tested were more efficacious than placebo among adults with major depressive disorder, the summary effect sizes were mostly modest. Among children, the effects were much less pronounced with the antidepressant fluoxetine, 'the only antidepressant that might reduce depressive symptoms'.[35] The evidence is still emerging and the conclusions remain debatable, but the growing view appears to be that the current pharmacological approach to anxiety and depression is, if not a fallacy, then a lot less efficacious than is often assumed and usually claimed. The scientific turn in the treatment of depression may not be quite as successful as first claimed. The wonder drugs don't (quite) work.

What really ails you?

This, however, is not the deepest problem with the recent turn to pharmacology to treat depression. That lies in the existential and anthropological

34 Irving Kirsch et al., 'Initial severity and antidepressant benefits: a meta-analysis of data submitted to the Food and Drug Administration', PLOS Medicine https://journals.plos.org/plosmedicine/article?id=10.1371/journal.pmed.0050045 (accessed 15 November 2023).

35 Andrea Cipriani et al., 'Comparative efficacy and acceptability of 21 antidepressant drugs for the acute treatment of adults with major depressive disorder: a systematic review and network meta-analysis', The Lancet https://www.thelancet.com/journals/lancet/article/PIIS0140-6736(17)32802-7/fulltext#seccestitle140 (accessed 15 November 2023). In addition to this, the systematic study of the serotonin theory of depression quoted earlier, having concluded that 'most studies found no evidence of reduced serotonin activity in people with depression compared to people without', went on to state that 'methods to reduce serotonin availability using tryptophan depletion do not consistently lower mood in volunteers'. Moncrieff et al., 'The serotonin theory of depression', Molecular Psychiatry.

assumptions that underlie the turn itself, something that can be glimpsed when we examine the deep causes of depression.

In late 2022, the UK's Office for National Statistics (ONS) released a study examining the link between depression among adults and the cost-of-living crisis.[36] The data covered the autumn of that year and reported that 16% of adults experienced 'moderate to severe depressive symptoms'. However, that figure masked considerable variety between groups.

According to the ONS, a quarter of adults in the most deprived areas of England reported experiencing moderate to severe depressive symptoms, compared to 12% in the least deprived. Nearly one in four (24%) of those who had difficulty paying their energy bills reported depressive symptoms, compared to 9% of those who found it easy to pay fuel bills. More than one in four (27%) adults who found it difficult to afford their rent or mortgage payments reported depressive symptoms, compared to 15% who had no such difficulties. Higher still, 37% of 'full-time' unpaid carers[37] reported depression, compared to 16% of non-carers. And, astonishingly (or perhaps not), 59% of people who were economically inactive on account of long-term sickness were depressed, compared to 23% of the unemployed, and 8% of the 'economically inactive because retired' group. The ONS report followed all these data with the warning, in bold, that 'this release looks at depression in the context of the rising cost of living. It does not suggest a causal link between the cost of living and rates of depression in the population.' Perhaps, but we defy anyone to read these statistics and deny that there might just be some kind of link between poverty, insecurity and depression.

This same ONS report mentioned how, although there did not appear to be a change in the overall rate of reported depression as the cost-of-living crisis struck in 2022, depression rates had increased significantly between 2019 and 2020 as Covid took hold. The data showed a marked fall in reported well-being and a comparable rise in levels of anxiety over the various

---

36 'Cost of living and depression in adults, Great Britain: 29 September to 23 October 2022', Office for National Statistics https://www.ons.gov.uk/peoplepopulationandcommunity/healthandsocialcare/mentalhealth/articles/costoflivinganddepressioninadultsgreatbritain/29septemberto23october2022#characteristics-of-adults-with-moderate-to-severe-depressive-symptoms-in-autumn-2022 (accessed 15 November 2023).

37 I.e. those caring for thirty-five or more hours a week.

waves and Covid lockdowns across 2020–21.[38] The threat of a global pandemic and repeated, government-enforced lockdowns disrupted people's mental health. Who'd have thought it?

This was particularly acute among children. For example, nearly a quarter (23%) of secondary school pupils who had experienced long Covid had a probable mental health disorder, compared with 14% of pupils who had not had long Covid. And this came on top of numerous other challenges to young people's mental health at this time. Pre-Covid ONS data reported that children living in 'families that struggle to function well' are more likely to have a mental disorder than those from healthy functioning families. What this meant in reality was that children of lone-parent families, children of parents who themselves reported mental ill health, children of parents who were in receipt of welfare benefits, and children who were living with step-siblings (presumably as a result of family break-up or upheaval) were all more likely to have a recognised mental disorder than those whose who were not living in any of these situations.[39] In addition to all these factors, it is now increasingly acknowledged that a culture saturated with idealised, often doctored, and highly sexualised body images has a deleterious impact on the mental health and self-esteem of children, especially adolescents and especially girls.[40] And, more generally, the data show that 'social media is a substantial cause . . . of depression and anxiety, and therefore of behaviours related to depression and anxiety, including self-harm and suicide' among teenagers.[41]

---

38 'Coronavirus (COVID-19) latest insights: well-being', Office for National Statistics https://www.ons.gov.uk/peoplepopulationandcommunity/healthandsocialcare/conditionsand-diseases/articles/coronaviruscovid19latestinsights/wellbeing#mental-health (accessed 15 November 2023).

39 'Children whose families struggle to get on are more likely to have mental disorders', Office for National Statistics https://www.ons.gov.uk/peoplepopulationandcommunity/healthand-socialcare/childhealth/articles/childrenwhosefamiliesstruggletogetonaremorelikelytohave-mentaldisorders/2019-03-26 (accessed 15 November 2023).

40 'The impact of body image on mental and physical health', House of Commons Health and Social Care Committee https://committees.parliament.uk/publications/23284/documents/170077/default (accessed 15 November 2023).

41 'More children using social media report mental ill-health symptoms', Office for National Statistics https://www.ons.gov.uk/peoplepopulationandcommunity/wellbeing/articles/more childrenusingsocialmediareportmentalillhealthsymptoms/2015-10-20(accessed15November 2023); Jon Haidt, 'Social media is a major cause of the mental illness epidemic in teen girls. Here's the evidence', After Babel https://jonathanhaidt.substack.com/p/social-media-mental-illness-epidemic (accessed 15 November 2023).

The list of deep causes of, or at least deep correlations with, mental ill health could be extended, but the point of all this is to underline quite how wide-ranging, and also how *ordinary*, so many of these connections are. While many mental disorders may be the result of profound genetic, neurological or developmental conditions, what emerges from these studies is how much mental ill health is linked with poverty, insecurity, unemployment, physical ill-health, toxic culture, social-media usage, broken relationships, and the like.

In effect, experiences of depression, particularly of 'mild to moderate' depression, are often triggered by the mundane, everyday burdens of life and, in particular, of life that has gone off track and lacks the material and relational resources to restore and sustain it. And this leads us back to our second opening question in this chapter: what has any of this to do with religion?

The religious turn

One of the stronger, and certainly one of the more frequently reported, findings of social science is that religion is good for mental health. 'Middle-aged atheists [are] the "unhappiest people" in Britain' according to *The Week*.[42] 'Religion [is] better for mental health than sport', according to *Newsweek*.[43] 'Religious people [are] much happier and have more "life satisfaction" than others', according to the *Daily Mail*.[44]

These media stories report on specific academic studies that spell out the connection, albeit usually in less flamboyant terms, offering, for example, 'a systematic review of recent research on adolescent religiosity/spirituality and mental health'.[45] There are literally hundreds of such studies, from

42 'Midde-aged atheists the "unhappiest people" in Britain', *The Week* http://www.theweek. co.uk/69192/middle-aged-atheists-the-unhappiest-people-in-britain (accessed 15 November 2023).

43 Conor Gaffey, 'Religion better for mental health than sport, study finds', *Newsweek* http:// europe.newsweek.com/religion-better-mental-health-sport-study-finds-331240 (accessed 15 November 2023).

44 Charlene Adams, 'Religious people much happier and have more "life satisfaction" than others, according to a new study', MailOnline http://www.dailymail.co.uk/news/article-2886974/ Study-Religious-people-happier-life-satisfaction-others.html (accessed 15 November 2023).

45 Y. J. Wong, L. Rew, K. D. Slaikeu, 'A systematic review of recent research on adolescent religiosity/spirituality and mental health', *Issues in Mental Health Nursing* 27(2) (2006), pp. 161–83.

dozens of countries, covering nearly all major religious traditions,[46] many of them collated and analysed by Harold Koenig, one of the world's leading psychologists in this area.[47] The frequency and strength of the correlation between religion and good mental health – so frequent and so widespread one might almost confuse it with causation – is truly impressive.

In spite of the frequency and strength of this connection, there is a complexity here that demands attention. In a way that has become familiar in this whole debate, the terms used in these studies – not only 'religion' and 'mental health', but also 'well-being', 'life-satisfaction', 'happiness', etc. – are capacious, and any simplistic linkage between them is misleading. In effect, the correlation between religion, well-being and mental health is not straightforward, and the risks of thinking otherwise range from the daft to the harmful.

A closer examination of the terms involved doesn't undermine the basic connection, but it does give it some nuance.[48] There are various different ways in which 'religion' may be understood and measured. Religion can mean *affiliation*, the extent to which you identify as 'belonging' to a particular religion. It can mean *religiosity*, the importance that you attach to religion in your life. It can mean *belief*, the extent to which you hold the creeds of a particular religion to be factually true. It can mean *group participation*, the extent to which you join in with what other people of that religion do. Or it can mean *personal participation*, the extent to which you perform the practices of that religion personally.

On the other side of the equation, academic studies in this area distinguish between people's subjective well-being (their own assessment of their levels of life-satisfaction, anxiety, depression, etc.) and their objective well-being (formal or clinical assessments of mental health), as well as measuring their physical health and 'health-supporting behaviours'.[49]

Disambiguated in this way, it is possible to get a more accurate understanding of the true relationship between 'religion' and 'mental health'.

---

46 See Nick Spencer et al., *Religion and Well-Being: Assessing the evidence* (London: Theos, 2016).

47 H. G. Koenig. *Religion and Mental Health: Research and clinical applications* (Cambridge, MA: Elsevier Academic Press, 2018).

48 This section draws heavily on Spencer et al., *Religion and Well-Being.*

49 Health-supporting behaviours are those habits and practices that prevent a subject from falling or feeling ill, and which are themselves often connected with mental health.

Looking at the categories in this level of detail, what we find is that simply labelling oneself religious ('Christian', 'Jewish', 'Muslim', etc.) has little impact on someone's mental health.

Slightly more substantively, *religiosity* has some impact on subjective well-being, although it has a less measurable effect on mental health. In effect, those who claim that religion is important to their lives are more likely, on balance, to be happier but not necessarily more likely to have better measures of objective mental health. In a similar vein, although *religious belief* is positively correlated with subjective well-being, its effects on mental health are less pronounced. Again, what you believe has some impact on how you feel, but less on any medical assessment of mental health.

The biggest difference to mental health is made by what you do and with whom. The overwhelming consensus among studies is that social participation has a strong positive correlation with both subjective and objective well-being. Regular, frequent religious service attendance has a consistently positive impact on well-being and mental health, while lower levels of attendance and other types of participation, such as volunteering, also have some effect. Along similar lines, personal and private forms of religious activity also show a strong positive correlation with objective mental health measures.[50] In effect, doing things like praying, meditating, practising mindfulness, and reading scriptures seems to be good for mental health. In Koenig's words, 'Studies consistently show how regular involvement in religious practices correlates with lower rates of depression, suicide, anxiety, and substance use disorder.'[51]

Changing the lens on mental health

The nuancing and qualifications of the research on religion and mental health are extremely important. However strong it is, the connection between the two is *not* universal, absolute or infallible. It is absolutely not the kind of link that should encourage people simply to throw away their

---

50 It is worth noting that in some studies, greater levels of distress were associated with more personal participation, though in the context it became clear that the private religious activity did not cause the negative impact on well-being, but was a response to it.

51 McLean Videos, 'Lecture – Religion, spirituality and mental health: research and clinical applications'; https://www.mcleanhospital.org/video/lecture-religion-spirituality-and-mental-health-research-and-clinical-applications (accessed 15 November 2023).

pharmacological crutches and walk. Neither prayer nor churchgoing, let alone religious self-identification, is a panacea for mental ill health and a mandate to come off the meds. Rather, the plethora of data linking certain religious behaviours and practices with better mental health can be taken as a prompt to reframe our approach to mental health and, in particular, to shift away from a narrowly medical or pathological interpretation to a more existential and spiritual one.

The word 'spiritual' here is apt to be misunderstood so it is important to be clear what we mean by it. What we emphatically *do not* mean is that mental health issues should be understood as a kind of spiritual or demonic possession, amenable to prayer or exorcism or anything like that. Mental health issues are experiences and diagnoses that can *impact* an individual's experience of spirituality, but are not caused by a lack of faith, possession or indeed a form of spiritual warfare.[52]

Rather, we are using spiritual in the sense of concerned with ultimate meaning and importance, and that, at least according to a Christian worldview, means right relationships. Humans are made for, fulfilled by, and only rest in right relationships. A Christian spiritual concern for the human good will focus on how we, as material beings, are embedded in relationships, which will either lift or crush the soul.[53]

We might explain it this way. There are many different ways of conceptualising and responding to the concept of the human: different human lenses through which we are seen and known. The science behind pharmacology deploys one of them and, given that it is essentially the same approach that underlies all medicine, which has proved to be astoundingly successful over the last 150 years, it should be no surprise that it has been considered potentially game changing. If we could heal the mind in the same way as we have been able to heal the rest of the body, we would be doing humanity a great service.

This approach is based, quite properly, on the conceptualisation of the human as a material organism. To understand what is wrong with the

---

52 Recent literature has highlighted that ascription of mental health issues to the demonic is not only biblically inaccurate but also deeply harmful. It is a form of spiritual stigma that creates a unique form of injustice for those with mental health issues; it damages relationships and leaves individuals isolated. See Hannah Waite's forthcoming work on this topic for more details.

53 Another word that is apt to be misunderstood, as we have seen in a previous chapter.

human, you need to grasp how it works, what are the connections, systems and processes, etc. that regulate the material organism; to identify where they are not functioning as they should; and to develop interventions that enable them to do so. In this instance, we ascertain a link between serotonin and mood, theorise a meaningful correlation between the two, and develop ways in which to redress any apparent imbalance.

Assuming, for the sake of argument, that the serotonin theory of depression is correct, there is nothing in principle wrong with this analysis and approach. It is, however, strictly limited. Because it is a scientific–medical approach, the causal chain it posits begins with low levels of serotonin and ends in reported depression. Intervention begins at point A; success or otherwise is visible at point B.

Human beings *are* material organisms, and mental illness is therefore a material phenomenon. However, we are also social or relational beings: our existence and our good is inextricably wrapped up with that of others. The serotonin understanding of depression is predicated on understanding the processes of the human organism in isolation from other organisms or indeed any wider context. Whatever the external factors are that have caused the reduction of serotonin are bracketed out of the analysis.

And yet, very often the causal link goes back beyond point A. As the sociological analysis of depression shows (even if the ONS backs away from this conclusion), there is a strong correlation between anxiety, depression and mental ill health on the one hand, and poverty, insecurity, family instability and relationship breakdown on the other. This approach places the material–medical understanding of the human within the wider emotional–social–relational–existential context. It recognises humans as material beings – there is no sense of alien invasive forces catalysing depression – but as material beings whose entire existence is embedded in and formed by their relationships with other material beings. In effect, it traces the causal link back beyond serotonin to whatever it is outside the organism that might be responsible for the stress that causes the disruption of neural connections in the first place.

Sometimes, we should stress, it will find nothing at the end of this link; nothing before point A. People today, as indeed throughout history, have reported feeling melancholy, despair, anguish and the like without finding any external reason for it. Sometimes, there are no reasons. Sometimes, the problem is internal to the machine.

However, often it is not, and the mental pain, like its physical twin, is a response to a negative external stimulus. The woman who experiences the symptoms of extreme anxiety because she lives with an abusive partner; the teenager who self-harms because advertising and social media have given her an image of the female body that causes her to feel intensely dissatisfied with her own; the child who has behavioural difficulties at school because he has become a prize in his parents' acrimonious divorce; the middle-aged man who lives in a state of perpetual exhaustion and yet still can't sleep because his employment is irregular, unpredictable, at risk and badly paid; the elderly couple who live in a state of permanent unease because they are unsure whether they have enough money to heat their house; the pensioner who is depressed because she has no one – family, friends or acquaintances – to visit her . . . all are depressed. All, were we to test them, would have worryingly low levels of serotonin in the brain. All might be prescribed SSRIs or perhaps some other pharmacological remedy, were they able to get a GP appointment. And none of their ultimate problems would be *solved* by such a prescription.

Looking at the landscape of mental illness through a scientific–medical lens alone risks missing the features and structures of real importance. They are fainter, more distant, lurking on the horizon, but ultimately of huge significance, and without reference to them we cannot understand where we are. In a similar vein, responding to what one finds there by means of antidepressants alone leaves those dominant features unchanged. If you think like a pharmacologist, every problem will look like it needs a pill. And continuing to do so, as we have for thirty years now, will cement a trend that is already worryingly prevalent in society in which, ironically, it is the antidepressant, rather than religion, that is the 'opium of the people'.

Meditation before medication

Writing about mental health has its perils, and we have been at pains throughout this chapter neither to play down any diagnoses of mental ill health nor to suggest that there is a simple non-pharmacological solution awaiting anyone who can tear their eyes aways from the pills. Mental ill health is a complex and sensitive subject and deserves to be treated as such.

However, it is a *human* subject rather than simply a medical one, and should be understood as such. And being a human subject means it is also a religious one. In this chapter we have tried to show how a religious dimension is relevant, and we want to conclude by reiterating that relevance and using it to gesture towards what this might mean for our ongoing treatment of mental health.

Two points stand out. First, as we have remarked throughout the book, the science and religion debate gets interesting when we home in on the concept of the human: how do we understand the human, and who gets to adjudicate on the question? The pharmacological turn in mental health treatment from the late 1980s onwards offered implicit answers to both of those questions:

1 We are material organisms that occasionally suffer from neurochemical imbalances.
2 Scientists become the adjudicators. If the problem lies in serotonin levels, then so does the solution.

The apparent success of this approach slowly eclipsed a broader, more humanistic (in the true sense of that word) conception of mental problems. That eclipse has not been total, by any means. However many people take antidepressants today, and however much that has grown in the last thirty years, we should remember that many more don't. There remain various ways in which we talk about anxiety and depression today, many of which don't simply gravitate to the medical. That recognised, the pharmacological conceptualisation of the human has been in the ascendancy for more than a generation, and there are few signs of that trend slowing.

To counter those who would find the tired old science and religion conflict narrative here, a religious conception of the human (or at least the one we have been arguing for in this book) is not opposed to the scientific one. It does not oppose a material or medical understanding of the human, so much as insist that it is incomplete – the truth, no doubt, but not the whole truth. Viewing and interpreting the human primarily, let alone exclusively, through a medical lens and divorcing us from the social and relational networks in which we live and move and have our being is to misconstrue the human, which can just as easily be understood as agential, social, economic, creative, spiritual, etc.

Each of these dimensions is relevant and important. As an example, take agency; the sense that we are able and free to determine and pursue our goals. The idea that mental health is effectively no different from back pain may have helped reduce the stigma around it, but hasn't necessarily helped people's agency in this matter, their sense that they can contribute to the solving of the problem. According to one study published in *Nature*:

> The general public widely believes that depression has been convincingly demonstrated to be the result of serotonin or other chemical abnormalities, and this belief shapes how people understand their moods, *leading to a pessimistic outlook on the outcome of depression and negative expectancies about the possibility of self-regulation of mood.*[54]

Telling people 'it's not your fault' can feel liberating, but if the other side of that coin is 'and so there's nothing you can do about it', the consequences are less happy. This is the subtle distinction between interpreting something as depression or as despair, mentioned above. Depression, being medical, risks robbing the person (tellingly redesignated as a 'patient') of their agency; you can't really do much about depression unless you are a qualified medical practitioner, with access to the right diagnostic tools and the right drugs. Despair, by contrast, is existential, and although that will not necessarily make a difference to how bad it feels, it does leave open the possibility that you have some chance, some role, some agency in addressing it.

Having recognised that, even if one particular dimension of the human (such as agency) is important, perhaps even necessary, that does not make it sufficient. Assuring people that they have agency *can* strengthen them, but telling them that the only way to deal with mental illness is through the

---

54 Moncrieff et al., 'The serotonin theory of depression', *Molecular Psychiatry*; emphasis added.

exercise of that agency is not helpful. Indeed, this whole 'pull your socks up and pull yourself together' approach can be as harmful as telling them that they are simply patients (as opposed to agents) who can only be healed through the administration of drugs by a medical professional. Humans are complex, multidimensional creatures, and any religious contribution to the debate over mental health will repeatedly draw our attention to this fact, and will insist that no single picture of the human will exhaust the true depth of our selves.

This, then, is the first way in which religion is relevant to the increasingly scientific mental health debate – shifting and broadening the language and conceptual framework away from a narrow, medical understanding to a wider and more plural, humanistic one. The second is somewhat more concrete. Some readers, when scanning through the data on the relationship between religion and mental health earlier on in this chapter, may well have responded: 'Yes, fair enough, but there's nothing here that couldn't also be said of non-religious activities. Playing sport, board games, going on rambles, volunteering: all of these are collective activities that fortify our well-being, without a shred of religion in them. Right relationships are not the preserve of the religious.'

They are right. To point to the consistent correlation between good mental health and religious practices, especially communal ones, is not to deny it for other similar practices. But pointing out that connection was never intended to prove some kind of either/or between religion and 'secular' activities. Nor was it an attempt to promote religion in some (self-defeating) instrumentalising way: 'Sign up for church and watch your mental health improve.' Rather, the connection highlights the fundamentally relational nature of the human and, therefore, of good mental health. To *be*, in the fullest sense of that slippery verb, is to be in communion, to be secure in relationships of gift, grace and generosity. By contrast, to have lost those relationships of gift, grace and generosity, or never to have enjoyed them in the first place, harms and ultimately destroys us.

It is no accident that mental ill health is so widely reported today among those whose relational networks either don't support them, actively harm them, or don't exist at all. And it is also no accident that the ethical commands and admonitions of the Old Testament law and prophets pay so much attention to the plight of the widow, the orphan, the poor, and the alien or refugee. These were the people who had fallen through the formal, familial, social safety net of the day. Their existence was socially and economically precarious because the relationships that should have secured and protected them were threadbare or non-existent.

Their situation would have caused them great stress. They would justifiably have felt anxious and depressed. The Office for Biblical Statistics would have reported higher than average levels of anxiety and depression among these groups. The Hebrew Healthcare Service would no doubt have diagnosed low serotonin levels, and the pharmacologists would have prescribed SSRIs by the wheelbarrow.

And yet, for most of these vulnerable people, the first response should be to love them, in a concrete, material, supportive way. It is to draw them into networks of support; to provide them with the stability, the confidence, the resources, the opportunities and the hope that they need.[55] To bring them back to their feet through gift, so they may one day be in a position to give themselves. If there is a cure for sadness, it is not scientific.

Sometimes, then as now, that might not be enough. As we said earlier, sometimes the problem lies within, and no level of relational re-establishment or emotional support will heal the damage. Sometimes the drugs, assuming they are the right ones, are needed. But that medical response should take place *within the context of a wider social response* that recognises and responds to the frail and vulnerable humanity of all of us.

Increasingly, it does. Ever more medical practitioners are beginning to recommend non-pharmaceutical treatments to help people with depression. They advocate social prescribing, which connects people to activities, groups and services in their community to meet the practical, social and emotional needs that affect their mental health and well-being.[56] Some of this even includes joining vaguely religious groups, such as choirs; the process of singing complementing the positive impact of the gathering. It's a kind of 'meditation before medication' approach.

---

55 For more details on this and to explore how this would look, see Hannah Waite, 'Named, shamed and blamed: exploring the experience of stigma in Christians with bipolar disorder' (doctoral dissertation, University of Aberdeen, 2021), pp. 221–32; and *Named, Shamed and Blamed: A theological exploration into the experience of stigma* (London: SCM Press, forthcoming).

56 'Social prescribing', NHS England https://www.england.nhs.uk/personalisedcare/social-prescribing (accessed 15 November 2023).

Social prescribing is a relatively new phenomenon – at least in this incarnation – and we wait to see its results. But its implicit understanding of the human person and location of the human in relationships is to be welcomed. It allows us to end this chapter where we started, with Bellamy's *Looking Backward*.

It is easy to mock the novel for being hopelessly wrong in its predictions. The America of the early twenty-first century was not a socialist utopia. The state did not happily employ all workers. Equality had not been achieved. Worse, those countries that had set off down that road in the twentieth century had ended up as economic, social, cultural and environmental catastrophes. In all these regards, Bellamy could not have been more wrong.

And yet, a careful reading of his novel shows that, in spite of the narrator's awe at 'music-by-telephone', the book did not actually locate perfect 'human felicity' in devices or 'stuff'. Rather, Julian West found himself in utopia because society was characterised by networks of cooperation and partnership that had transformed everyday life. Writing in an age in which utopia was frequently predicted as the inevitable result of technological progress, Bellamy was subverting the techno-utopian narrative. Yes, the 'radio' might be a source of happiness, but it was only to be achieved as a result of humans working together in collaboration, almost in communion, to achieve shared goals. This, ultimately, is where true 'human felicity' lies.

7

The unformed body

Why abortion?

Why would you do it? Why would you write a book that ranged from aliens to AI, from scientific immortality to animal personhood, all with the intention of steering the encounter between science and religion away from cantankerous discord and towards fruitful dialogue, only to include a chapter on abortion? There is surely no subject more divisive and less amenable to dialogue, let alone compromise. Whatever you say, you are going to upset someone.

In truth, the decision is made for us, and the reason for including a chapter on the topic is as manifest as the temptation to sidestep it altogether. In his book *Morals Not Knowledge: Recasting the contemporary U.S. conflict between religion and science*, Professor of Sociology at University of California San Diego, John Evans, teases apart 'elite' discourse on science and religion from 'public' or 'popular' discourse.[1] The former, he argues, is focused on disagreements over knowledge – what we know and how we come to know it. It's the kind of thing that intellectuals get excited about, and draws the science and religion conversation onto questions of cosmology, evolution, miracles, eschatology and the like. It's one of the reasons, as we indicate in our introduction, why the science and religion debate often fixates on these issues.

Popular discourse, by contrast, tends to locate the encounter and the conflict (when it finds one) on moral grounds, such as which institutions, 'religious' or 'scientific', get to set the moral purpose and meaning of a society, or how medical technology should be used and regulated. In effect,

---

1 John Evans, *Morals Not Knowledge: Recasting the contemporary U.S. conflict between religion and science* (Berkeley, CA: University of California Press, 2018).

the general public tends to view science and religion through the lens of the kind of things they see in the news. Abortion is one of those things.

In summer 2022, the US Supreme Court overturned its own 1973 decision of *Roe v. Wade*, thereby removing the constitutional right for women to have an abortion and placing the issue back into the hands of state legislatures.[2] The reaction was hysterical, with jubilation on one side and fury on the other. Much of that reaction, especially the furious part, focused on the fact that an unprecedented six members of the Supreme Court were Catholics.[3] '[Is] the U.S. Supreme Court now a Roman Catholic institution?' asked one online magazine, without tongue obviously in cheek.[4]

There were other religious connections. Five of the six Catholic justices were nominated by Republican presidents, two of them by Donald Trump, who had also been responsible for the nomination of a third justice, Neil Gorsuch, a mainline Protestant.[5] Over the previous half century, the Republican party had simultaneously become both decisively pro-life and prominently religious, having been very successful in capturing the country's religious vote, in part among Catholics[6] and in much larger part among evangelicals. Donald Trump had made a great play for the evangelical vote in 2016, and intimated that Supreme Court nominations would be the reward for evangelical support. It worked. Fully 81% of white evangelicals supported Trump, a higher proportion than even for George W. Bush in 2004.[7]

---

2   *Dobbs v. Jackson Women's Health Organization*, No. 19-1392, 597 U.S. 215 (2022).

3   The other three members comprised two Protestants and one Jew. Frank Newport, 'The religion of the Supreme Court justices', Gallup https://news.gallup.com/opinion/polling-matters/391649/religion-supreme-court-justices.aspx (accessed 16 November 2023).

4   'The U.S. Supreme Court: now a Roman Catholic institution?' *The Globalist* https://www.theglobalist.com/the-u-s-supreme-court-now-a-roman-catholic-institution (accessed 16 November 2023).

5   Gorsuch's religious beliefs are not entirely clear but he appears to be an Episcopalian with liberal leanings. Daniel Burke, 'What is Neil Gorsuch's religion? It's complicated', CNN Politics https://edition.cnn.com/2017/03/18/politics/neil-gorsuch-religion/index.html (accessed 16 November 2023).

6   US Catholics had been disproportionately Democrat up until the 1960s but less so after that, and remain evenly split today. '8 facts about Catholics and politics in the U.S.', Pew Research Center https://www.pewresearch.org/short-reads/2020/09/15/8-facts-about-catholics-and-politics-in-the-u-s (accessed 17 November 2023).

7   'How the faithful voted: a preliminary 2016 analysis', Pew Research Center https://www.pewresearch.org/short-reads/2016/11/09/how-the-faithful-voted-a-preliminary-2016-analysis (accessed 17 November 2023).

In addition to the composition of the Supreme Court, and the raw theo-politics behind abortion, there is an obviously religious dimension to campaigning and public opinion on the issue. The fight against *Roe v. Wade* had been started, steered, funded and powered by Catholics, who were latterly joined by evangelicals. Polling repeatedly shows a big difference of opinion on the topic by religious affiliation. Whereas 84% of religiously 'unaffiliated' Americans think that abortion should be legal in all/most cases, 74% of white evangelical Protestants think it should be *illegal* in all/most cases.[8]

The difference is not limited to America. According to the Theos/Faraday research, 72% of non-religious adults in the UK say abortion is acceptable, compared to 46% of self-affiliating Christians. Across Europe there is an obvious correlation between how secular a nation is and its views on abortion. Sweden, Denmark, Finland, Belgium, the Czech Republic and the Netherlands are the continent's most pro-abortion countries, while Greece, Poland, Russia, Ukraine and Georgia are its least.[9] In short, wherever you are and whichever way you look at it, abortion feels like a religious issue.

How genuine is this? Many people have claimed that what looks like religion is really just politics. They point out that abortion was not that much of an issue for US evangelicals at first.[10] They observe that, however certain US evangelicals are on the issue, other religious groups are far more ambivalent, with even Catholics divided in their views.[11] They further point out that there is a range of different opinions on the subject within most religions and denominations.

---

8 'Public opinion on abortion', Pew Research Center https://www.pewresearch.org/religion/fact-sheet/public-opinion-on-abortion (accessed 17 November 2023).

9 'Eastern and Western Europeans differ on importance of religion, views of minorities, and key social issues', Pew Research Center https://www.pewresearch.org/religion/2018/10/29/eastern-and-western-europeans-differ-on-importance-of-religion-views-of-minorities-and-key-social-issues (accessed 17 November 2023).

10 Some go further and claim that the subject is really just a convenient weapon with which evangelicals can fight a wider culture war. Jessica Glenza, '"Historical accident": how abortion came to focus white, evangelical anger', *The Guardian* https://www.theguardian.com/world/2021/dec/05/abortion-opposition-focus-white-evangelical-anger (accessed 17 November 2023).

11 Of mainline US Protestants, 60% think abortion should be *legal* in all/most cases, compared with 38% who think it should be illegal. Of US black Protestants, 66% say legal vs 28% illegal. Of Catholics, 56% say abortion should be legal in all/most cases compared with 42% illegal.

This is an important corrective, and it is certainly right to try to bring a bit of nuance into the debate by acknowledging that, however much abortion is felt to be a religious issue, it is also mixed up with a great deal else, not least when the conversation shifts from its morality to its legality. Whatever else is going on under the surface of public opinion in the USA and elsewhere, it is more than *just* religion.

That said, there is no getting away from the fact that, however complicated and varied religious opinions are here, abortion does have a profoundly religious dimension to it. Jewish and Christian groups were noted in antiquity for prohibiting abortion and infanticide amidst a pagan culture that saw little problem with either, particularly when applied to sick, weak or female newborns.[12] The Catholic Church has been consistent in its condemnation of induced abortion for two millennia, albeit with some variation of opinion on the point at which the foetus became 'formed' or 'ensouled', only after which point did abortion become murder (more on which below).

Today, Catholic teaching on the issue is clear. 'Human life must be respected and protected absolutely from the moment of conception.'[13] Anglican teaching occupies a similar, if slightly more tractable, position, combining 'principled opposition with a recognition that there can be strictly limited conditions under which abortion may be morally preferable to any available alternative'.[14] Jewish and Islamic teaching is generally against abortion, although both traditions admit a range of voices which allow exceptions to the rule for a variety of reasons.[15]

In short, however political (or at least politicised) abortion has become, it is – and is certainly perceived as being – a genuinely religious issue of longstanding, major and, after the events of 2022, ever more contentious public concern to religious believers.

---

12 Andreas Lindemann, '"Do not let a woman destroy the unborn babe in her belly": abortion in ancient Judaism and Christianity', *Studia Theologica - Nordic Journal of Theology*, 49(2) (1995), pp. 253–71.

13 *Catechism of the Catholic Church*, para. 270.

14 General Synod July 2017: Answer to question with regard to marking 50th anniversary of 1967 Abortion Act.

15 See Elliot N. Dorff, 'Jewish bioethics: the beginning of life', in Elliot N. Dorff and Jonathan K. Crane (eds), *The Oxford Handbook of Jewish Ethics and Morality* (Oxford: Oxford University Press, 2013), pp. 313–29.

Abortion and the progress of science

That abortion is also a scientific issue may strike readers as either obvious or obscure. The procedure is obviously scientific in as far as it is modern medical science that has made abortion not just possible but a relatively straightforward, cheap, quick and safe procedure, when it used to be extremely dangerous and often fatal. Quite simply, without science, there is no abortion.

Beyond that, however, it may not be immediately clear why this is a particularly scientific issue, still less one that will change because of scientific progress in the twenty-first century. After all, the stages of pregnancy have been well understood for centuries, and the science of obstetrics seems unlikely to make the kind of advances that we expect to see in genetics, astrobiology or pharmacology. What has the future of abortion to do with the future of science?

The answer to this is that our ability to 'see' into the womb, to understand and to intervene in the course of pregnancy has developed enormously over recent decades and will continue to do so in coming years. Previously unseen by, and largely unknown to, the wider human community, the unborn are increasingly visible, known and present to us. And as this progress casts light on the unborn themselves, it may also change the way we think of them.

Ultrasound technology was first employed for embryological diagnostic use in the mid-1950s. Amniocentesis, the sampling of amniotic fluid to screen for abnormalities, arrived about a decade later, as did percutaneous umbilical blood sampling. Since then, our ability to 'see' pregnancy has become ever more impressive, less invasive, more comprehensive and more 'democratic'. The first 3-D ultrasound was used to take three-dimensional images of a foetus in the late 1980s. Chorionic villus sampling, a form of prenatal diagnosis for chromosomal or genetic disorders, was developed at the same time. Real-time or 4-D ultrasound developed in the 1990s.[16]

From the early 2010s, expectant mothers have been able to access non-invasive prenatal testing to screen for chromosomal abnormalities and

---

16 S. Campbell, 'A short history of sonography in obstetrics and gynaecology', PMC, National Library of Medicine https://www.ncbi.nlm.nih.gov/pmc/articles/PMC3987368 (accessed 17 November 2023).

other factors. Since then, researchers have developed sensors that can be worn for extended periods of time, which allow a pregnant woman to track her baby's sound and movements, thereby enabling close monitoring beyond the usual realm of the hospital.[17] This is especially useful during high-risk pregnancies but is not limited to them. A growing number of biomedical companies are marketing devices for what is known as 'remote clinical diagnosis and screening', which enable expectant parents to monitor the health of their unborn child on an ongoing basis.[18]

This enhanced ability to see into pregnancy is allowing scientists to assess the nature and health of unborn children far more comprehensively than has previously been the case. Ultrasound scans have long been able to test for nuchal translucency, the area of fluid behind a foetus's neck, or nasal bone determination, both of which can give an indication of chromosomal abnormalities such as Down's syndrome or Patau's syndrome. Maternal blood tests can have the same result. Foetal growth and anatomy can be monitored or assessed by 3-D or, if necessary, 4-D ultrasound tests, as well as patterns of foetal activity and behaviour. Tests for hormones like estriol and inhibin allow further assessment of the baby's health. And all this can now be supplemented by genetic screening for conditions like cystic fibrosis, Duchenne muscular dystrophy, sickle cell disease, haemophilia A, Tay-Sachs disease and thalassemia. In effect, obstetrics is now able not only to see, but to evaluate the health of unborn babies with something approaching the accuracy it can with newborn babies.

Furthermore, it is also capable, in some instances, not simply of assessing foetal health but intervening in it. Foetal surgery is a relatively new branch of medicine. It is not often needed, either because the foetal condition cannot be treated during pregnancy or because it does not need to be. It remains highly complex and risky. Nevertheless, it is increasingly possible and common. Some foetal surgery is 'minimally invasive', involving minor incisions and procedures on the foetus while in the womb. Other surgery is 'open', involving a much more substantial procedure even up to the point of the foetus being removed from the womb, as it would be during a

---

17 Bridie Kennerley, 'New technology can keep an eye on babies' movements in the womb', Imperial College London https://www.imperial.ac.uk/news/187286/new-technology-keep-babies-movements-womb (accessed 17 November 2023).

18 For example 'Pulsenmore' https://pulsenmore.com (accessed 17 November 2023).

caesarean section, anaesthetised, left dependent on the placenta, and then replaced after the procedure. Conditions such as spina bifida, in which the baby's spinal cord does not develop properly, can be treated in this way.[19]

More futuristically, science has aspired towards creating an artificial womb, in which foetuses might develop outside the mother's body altogether. Remarkably, the patent for such a so-called 'exo-womb' was taken out in 1954.[20] There has not been a great deal of progress since then, although scientists have successfully experimented with '*ex utero* embryogenesis' for mice[21] and lambs.[22] Moreover, it is fair to say that there are one or two ethical queries around the very notion of the motherless womb. At present, the focus is on developing an artificial womb that would help very premature babies develop in such a way as to reduce the risk of subsequent health problems. But more fantastical ambitions seek to separate motherhood and pregnancy altogether. The biologist J. B. S. Haldane, who coined the term 'ectogenesis', meaning the development of a foetus outside the body, once predicted that, by the end of the twenty-first century, only a small minority of babies would 'be born of woman', while a more recent article in the *Guardian* claimed that 'there is a case for an artificial womb being a better option than a woman's'.[23]

Finally, medical science is increasingly able to keep premature babies alive at ever-earlier stages of pregnancy. A premature or preterm birth is classified as any before thirty-seven weeks; an extreme one as before twenty-eight weeks. All preterm births risk complications – the earlier the birth, the greater the risk – but the chances of dealing with these improve

19 'Dozens of unborn babies receive op on NHS to stop paralysis', NHS England https://www.england.nhs.uk/2021/05/dozens-of-unborn-babies-receive-op-on-nhs-to-stop-paralysis (accessed 17 November 2023).

20 Patent 2,723,660: ARTIFICIAL UTERUS, taken by Emanuel M. Greenberg, New York, N.Y., Application July 22, 1954, Serial No. 444,958 6 Claims. (C. 128-1) 1498407273133145063-02723660; https://patentimages.storage.googleapis.com/ce/98/f3/ec88cc9bda874d/US2723660.pdf (accessed 17 November 2023).

21 Alejandro Aguilera-Castrejon et al., 'Ex utero mouse embryogenesis from pre-gastrulation to late organogenesis', *Nature* https://web.archive.org/web/20220801215514/https:/www.nature.com/articles/s41586-021-03416-3 (accessed 17 November 2023).

22 Emily A. Partridge et al., 'An extra-uterine system to physiologically support the extreme premature lamb', *Nature* https://www.nature.com/articles/ncomms15112 (accessed 17 November 2023).

23 Aarathi Prasad, 'How artificial wombs will change our ideas of gender, family and equality', *The Guardian* https://www.theguardian.com/commentisfree/2017/may/01/artificial-womb-gender-family-equality-lamb (accessed 17 November 2023).

every year, as does the survival rate of extreme preterm births. In Western nations, babies born at twenty-four weeks have around a 50% chance of survival, and those at twenty-three weeks about 25%.

Considering that sixty years ago parents could still be surprised by the arrival of twins at birth, these are extraordinarily impressive advances. The fact that it is now possible to conduct brain surgery successfully on unborn babies is nothing short of jaw-dropping.[24] Science has not only made the ending of a pre-born's life much easier and safer than it ever has been, but it has also made enormous progress in understanding, and potentially healing and saving, the same life. In so doing, it has also sharpened up the ethical tensions that have long hovered around the status of the foetus.

Why science can't just sort this out

If science is making progress of this nature in understanding, and intervening more successfully in pregnancy, it is only fair to ask whether it is also now in a position to step into and resolve those debates. Scientists know so much more about the processes of pregnancy, from the fusing of chromosomes to make a zygote to the unprecedentedly safe delivery of newborns, are they not also better positioned to settle the debates that swarm around abortion? Doing so would certainly obviate the need for any religious contribution to them.

There are certainly some high-profile figures who have argued just this, such as the popular historian and public intellectual, Yuval Noah Harari. Writing about abortion in *Homo Deus*, Harari reasoned that although devout Christians oppose abortion and many liberals support it, 'the main bone of contention is factual rather than ethical'. Christians and liberals both 'believe that human life is sacred' and murder is a crime. They simply disagree about 'certain biological facts', such as whether human life begins at the moment of conception, at the moment of birth or at some intermediate point. That being so, Harari says, scientists should resolve the issue as they are 'more qualified

---

24 Technically, this operation was on the Great Cerebral Vein (sometimes known as the Vein of Galen), which carries blood from the brain to the heart, but as the condition tackled by the surgery can lead to brain injuries, the operation was widely reported under the rubric of brain surgery. See, for example, Nadia Kounang and Amanda Sealy, 'Doctors performed brain surgery on a baby before she was born and now she's thriving', CNN https://edition.cnn.com/2023/05/04/health/brain-surgery-in-utero/index.html (accessed 17 November 2023).

than priests to answer factual questions such as "Do human foetuses have a nervous system one week after conception?" [or] "Can they feel pain?"[25]

Although Harari doesn't say as much, this argument is a version of Stephen Jay Gould's 'non-overlapping magisteria', which we have gently critiqued in this book. (In actual fact, it's a rather less generous version because Gould did at least envisage a magisterium of values to which religion belonged, whereas it is doubtful whether Harari acknowledges any such magisterium, let alone any contribution religion can make to it.) By this understanding, the whole arena of conception, pregnancy, foetal development and abortion is one of facts and facts alone, and as scientists are in the business of determining facts, they are therefore able to adjudicate decisively on this topic. In effect, the moral status of the kind of entities we are dealing with here can be decided by a better grasp of their biology.

Understanding why this is wrong is instructive as it helps map out the way in which abortion is *necessarily* a science and religion issue. In spite of what Harari argues, 'devout Christians' and 'liberals' do usually agree about the 'biological facts' pertaining to pregnancy. Both accept, for example, the scientific understanding of when the foetal brain, heart, spine and nervous system develop. There is no chasm of factual disagreement between opposing parties on this issue.

It is, of course, possible that certain factual disagreements do remain, but if they do, it is usually because there is ongoing scientific disagreement about them. For example, there is some dispute about the nature and extent of prenatal perception and, in particular, the point at which a foetus can be said to feel pain. Some argue that because the cortex and thalamo-cortical tracts, which only become fully functional in the third trimester of pregnancy, are necessary for pain experience, the unborn child cannot experience pain before that stage. Others claim that a functioning cortex and thalamic connectivity are not necessary, and that there is evidence of foetal response to stimuli before twenty-four weeks, meaning we cannot rule out the possibility of prenatal perception in the second trimester.[26] In the light of this, there is a good chance that 'devout Christians' and 'liberals' will

---

25 Yuval Noah Harari, *Homo Deus: A brief history of tomorrow* (London: Harvill Secker, 2016), p. 221.

26 Stuart W. G. Derbyshire and John C. Bockmann, 'Reconsidering fetal pain', *Journal of Medical Ethics* https://jme.bmj.com/content/46/1/3 (accessed 17 November 2023).

disagree on this issue, but that is only because the scientists on whose work they draw also disagree. We can safely assume that, as evidence mounts, the gap will close and such disagreements will wither.

If there is no major, systemic factual disagreement between different parties on this issue, where does the difference lie? To pick up on Harari's examples, science is able to discern when a human foetus develops a nervous system. It may be able to determine at what point he or she feels pain. It might have an idea, one day, of if and when a pre-born becomes conscious of their own existence. And it can certainly identify anatomical, chromosomal and genetic abnormalities in foetal development, correct some, and give an indication of the potential impact of others on the newborn's life prospects.

What science cannot do is determine the ethical or existential significance of any of these biological facts. It cannot adjudicate on whether, or to what extent, the stage of foetal development or the ability to feel pain (or the existence of consciousness, or the chances of a healthy life, or the ability to survive outside the womb, etc.) are morally significant facts that have any bearing on the right of an unborn human to life. In short, it can establish biological facts with ever greater accuracy, but it cannot say what those facts *mean*, or even whether they matter.

This point was made by the 'Warnock Report into Human Fertilisation and Embryology' as long ago as 1984.[27] Some people, the report stated, hold that an embryo is human and alive and therefore 'should not be deprived of a chance for development' (which would therefore preclude its use in IVF). Others, 'while in no way denying that human embryos are alive . . . hold that embryos are not yet human persons' and that therefore they might be used in fertility research. As the report goes on to say:

> Although the questions of when life or personhood begin[s] appear to be questions of fact susceptible of straightforward answers, we hold that the answers to such questions in fact are complex amalgams of factual and moral judgements.

---

27 *Report of the Committee of Inquiry into Human Fertilisation and Embryology*, para. 11.9; https://www.hfea.gov.uk/media/2608/warnock-report-of-the-committee-of-inquiry-into-human-fertilisation-and-embryology-1984.pdf (accessed 17 November 2023).

Harari's belief that the question of human life is amenable to 'biological facts' is simply a consequence of a limited, positivist approach to knowledge, holding to the idea that science alone can discern truth, and if science can't, then there isn't a truth there to be discerned. Unfortunately for him, Harari's 'biological facts' cannot so easily be detached from the wider moral considerations.

Moreover, as we have emphasised throughout this book, such moral considerations are always embedded within, and cannot be considered without attention to, wider existential contexts, 'forms of life' that give frame and meaning to the moral concepts we use. In effect, the debate over abortion must draw on the kind of metaphysical ideas with which all worldviews, religious and non-religious alike, ultimately concern themselves. As the philosopher, Antony Kenny, wrote in an essay on 'The beginning of individual human life', however much politicians and lawyers might try, ultimately this subject 'cannot evade . . . the question of personhood', and that is unavoidably 'a metaphysical question', the answer to which necessitates concepts like 'actuality and potentiality, identity and individuation'.[28]

Why 'choice' is not enough

To some readers, all this may come across as a demonstration of the patently obvious. Such people never doubted that abortion was a scientifically facilitated procedure that demanded religious attention, one that necessarily draws on *both* 'biological facts' derived from science, *and* metaphysical concepts and commitments informed by worldviews. These voices, however, have hardly been the only ones in this debate. In the face of the voices that like to claim that science is capable of settling these questions; or that this is simply none of religion's business ('Keep your rosaries off my ovaries'); or, most prevalently, that this is, properly speaking, simply a matter of 'choice', it is important to stress why and how this discussion cannot but involve scientific and religious considerations.

This last objection – choice – is so widespread and so popular that it is worth responding to it separately. For those convinced of the moral and

---

28 Anthony Kenny, 'The beginning of individual human life, *Daedalus* 137(1), On Life (Winter 2008), pp. 15–22; https://www.jstor.org/stable/20028161?seq=8 (accessed 17 November 2023).

legal acceptability of abortion, the notion of 'choice' is the go-to term. A woman's right to choose is treated, by one side of the debate, with the same finality as a foetus's right to life by those on the other side.

It is perhaps unfair to criticise slogans. They are, after all, intended to be short, catchy and popular, rather than nuanced, balanced or subtle. Nevertheless, the question-begging way in which 'choice' is invoked to close down this moral debate is especially problematic. This is something that has been pointed out by philosophers on both sides of the debate.

Half-way through his magnum opus, *A Secular Age*, Charles Taylor comments on how unsatisfactory the instinctive and allegedly decisive appeal to 'choice' is in this debate. 'I can think of a number of reasons against the idea of forbidding by law . . . first-trimester abortions,' he wrote. One might cite the fact that the 'burden' of bearing the child falls 'almost totally on the pregnant woman', or there is a 'high likelihood' that the law would be widely evaded, which would then lead to 'operations carried out in much more perilous conditions'. These are serious, if contestable, reasons to permit aborting a foetus in the first twelve weeks of pregnancy. However, he continues, leaving the reasoning simply at the door of 'choice' is not enough, 'unless one would like equally to legitimate the choice of prospective parents to selectively abort female foetuses to reduce their eventual dowry cost'. Choice, he concludes, 'is a word which occludes almost everything important: the sacrificial alternatives in a dilemmatic situation, and the real moral weight of the situation'.[29]

On the other side, atheist to Taylor's Catholic, and 'pro-choice' to Taylor's more generally pro-life position, the British philosopher Julian Baggini has written about how the decision by the 'pro-choice lobby' not to 'directly rebut' their opponents' arguments, but instead to base their case on the woman's right to choose, 'is a serious philosophical misstep'. As he goes on to point out:

> a woman only has a right to choose if that choice is ethically permissible. Otherwise, a woman has no more right to choose an abortion

---

29 Charles Taylor, *A Secular Age* (Cambridge, MA: Harvard University Press, 2007), pp. 478–9.

than she does to shoot an irritating neighbour. No appeal to freedom of choice can transform an act of murder into a surgical procedure.[30]

Baggini goes on to try to make that philosophical case; Taylor does not. The point, however, is that both recognise that the invocation of 'choice' as a way of circumventing the ethical and existential questions that surround pregnancy and abortion is not good enough.

The inadequacy of this stance is far from just theoretical, and can be seen in vivid technicolour in two sub-areas of this debate, one of which Taylor alludes to, both of which have grown in prominence over recent years. The first is sex-selective abortion. This remains common across the world, as does sex-selective infanticide, just as it has been through history. 'If you happen to be pregnant again, if it is a boy, leave it; if it is a girl, throw it out,' one absentee husband in Alexandria famously wrote to his Roman wife.[31] Chilling as we are likely to find this advice, it is hardly unknown today, particularly in areas of East and South Asia.[32] The American writer, Mara Hvistendahl, has estimated that there could be as many as 160 million missing women and girls across the globe on account of sex-selective practices.[33] Moreover, there is growing anecdotal evidence (official data are, understandably, hard to come by[34]) that the phenomenon may be happening in the UK and other Western countries, facilitated by the availability of the non-invasive prenatal testing mentioned earlier.[35]

The British Labour Party was so shocked by this that it called for the sex of unborn children, as revealed by early non-invasive prenatal testing, to be kept from expectant parents, for fear they might choose to abort the

30 Julian Baggini, 'What philosophy can tell us about the right to abortion', *Prospect* https://www.prospectmagazine.co.uk/ideas/philosophy/38753/what-philosophy-can-tell-us-about-the-right-to-abortion (accessed 17 November 2023).

31 Stephanie West, 'Whose baby? A note on P. Oxy. 744', *Zeitschrift für Papyrologie und Epigraphik* 121 (1998), pp. 167–72.

32 At least with regard to abortion, rather than infanticide, though that too remains common.

33 Mara Hvistendahl, *Unnatural Selection: Choosing boys over girls, and the consequences of a world full of men* (New York, NY: PublicAffairs, 2011).

34 'We have no evidence that sex related abortions are taking place in Great Britain. The latest analysis by the Department found that the United Kingdom gender ratio over the period 2013 to 2017 was 105.4 male to 100 female births, which is within the normal boundary.' Written questions, answers and statements, UK Parliament https://questions-statements.parliament.uk/written-questions/detail/2020-01-21/6069 (accessed 17 November 2023).

35 'I aborted after they told me it was a girl', *Victoria Derbyshire*, BBC 2 https://www.bbc.co.uk/programmes/p06lffpy (accessed 17 November 2023).

foetus on discovering it was female.[36] By the logic of 'choice', however, there is nothing obviously wrong with such a decision. If maternal (or parental) choice is enough to legitimise abortion, there is no reason why it should not be enough to legitimise specific kinds of abortion. Put the other way round, if I cannot mount any legitimate objection against a woman's choice to abort a foetus, I cannot mount any legitimate objection against the same woman's choice to abort a female foetus. Unless one accords some inherent moral status to the baby in the womb, citing their sex as a reason for protection is not possible.

A second and comparable problem is in the treatment of unborn children with disabilities. In 2022, the British disability rights campaigners Heidi Crowter and Máire Lea-Wilson lost their Court of Appeal challenge over the status of late-term abortions on grounds of serious foetal abnormalities. Abortion is not permitted under English law after twenty-four weeks, except in cases where there is deemed a substantial risk that if the child were born it would suffer from such physical or mental abnormalities as to be seriously handicapped. Astonishingly, Down's syndrome is included under this exception, as is having a cleft lip, cleft palate or a club foot. The judges rejected their appeal on the grounds that it raised substantive issues that only parliament could decide.

So sacred is the 'right to choose' that even some disability rights campaigners sided *against* Crowter (who has Down's syndrome) and Lea-Wilson (whose son does).[37] However, as with sex-selective abortion, no society that claims to view and treat people with disabilities in the same way as those without can seriously justify what is a transparently discriminatory approach. If we judge a child born with Down's syndrome to be worth protecting, indeed not just protecting but helping, nurturing, and guarding against discrimination, it is not clear why we fail to do the same when that same child is a foetus. Appealing to 'choice' is simply ethically evasive. Both these cases, the like of which we are almost certain to hear more of in coming years, underline how, unless we choose to evade all

---

36 Amber Haque, 'Labour calls for ban on early foetus sex test', BBC News https://www.bbc.co.uk/news/health-45497454 (accessed 17 November 2023).

37 Matthew Weaver, 'Woman with Down's syndrome loses court of appeal abortion law case', *The Guardian* https://www.theguardian.com/society/2022/nov/25/heidi-crowter-woman-downs-syndrome-loses-court-of-appeal-abortion-law-case (accessed 17 November 2023).

moral evaluations by taking refuge in the idea of choice, the heart of this issue demands wrestling with the existential status of the child in the womb.

To be clear, it is equally important to recognise that this need not be the *only* factor brought into our moral evaluation. As Taylor states, and as the Church of England's position intimates, it is quite proper to introduce other considerations alongside the status of the foetus when thinking through this issue. The circumstances of conception (e.g. was coercion involved?) and the genetic inheritance and the prospective quality of life of a severly disabled newborn are both salient factors, as is the likelihood of any restrictions being circumvented in still more dangerous ways. Simply because one accords a certain moral status to the unborn child, that does not mean excluding every other moral consideration. What it does mean is that we cannot altogether avoid wrestling with the question of the moral status of the foetus – especially now that the US Supreme Court's decision has thrown the issue back into the arena of politics, civil society and public moral argument; *and* scientific progress has augmented our ability to see, understand and intervene in pregnancy.

Why 'life' is not enough

For all that we have criticised the simplistic and evasive resort to 'choice' in the debate, we also recognise that the anxiety (felt by those who want to argue *for* abortion) at the prospect of a religiously inflected debate on the issue is not without reason. The prospect of campaigners proclaiming on this issue by quoting Scripture or instinctively appealing to the sanctity of life, without further explication, is not an appealing one. 'Pro-life' can be as thin a slogan as 'pro-choice'. If religious advocates want to restrict or abolish the right to abortion, some of them at least will need to up their ethical game.

This will involve some honesty. In his book *The Moral Vision of the New Testament*, Richard Hays concludes with a short chapter on abortion. In it, he points out, bluntly, that 'the Bible contains no texts about abortion'.[38] Those texts that are commonly cited by the pro-life side of the debate are

---

38 Richard B. Hays, *The Moral Vision of the New Testament: Community, cross, new creation: A contemporary introduction to New Testament ethics* (New York, NY: HarperOne, 2013), p. 446.

question-begging and deal not with the status of the foetus but with (sometimes only distantly) related issues.[39]

Moreover, as Hays points out, 'sacredness of life' is, in fact, itself 'a sacred cow that has no basis in the New Testament', as he goes on to explain by quoting ethicist Stanley Hauerwas:

> The Christian prohibition against taking life rests not on the assumption that human life has overriding value but on the conviction that it is not ours to take. The Christian prohibition of abortion derives not from any assumption of the inherent value of life, but rather from the understanding that as God's creatures, we have no basis to claim sovereignty over life.[40]

If religious contributors want to argue 'pro-life', they need to do more than proof-quote the Bible or use phrases like 'sanctity of life'. Instead they need to grapple with the attendant question of what kind of religious public reasoning is legitimate in debates of this nature, not to mention, in the USA at least, ironing out a few little local anomalies regarding attitudes to gun ownership and the death penalty.[41]

Beyond this, it is worth noting, as we mentioned above, that Christian tradition on this issue has not been quite as univocal as some modern proponents would like it to have been. To be clear, the Church has rarely if ever tolerated, still less advocated, induced abortion. From the collection of early Christian teaching known as the *Didache*, dating from perhaps the late first century, the Church has taught that 'you shall not murder a child by abortion'.[42] The inclination of some contemporary liberal Protestant

---

39 Exodus 20:13; Psalm 139:13–16; Luke 1:44; Galatians 5:19–20; Matthew 19:14. The Exodus text is simply about murder. Psalm 139 is about God's care and foreknowledge. The Luke verse has only Christological significance and is not interested in the question of prenatal personhood. Paul's inclusion of *pharmakeia* in his list of the works of the flesh in Galatians 5 is not about abortifacients as some claim. And Jesus is talking about living children in Matthew 19. See Hays, *The Moral Vision of the New Testament*, pp. 446–8.

40 Hays, *The Moral Vision of the New Testament*, p. 454, quoting Stanley Hauerwas, *A Community of Character: Toward a constructive Christian social ethic* (Notre Dame, IN; London: University of Notre Dame Press, 1981), pp. 225–6.

41 On religious public reasoning, see Jonathan Chaplin, *Talking God: The legitimacy of religious public reasoning* (London: Theos, 2008).

42 *Didache* 2.2.

denominations to defend abortion is, as Hays points out, a significant departure from the Church's historical teaching.

That said, Christian teaching on the point at which the foetus is formed or 'ensouled', only after which point abortion is considered murder, has not been entirely consistent.[43] For some church fathers, any form of abortion at any stage was illicit. Tertullian wrote that 'it is not lawful to destroy what is conceived in the womb even while the blood is being drawn into a human being' (meaning in the earliest stages of pregnancy), while Basil of Caesarea stated that 'any fine distinction as to its [i.e. the foetus] being completely formed or unformed is not admissible'.[44]

For others, however, in the words of Gregory of Nyssa, 'it would not be possible to style the unformed embryo a human being, but only a potential one'.[45] St Augustine was one of a number of church fathers who held that the foetus remained 'unformed' in the earliest stages of pregnancy, during which period 'the law of homicide would not apply, for it could not be said that there was a living soul in that body, for it lacks all sense'.[46] Aquinas, drawing on the influence of Aristotle, believed the ensoulment of the foetus occurred forty days after conception, although there is much debate on what that meant in terms of the status of the foetus before that point.[47]

Such examples are given not to cast doubt over the position held by mainstream churches today, which is, for the most part, clear. Rather they are intended to illustrate the point that just as invoking 'choice' is no immediate solution to the ethical questions arising in this area, neither is simply invoking 'life'. Mainstream Christian thought has had to reason its way to its current position, and it must continue to do so if it wishes to advocate that position to a rather sceptical and hostile culture. The question, what

---

43 The following discussion draws on G. R. Dunstan, 'The moral status of the human embryo: a tradition recalled', *Journal of Medical Ethics* 1 (1984), pp. 38–44.

44 Tertullian, *Apologia*, 9.8; Basil of Caesarea, Ep. 188, *Ad Amphilochium*, II. Dunstan does point out that 'Tertullian was by no means accounted orthodox in other of his controversial opinions, particularly in his "transducianism" or peculiar belief that the soul (anima) derived from the parental seed, a belief that would give added importance to the early embryo'. Dunstan, 'The moral status of the human embryo', p. 40.

45 St Gregory of Nyssa, *Adversus Macedonianos*.

46 Augustine of Hippo, *Quaestionum in Heptateuchum*, I; II; n. 80.

47 See, for example, Fabrizio Amerini, *Aquinas on the Beginning and End of Human Life* (Cambridge, MA: Harvard University Press, 2013).

is it about foetal life that gives it a status that requires protection, is a live and legitimate one.

For and against

One way of answering this is to engage with the opposing view; in other words, the reasons (when they are given) as to why the unborn child might *not* deserve our protection. Five factors stand out: (ab)normality, rationality, viability, sentience and existence.[48] The purpose and value of drawing out these factors is not to endorse them, but rather to illustrate the different ways in which it is possible to ground the value of life.

The first of these asserts that it is the absence of (ab)normalities – whether genetic, chromosomal or developmental – that is relevant to the question of foetal protection. If the pregnancy is normal, all well and good. If, however, there are abnormalities, and especially those that are understood to adversely affect the life and health of the newborn, then the protection afforded the unborn may be legitimately withdrawn.

The second contends that it is by dint of his or her lack of rationality that the foetus forfeits the right to full protection. The argument is similar to that which accords fundamental value to the perceived richness of mental life, and so, for example, perform medical experimentation on, say, mice or other less cognitively complex mammals rather than on primates. What we value is the ability to understand, plan, and independently navigate the world.

The third argues that it is the ability of the foetus to survive outside the womb that is of key relevance. The fact that a newborn is currently completely unable to survive before twenty-one weeks,[49] and is still unlikely to survive before twenty-four weeks, is taken to mean that he or she does not, at those stages, exist as an independent organism, which is a prerequisite for the protection of wider society. In effect, where there is no viable, independent life, there is no right to life.

The fourth reason, sentience, is related to the foetal ability to feel pain, which we discussed earlier. Its salience in this matter relates to the

---

48 The following section draws on Michael Banner's chapter on abortion in *Christian Ethics and Contemporary Moral Problems* (Cambridge: Cambridge University Press, 1999).

49 The current record for more premature delivery stands at twenty-one weeks and one day.

connection between suffering and moral evil, and the belief that 'where there is no pain because there is no sentience . . . the killing is not wrongful'.[50] The fact that the foetus does not feel pain – assuming that it does not; the matter, as we have discussed, remains contentious – is judged to legitimise abortion, although the broad coincidence between the point of viability and the point of sentience helps reinforce this point.

The fifth reason places the relevant value on the point at which the new life can be said to exist as an, albeit dependent, being. Modern science has enabled us to understand the exact processes involved in conception much better, but that has not stopped different parties from identifying the point of existence at different moments. That can be the initial fusing of chromosomes to make a zygote, or the successful implantation of the blastocyst in the uterine wall (as many as a third of fertilised eggs are not successfully implanted), or the point at which monozygotic twins are formed and therefore, by definition, the point at which we can be sure of the single or multiple identity of the new life/lives.

As Yuval Noah Harari rightly says, science certainly has a role here, in as far as it is capable of determining questions around foetal abnormality, viability, sentience, etc. However, it cannot determine which of these should be deemed the salient factor, or, in Harari's terms, which of these constitutes the essential core of life that demands protection.

The historic understanding of this issue, within Christian theology at least, is that none of them, with the potential and partial exceptions of the first and last, constitutes a sufficient reason to withdraw the protection we normally owe to human life. To take each in turn, albeit necessarily briefly, society has made great steps in the last fifty years in revising its attitude to disability, in particular to the idea that disability makes someone less human, less valuable, or that it renders their life less livable. Yet, this view strangely persists before the moment of birth. As the philosopher of disability, Joel Michael Reynolds, has pointed out, this area of debate habitually conflates the lived experiences of disability with that of people who suffer endemic pain and suffering. To be disabled is not, contrary to the cliché, to live in constant misery.[51] To be clear, there is evidence of a correlation

---

50 Banner, *Christian Ethics and Contemporary Moral Problems*, p. 109.
51 Joel Michael Reynolds, *The Life Worth Living: Disability, pain, and morality* (Minneapolis, MN: University of Minnesota Press, 2022).

between physical disability and depression,[52] and it may well be possible to mount the argument that some disabilities are so severe, painful and beyond amelioration that life becomes objectively not worth living. Wherever one comes down on this issue, however, a straightforward link between normality and the right to protection is surely unsustainable.

Second, although the capacity to think rationally is undoubtedly valued in the Christian tradition, nowhere is it judged to be the fundamental quality of human life (as we noted in a previous chapter). Quite apart from the fact that most foetuses can be expected to attain capacity for rational thought at some point in their post-natal development, there is a powerful strand in most ethical systems that insists on the duty of care to those who are permanently cognitively impaired, or are losing their rationality at the end of life. Reason is a good, and humans are usually rational, but their humanity does not reside in that rationality.

Third, the criterion of viability seems to rest on a normative conception of the human as independent and autonomous. However, this is an odd and, it has to be said, historically anomalous view.[53] 'All sorts of people are "viable" only through their reliance on others, even if this reliance is not as intimate or extensive as the reliance of a foetus on its mother.'[54] The understanding of the human as naturally and necessarily autonomous is a function of a liberal anthropology that, facilitated by unprecedented access to energy and resources, has become the norm in Western culture. But even here, a cursory examination of almost every stage of life shows genuine and profound dependency throughout. If viability means the capacity to live and flourish without being dependent on another, is anyone truly viable? Indeed, would anyone want to be? There is a reason why loneliness is so prevalent in Western societies, and also why it is considered so awful.

Fourth, while there is no doubt that the ability to feel pain does change ethical calculations, it does not follow that the inability to feel it automatically decides those calculations. Quite apart from the same point that applied to rationality, namely that a foetus will, in the normal run of events,

---

52 See, for example, 'Relationship between physical disability and depression by gender: a panel regression model', PMC, National Library of Medicine https://www.ncbi.nlm.nih.gov/pmc/articles/PMC5130183 (accessed 17 November 2023).

53 It is also a view that would be made redundant by the development of artificial wombs, though that is not an argument we pursue here.

54 Banner, *Christian Ethics and Contemporary Moral Problems*, p. 108.

develop sentience, it is surely a misstep to equate moral responsibility with the ability to feel pain. Operating on an anaesthetised patient does not absolve the surgeon of moral duties. Many environmental ethical arguments pivot on our responsibility to future generations. Indeed, there have been substantial (and very popular) books published entirely on 'what we owe the future'.[55] But such future generations cannot, by definition, feel pain. Indeed, they don't even exist yet. It they have some moral claim on those of us who are alive, it is not because they are sentient. Accordingly, as Michael Banner has pointed out, 'if we do have an obligation to future generations in spite of their lacking present capacities including sentience, it is difficult to understand how the early foetus' lack of sentience should disqualify it from moral regard'.[56]

Finally, the nature of existence is clearly the most difficult to determine precisely, which is possibly why there has been greater uncertainty about the moral status of the very early foetus in the Christian tradition. On the one hand, it is argued that if there is *any* chance of a human life developing, and once an egg and sperm combine there is certainly a good chance, it should be protected, such as by banning substances that induce abortion or perhaps even the use of contraception at all. On the other hand, the fact that a good proportion of zygotes do not develop into a foetus at all, and a small proportion of them develop into more than one, means that what we are protecting is far from clear.

Different readers will naturally have different views on this last factor, as indeed they will on the previous four, and no survey of these arguments, let alone one as necessarily brief as the one in this chapter, can hope to cover all the relevant points, still less steer the discussion towards a satisfactory conclusion. That is not our intention. What we are hoping to do with this chapter is to underline the ways in which the question of abortion is not only popularly seen as a scientific and religious issue, but is genuinely and necessarily such an issue; and the issue is sharpened and refocused by the developments in obstetrics, which have, as it were, drawn the unborn closer into the camp of the living.

---

55 Such as William MacAskill's *What We Owe the Future: A million-year view* (London: Oneworld, 2022).

56 Banner, *Christian Ethics and Contemporary Moral Problems*, p. 110.

'Your eyes saw my unformed body'

My frame was not hidden from you
    when I was made in the secret place,
    when I was woven together in the depths of the earth.
Your eyes saw my unformed body . . .

The above words from Psalm 139 will be familiar to anyone who has engaged in debates over abortion, as a text favoured by those on the pro-life side of the argument. Richard Hays is right in pointing out that these verses, quite apart from being poetry rather than ethical instruction, are 'in no way explicitly concerned with abortion'.[57] However, that hardly means they are irrelevant to the debate. On the contrary, they are of a piece with the wider scriptural witness that views children as a blessing to be grateful for rather than a problem to be solved, and that insists on God's love for even the 'invisible' members of society. It is from these strands, alongside the fundamental, ubiquitous but much-debated 'image of God', that the historic Christian case against abortion has been woven.

These verses acquire a particular pertinence for a contemporary debate that is now informed, and may ultimately be transformed, by our new-found scientific ability to see such 'unformed bodies' – indeed, in some instances, even to help the process of their being knit together in the womb. For a little over a half century now, that 'frame' has no longer been fully hidden and visible to God alone. Now we humans too can see life being 'woven together' in the darkness. Now we too can see the unformed body.

From having been invisible, unknown, and thus, rightly or wrongly, considered outside the community of human persons, the unborn are increasingly known, seen and 'among us'. That ability has given us – burdened us – with the kind of moral decisions unknown in history. Science has enabled us to *know* the unborn in a way none of our ancestors ever did, and that knowledge has brought with it the ability, indeed the necessity, to make choices that were simply not there for those who came before us. As ethicist

57 Hays, *The Moral Vision of the New Testament*, p. 448.

James Mumford has commented, 'Parents of previous generations never had to live with this "poisoned chalice of knowledge and choice".'[58]

Choice, as we have argued in this chapter, implies – demands – careful ethical evaluation. Invoking 'choice' alone is not enough. By the same reckoning, invoking 'life' alone is not enough, either. There are always ethical evaluations concerning the nature and value of 'life', the kind that science, no matter what public intellectuals like Harari claim, cannot answer. Scientists can clarify and refine information around the existence, sentience, viability, rationality and normality of an unborn child. But they cannot determine which, if any, of those is salient to the question of why a life is judged valuable and worthy of protection.

To be clear, and to repeat a common refrain from this book, religion cannot determine those questions. They are inherently dilemmatic and agonistic. They do not admit 'answers' of this kind. The point is, the questions themselves, being born of scientific progress, now live on religious territory, or at least territory on which religious belief has long been at home. They are questions, like so many in this book, that rest ultimately on what and how we think of the human; questions that are only set to grow in significance and urgency as the twenty-first century progresses.

58 James Mumford, 'The tragedy of selective abortion in Britain', *Spectator*, 15 June 2023.

8
Editing our way to the post-human future

God's most sacred gift

Four years after Bill Clinton stood outside the White House and enthused about alien life, he was back there to talk about human life.[1] The International Human Genome Project and Celera Genomics Corporation had just completed the world's first full sequencing of the human genome, and Clinton was congratulating the scientists on their achievement. 'Today, we are learning the language in which God created life,' he said, using an ancient metaphor. 'We are gaining ever more awe for the complexity, the beauty, the wonder of God's most divine and sacred gift.'[2]

It is no surprise that when we talk about genetics, and in particular the human genome, our rhetoric naturally slides towards the transcendent. The subject seems to require a vocabulary that is deep and metaphysical. How else can we describe the profundity of creation itself?

That language often comes from specific religious stories, such as those that lie just beneath the surface soil of Western modernity. The creation days of Genesis 1, the idea of Eden, the power and potential of Adam, the tree of knowledge: all have been used to convey the significance of the new

---

1 Technically, we know that Clinton was in the East Room and was on a teleconference with Blair (and others) rather than on the White House lawn, but we thought we would allow ourselves a tiny bit of poetic licence here.

2 June 2000 White House Event, National Human Genome Research Institute https://www.genome.gov/10001356/june-2000-white-house-event#:~:text=We%2520must%2520en-sure%2520that%2520new,open%2520the%2520doors%2520of%2520privacy (accessed 17 November 2023).

science.[3] The framing can be generically theological rather than specifically scriptural. Clinton, referring to the 'language of God' (also the title of a book by a future head of the Human Genome Project), drew on the ancient metaphor of God's two books – of words (Scripture) and of works (nature) – and Galileo's statement that mathematics was the language in which God had written the universe. Images and narrative can also come from other religious traditions, as the oft-cited references to Prometheus testify, or, indeed, from more secular sources.[4] Even the commonly deployed metaphor of 'mapping' the genome evokes a very secular sense of transcendence, in which humans rise above their immediate condition and enjoy a god-like view from which they may survey and appraise creation. Such is the magnitude of the issue at hand, our language instinctively drifts away from the sober precision of the scientific paper and reaches for words, images and stories that are saturated with a sense of transcendence and existential significance.

There is nothing unusual or suspect in all this. Models, metaphors and narratives are common currency in science, not least when scientists want to communicate their ideas and discoveries to a general audience. It is perfectly natural for the language of genetics to reach for 'deep' metaphors of this kind to communicate something of what is going on.

The trouble comes when the metaphors do the thinking for us and, in particular, when they do the *fearing* for us. This is a real problem in the field of human genetic editing. All too often, our instinct for religious metaphors fuses with our partial understanding and anxiety, and results in the phrase 'playing God'. The metaphor was used of the birth of Louise Brown, the first baby to be born by *in vitro* fertilisation in 1978.[5] It was used of He

---

3 Horace Freeland Judson, *The Eighth Day of Creation: Makers of the revolution in biology* (Cold Spring Harbor, NY: Cold Spring Harbor Press, 1996); Lee M. Silver, *Remaking Eden: Cloning and beyond in a brave new world* (New York, NY: Avon Books, 1998); Steve Jones, *The Serpent's Promise: The Bible retold as science* (Boston, MA: Little, Brown and Company, 2014).

4 Discussions about manipulating the human genome commonly invoke Mary Shelley's *Frankenstein*, a quintessentially 'modern myth', albeit one thick with biblical allusions. Victor Frankenstein is (probably) named after John Milton's frequent epithet of 'the victor' for God, in *Paradise Lost*, a book quoted as the novel's epigraph, and read by the monster. The monster is resonant with images of *Paradise Lost*'s Satan, and compares himself both to Adam and to Lucifer. For modern myths see Philip Ball, *The Modern Myths: Adventures in the machinery of the popular imagination* (Chicago, IL: University of Chicago Press, 2021).

5 '"Test-tube baby" Brown hails pioneers on 35th birthday', BBC News https://www.bbc.co.uk/news/health-23448665 (accessed 17 November 2023).

Jiankui's surprise cloning of human babies forty years on. And it has been used to crystallise opposition to genetic editing of any kind many times in between. In the words of Leon Kass, former chair of the US President's Council of Bioethics, in the 2003 document *Beyond Therapy: Biotechnology and the pursuit of happiness*, 'Not everyone cheers a summons to a "post-human" future. Not everyone likes the idea of "remaking Eden" or of "man playing God."'[6]

The problem with the 'playing God' metaphor is not that it might act as a brake on technological progress. The precautionary principle is not a bad one, especially in a field vulnerable to techno-utopianism. Rather, the problem is that it traps us in a restrictive all-or-nothing approach, which is then mapped onto a science-or-religion dichotomy; a choice which was elegantly captured by an ABC News headline in response to He Jiankui's work: 'Genetically edited babies – scientific advancement or playing God?'[7]

Framed this way, we are faced with stark alternatives: scientifically grounded progress or religiously justified opposition? The public is forced to choose, and the religious public often turns out to be disproportionately hostile to the science.[8] The scientists are forced to justify themselves and, not surprisingly, when criticism is viewed as absolute and fundamentally religious, they are inclined to downplay its significance. If playing God is the alternative, we'll take scientific advancement, thank you.

Ultimately, the phrase pits religion against science in the kind of blunt, unproductive, zero-sum way we have been trying to critique in this book. Worse, it does so for a subject, and at a moment, when both are needed. Because the rapidly developing science of human gene editing poses precisely the kind of questions about the nature, purpose, value and ends of the human that science itself is ill-equipped to answer. It positively invites

6 *Beyond Therapy: Biotechnology and the pursuit of happiness* (Washington, DC: The President's Council on Bioethics, October 2003), p. 7; https://biotech.law.lsu.edu/research/pbc/reports/beyondtherapy/beyond_therapy_final_report_pcbe.pdf (accessed 17 November 2023).

7 Dr Sumir Shah, 'Genetically edited babies – scientific advancement or playing God?', ABC News https://abcnews.go.com/Health/genetically-edited-babies-scientific-advancement-playing-god/story?id=59425909 (accessed 17 November 2023).

8 See, for example, 'Biotechnology research viewed with caution globally, but most support gene editing for babies to treat disease', Pew Research Center https://www.pewresearch.org/science/2020/12/10/biotechnology-research-viewed-with-caution-globally-but-most-support-gene-editing-for-babies-to-treat-disease/?utm_source=AdaptiveMailer&utm_medium=email&utm_campaign=20-12-10%2520International%2520Biotech%2520and%2520Evolution%2520GEN.%2520DISTRIBUTION&org=982&lvl=100&ite=7604&lea=1679281&ctr=0&par=1&trk= (accessed 17 November 2023).

dialogue with religion that can be rich and beneficial. The question is not so much about whether or not we should 'play God', but more what kind of god we should seek to imitate.

The rapid rise of gene editing and the ethical questions it raises

One of the conceptual problems that dogs our attitude to human genetic editing is that we see it as something unprecedented and uniquely modern. In one respect it obviously is. As we shall note presently, our capacity to understand and edit the human genome has advanced enormously in the last thirty years. But in another, it is as old as the hills, and the category of human genetic editing belongs within the much broader and more ancient category of humans exercising control over creation.

Humans modify themselves, each other, and their shared environment constantly; sometimes intentionally, sometimes unintentionally. Aside from the obvious point that every human is the result of a genetic experiment between their parents, civilisation developed on the back of the extended programme of gene modification that was the agricultural revolution.[9] Humans radically transformed the natural environment through farming and domestication; the process of which transformed us. In addition, we are also all involved in the ongoing business of altering how our genes are expressed. The way in which we engage with one another, and in particular the way we treat the young of the species, affects the manner in which genes are 'switched on and off' (see below), sometimes in profound and permanent ways.[10] Recent progress in genetic editing is part of this longer story of the exercise of human intelligence, agency and responsibility.

---

9 Properly speaking, gene editing involves changing an organism's DNA by making alterations to its genetic code, whereas genetic modification is the process of changing DNA by introducing elements of DNA from a different organism. We have tended to talk about gene editing in this chapter.

10 Laura Spinney, 'Epigenetics, the misunderstood science that could shed new light on ageing', *The Guardian* https://www.theguardian.com/science/2021/oct/10/epigenetics-the-misunderstood-science-that-could-shed-new-light-on-ageing (accessed 17 November 2023). For children see, for example, Felix Dammering et al., 'The pediatric buccal epigenetic clock identifies significant ageing acceleration in children with internalizing disorder and maltreatment exposure', ScienceDirect https://www.sciencedirect.com/science/article/pii/S2352289521001028 (accessed 17 November 2023).

That acknowledged, the speed and manner in which we are now able to modify the genome, accelerating the process from generations to days, is unprecedented. Our ability to insert, delete, modify or replace genetic material directly and with precision and control is a legacy of decoding the genome in the 1990s. However, it has been accelerated and transformed in the last ten years, since Jennifer Doudna of the University of California, Berkeley, and Emmanuelle Charpentier of the Max Planck Institute for Infection Biology, developed a technique for gene editing that came to be known as CRISPR-Cas9.

CRISPR stands for Clustered Regularly Interspaced Short Palindromic Repeats and refers to repeated sequences of DNA found in the genome that derive ultimately from bacteriophages (viruses that infect and replicate only in bacterial cells) that once infected single-celled organisms. Cas9 (from CRISPR associated protein 9) is an enzyme that is capable of splitting DNA. The way in which CRISPR-Cas9 works is highly complex (and way beyond the expertise of your authors), but metaphors (again) help here. The two most commonly used are 'arrow and target' and 'cut and paste'. According to the first, CRISPR provides the target at which geneticists can shoot Cas9. According to the second, Cas9 then acts as a pair of scissors, cutting the DNA at the appropriate point to remove, deactivate or insert a prescribed sequence of nucleotides as desired, and then reconnect the severed DNA.

The technicalities aside, the consensus is that CRISPR-Cas9 will transform the business of gene editing. The technique will allow scientists to change the genome of plants, animals and ourselves with accuracy, speed, relative ease and comparative economy. In under a decade, genetic editing has slipped from aspiration to imminent prospect.

This acceleration has catalysed some serious ethical questions, which is usually where religious ideas are invited, alongside other guests from civil society, to take a seat at the table. Perhaps the most familiar of these arises from the difference between somatic and germline modification. A somatic cell is any cell in your body that is non-reproductive (i.e. any cell other than egg, sperm or zygote). A germ cell is, predictably, one that is involved in reproduction. Accordingly, somatic genome editing involves changing the DNA of a patient in a way that remains restricted to that individual and is not passed on to their children, whereas germline editing involves changes that affect *all* cells, including egg and sperm cells, so that they become

172

heritable. Naturally, somatic genome editing is far less controversial than germline editing. The ethical questions raised by making genetic changes that are extended to unnumbered, unborn descendants, who have had no say in the decisions that affect them, are rather more complex.

This was one of the issues at stake in the He Jiankui controversy in 2018. Jiankui is a Chinese biophysicist who announced, first on YouTube (!) and then at the Second International Summit on Human Genome Editing, that he had genetically modified the embryos of twin girls so that they would be resistant to a particular strain of HIV. The modification being a germline one, their apparent HIV-immunity would be passed on to their offspring in perpetuity. Scientists around the world reacted badly, and Jiankui was heavily criticised and subsequently sentenced to three years in prison by the Chinese authorities.

However, the fact that Jiankui effected a germline modification was only one of the reasons for the outrage; criticisms of his work also pointed to a second major ethical concern. For example, Jiankui's apparent indifference to transparency, scrutiny or accountability to the wider scientific community, to ethical norms, and to any serious regulatory framework was also condemned for the very good reason that genetic editing remains *risky*.

Once again, metaphors can illustrate the nature of the ethical challenge here. The metaphor of 'code' is frequently used to describe genetics: 'decoding the gene', 'breaking the code of life', etc. However, DNA does not operate like a code, in which a discrete and finite set of inputs maps directly onto a discrete and finite set of outputs. In spite of the media's propensity to use the phrase 'a gene for . . . ', there is only rarely a direct and absolute correlation between a gene and an identifiable human condition or characteristic. Genetic 'code' does not work like Morse code.

'Language' is a rather better metaphor here because, in spoken or written language, there is no necessary, clear and direct equivalence between a word and its meaning. Rather, words take on subtle and sometimes very significant differences depending on their context. They work together in collaboration, in ever-spreading webs of relationship, to generate meaning, rather than in code-like isolation.

The fact that genes operate more like a language than a code helps explain why Jiankui's isolation and secrecy was so dangerous. It was not only the unknown long-term implications of germline modification that were alarming. It was the immediate success and effect on the girls themselves. In a field as complex as gene editing, it is extremely hard to be absolutely sure that a treatment will be effective and that there will be no unanticipated and/or potentially harmful side-effects. This is why it requires collaboration, scrutiny and oversight, not simply by other scientists and by regulators, but also by policymakers and ultimately the general public. The science must be embedded in widespread ethical consultation, in order to minimise immediate risks, as well as to evaluate longer-term ones.

A third area that demands particular ethical attention lies in the potential for genetic editing to exacerbate existing health disparities. This can be seen in the example of sickle cell anaemia. This is a severe, inherited disease in which a single gene defect disrupts the production of red blood cells, starving the body of oxygen and resulting in anaemia, organ failure, tissue damage and early death. Being a 'monogenic' disease, it is in theory amenable to gene therapy and there has been much excitement about the potential to treat a condition that has been understood – but incurable – for decades.[11]

However, on account of the fact that sickle cell traits appear to have helped survival against malaria, the disease is especially prevalent in sub-Saharan Africa and among black-minority communities elsewhere. Given the cost of gene therapy – CRISPR-Cas9 has made it a great deal cheaper but that doesn't mean it's cheap – the case of sickle cell anaemia offers a potent example of a condition in which the people who most need the treatment also happen to be those who are least likely to be able to afford it. In the light of the initially prohibitive costs of most new medical treatments, this is not an unusual problem. But the sheer potential of human genome editing, combined with the variety of ends to which the technology can be turned, means that it is a particularly acute one in this case.

From health to intelligence: what goods are we after?

Situating the rapid rise of human genetic editing within the bigger story of human control over nature does something to take the 'scientific

---

11 Mark Zipkin, 'CRISPR's "magnificent moment" in the clinic', *Nature* https://www.nature.com/articles/d41587-019-00035-2 (accessed 17 November 2023).

advancement or playing God?' sting out of the subject. In a similar way, foregrounding the ethical questions that have been catalysed by CRISPR-Cas9 can also help calm fears about 'scientific advancement' running ahead of familiar norms. Both, in their own way, help to defuse the 'playing God' problem and hold out the possibility of a sensible conversation between science and religion on this topic.

That recognised, human genome editing does more than simply open up the kind of familiar ethical deliberations that admit a religious perspective among many others. As noted at the start of this chapter, the way the language so often gravitates towards depths, myths and metaphors of transcendence indicates how the whole issue might be of particular interest and relevance to religious thought.

We can begin to understand this by looking at the problem that He Jiankui was trying to solve. Amidst the chorus of criticism his intervention provoked, no one condemned him for trying to engineer genetic immunity to AIDS. Nobody thinks this itself is an illegitimate goal. It was just the way he went about it that was wrong.

Bill Clinton did not mention AIDS in his 2000 speech, but he did place a similar emphasis on the potential for healing that was now afforded by the newly mapped genome. The achievement, he said, will 'revolutionize the diagnosis, prevention and treatment of most, if not all, human diseases' so that in coming years, doctors will be able to cure 'Alzheimer's, Parkinson's, diabetes and cancer by attacking their genetic roots'. A quarter of a century on, this is where the energy is focused.

The task is still in its infancy but there are many promising signs. Scientists have been able to edit defective T cells, the frontline in the body's defences against cancer, so that they can successfully combat the disease in certain patients.[12] Sickle cell disease has, as noted, shown signs of being amenable to CRISPR-Cas9 therapy. Gene editing has made steps towards controlling the symptoms of Huntington's disease, a neurodegenerative disorder (and another monogenic condition) that is characterised by

---

12 Robin McKie, 'Revolutionary gene therapy offers hope for untreatable cancers', *The Guardian* https://www.theguardian.com/science/2022/dec/11/revolutionary-gene-therapy-offers-hope-untreatable-cancers (accessed 17 November 2023).

loss of coordination and cognitive capacity.[13] There are similar hopes for the treatment of Duchenne muscular dystrophy, a disorder causing muscle degeneration, loss of mobility and early death.[14]

The point about all these diseases is that they clearly and incontestably affect the normal functioning activities of a human body in negative ways. There is no question about the goods that gene editing is trying to achieve here. This does not necessarily mean they are uncontroversial. T-cell modification is a somatic treatment which makes both the goal and process obvious goods.[15] By contrast, the germline modification inherent in treating Huntington's kicks up all the long-term questions mentioned above.

Such questions of method aside, there is justifiable confidence about the fundamental good being pursued in these cases. The ends sought are demonstrably and incontestably worthy ones. There is no clear line between these particular and unarguable goods, and other more debatable ones. Put another way, there is a sliding scale between eradicating diseases and eradicating disabilities, and between eradicating disabilities and enhancing abilities, and the further we travel along that scale the more debatable the good in question becomes.

A few examples draw out the challenge here. There is evidence that, in some instances, blindness may be treatable through gene editing.[16] While there is no question that vision is a good and blindness a disability, there is also no question that being blind does not necessarily stop someone from living a rich, fulfilled and happy life, and contributing to the wider public good. Whereas few would countenance denying gene therapy to a blind person on the grounds that blindness isn't necessarily life-destroying, it is

---

13 Scott LaFee, 'CRISPR technology improves Huntington's disease symptoms in models', Neuroscience News https://neurosciencenews.com/crispr-huntingtons-22059/#:~:text=-Summary%253A%2520Using%2520CRISPR%2520gene%2520editing,not%2520disrupt-ing%2520other%2520human%2520genes.&text=Huntington%2527s%2520dis-ease%2520(HD)%2520is%2520a,movement%252C%2520coordination%2520and%2520cognitive%2520function (accessed 17 November 2023).

14 Esra Erkut and Toshifumi Yakota, 'CRISPR therapeutics for Duchenne muscular dystrophy', PMC, National Library of Medicine https://www.ncbi.nlm.nih.gov/pmc/articles/PMC8836469 (accessed 17 November 2023).

15 Indeed, it is a somatic treatment that can, in theory, be conducted *ex vivo*, editing the relevant cells outside the body and verifying the success of the modification before reintroducing them to the patient, which makes it even safer.

16 Moya Sarner, 'They said I'd go blind. Now gene therapy has changed that', *The Guardian* https://www.theguardian.com/science/2019/jan/19/they-said-i-would-go-blind-gene-therapy-has-changed-that (accessed 17 November 2023).

nonetheless true that the good sought by curing blindness is not the same as the good of curing cancer or Huntington's.

Or take shortness of stature. Dwarfism is commonly defined in adult humans as having a height of less than 147 cm. It takes different forms, has different causes and can sometimes be treated by growth hormone therapy.[17] Recent research has shown that some forms of dwarfism that are resistant to growth hormones may be amenable to gene therapy. As an article in *Drug Target Review* put it, '[A] single-dose injection of a virus carrying the "good" gene can potentially be used to cure growth-hormone resistant dwarfism, also known as "Laron Syndrome".'[18] The scare quotes around the word "good" are (rightly) telling, because although many people with dwarfism do support treatment that increases their height, some do not, and most (all?) would reject the idea that being under 147 cm is a disease to be cured, let alone one comparable with Huntington's. Treating dwarfism might be judged good, but that does not mean dwarfism itself is bad.

Our attitude and treatment of vision and height are often shaped according to what is 'normal' for us. Humans can normally see and, in the UK today, they are normally above 147 cm tall. In the light of this, it is considered acceptable to modify those conditions, genetically or otherwise, because they are (1) abnormal and (2) judged (by some) to be disabling. But there are problems with this approach.

In the first instance, while vision is normal for people, perfect vision is not (nearly three-quarters of the British wear corrective eyewear or have had laser eye surgery). This being so, it is fair to ask what 'restoring vision' actually means, and whether it should also apply to those who, although not blind, have impaired vision in other ways. In other words, what exactly is the bad that is being solved here, or the good that is being sought?

In the second instance, as disability rights campaigners have pointed out for decades, basing social norms on what is 'normal' for humans merely serves to exclude those with particular needs. Being abnormal does not constitute having a 'bad' that one needs to correct. The pain that people with dwarfism suffer is, in some measure, down to public attitudes,

---

17 Proportionate dwarfism is characterized by either short limbs or a short torso, whereas in disproportionate dwarfism either one or the other is out of size.

18 Ria Kakkad, 'Gene therapy: a potential cure for growth-hormone resistant dwarfism', Drug Target Review https://www.drugtargetreview.com/news/103053/gene-therapy-a-potential-cure-for-growth-hormone-resistant-dwarfism (accessed 17 November 2023).

practical inconveniences and social prejudices, rather than the condition itself. In other words, although deploying gene editing in cases like these can be said to serve goods, they are contentious goods.

They become more contentious still when we consider other important human characteristics, like intelligence or mental well-being. Intelligence is widely judged to be a good. The word 'unintelligent' is rarely used as a term of praise. It is also highly heritable, with recent studies 'successfully identifying inherited genome sequence differences that account for 20% of the 50% heritability of intelligence'.[19] While some scientists have claimed that 'Crispr could in principle be used to boost the expected intelligence of an embryo', many dispute this and there is no sign that this kind of modification is on the horizon.[20] Intelligence itself is a varied and debatable phenomenon and, genetically speaking, too complex, polygenic, poorly understood and risky to be a candidate for gene therapy any time soon – possibly ever. Discussion of gene editing for intelligence is, therefore, hypothetical in the way that discussion for Huntington's or dwarfism is not.

But it is a useful hypothetical because if it were possible to use CRISPR-Cas9 to improve someone's intelligence, we would need to have an answer as to whether it would be right to do so. Intelligence is strongly correlated to educational, occupational, financial and health outcomes in life. Lack of intelligence might be considered a disability in as far as it prevents people from accessing roles and functions in society for which they might otherwise be well suited. Assuming gene editing for intelligence avoided the obvious dystopian nightmare of creating an upper caste of the intellectually elite, why should we not improve people's intelligence genetically? Or, more precisely, why should we not seek to improve the intelligence of those at the lower end of the normal distribution curve, so that they had better life chances?

Instinctively, most of us revolt against this idea, but our antipathy is often vague. If intelligence is a good, why not pursue it through all means possible? It is worth remembering that many rural communities resisted the idea of educating children when public education was introduced in the

19 Robert Plomin and Sophie Stumm, 'The new genetics of intelligence', Nature Reviews Genetics https://www.nature.com/articles/nrg.2017.104 (accessed 17 November 2023).

20 Jim Kozubek, 'Can CRISPR-Cas9 boost intelligence?', Scientific American Blog Network https://blogs.scientificamerican.com/guest-blog/can-crispr-cas9-boost-intelligence (accessed 17 November 2023).

nineteenth century, for fear (correct as it turned out) that it would remove them from the land, their families and their settled way of life. Might our current resistance to genetically enhanced intelligence one day look like their resistance to educationally enhanced intelligence?

Or take the example of mental ill health. We have already, in another chapter, explored the significant medical turn that there has been in our approach to mental health over the last thirty years. That turn has been pharmacological in nature, but some have argued that it may – perhaps *should* – become genetic. Some mental health conditions, like bipolar disorder and schizophrenia, have comparatively high levels of heritability, some of which can be traced to particular genes.[21] Other mental health conditions are thought to be partly the result of the impact of earlier trauma, affecting the way in which genes express themselves later in life, rather than altering the genes themselves (this is what we were referring to earlier when we mentioned how the way in which we engage with one another can affect the manner in which genes are 'switched on and off' – epigenetics).[22] In either instance, the discoveries open the possibility of treating mental ill health genetically, albeit with the same reservations that apply to treating intelligence genetically. Mental ill health is a clear 'bad', and far less contentiously so than low intelligence. If we can treat it pharmacologically, why not do so genetically?

This necessarily brief discussion of genetic editing for diseases, sight, stature, intelligence and mental health highlights the crucial question that underlies this scientific advancement and begins to delineate the nature of the potential science and religion conversation here. The decoding of the human genome and the potential opened up by CRISPR-Cas9 has put on the table a range of difficult questions about the goods we should be seeking. Some are wholly uncontentious. Others are much more complex. But underlying them all are wider questions about what human qualities and characteristics we should value – life, health, sight, stature, intelligence,

---

21 Duncan S. Palmer et al., 'Exome sequencing in bipolar disorder identifies *AKAP11* as a risk gene shared with schizophrenia', Nature Genetics https://www.nature.com/articles/s41588-022-01034-x (accessed 17 November 2023). However, the study strongly emphasises that bipolar disorder is a polygenetic condition.

22 Ida Emilie Steinmark, 'Does gene editing hold the key to improving mental health?', *The Guardian* https://www.theguardian.com/science/2023/feb/26/does-gene-editing-hold-the-key-to-improving-mental-health (accessed 17 November 2023).

confidence, appearance, etc. In essence, it poses to us the question, what ends do we want to pursue, what kind of creature should we be? And this is a question that science is, by definition, ill-equipped to deal with.

Reintroducing ends

The lawyer and statesman Francis Bacon was once, and sometimes still is, known as the father of science. This was not because his scientific contributions were substantial or impressive – they were not – but because he set out the principles of inductive reasoning that underpinned the scientific method as it developed in the seventeenth century.

Bacon was not working in a vacuum. In spite of the popular belief that the phrase is an oxymoron, the tradition of 'medieval science' (or, more properly, 'medieval natural philosophy') had been a live one for centuries. However, for much of that time, it had been based not on the inductive approach that Bacon advocated, but on the authority of the Greek philosopher Aristotle.

Aristotle had argued that all things in the changeable, terrestrial realm in which humans lived were amenable to four kinds of explanation, or had four 'causes'. The material cause of something concerned the substance from which it is made. The formal cause referred to its shape or form. The efficient cause was about the immediate source of its being. And the final or teleological cause referred to the ends or purpose for which it existed. Thus, a table could be made of wood (material cause) that was shaped in a certain way (formal cause) by a carpenter (efficient cause) in order to have a surface to eat from (final cause). A human being comprised flesh, bones and blood (material), which took the form of the soul (formal), having been created immediately by their parents (efficient), in order ultimately to contemplate God (final).[23]

Bacon was not impressed by this, or indeed by any scholastic philosophy.[24] Natural philosophy, he argued, should be interested in material and

---

23 This particular understanding of a human is Aristotelian as adopted and adapted by Aquinas.

24 He lamented in *The Advancement of Learning* (1605), I.vi.2, the 'degenerate learning' of medieval scholastic philosophers who had an 'abundance of leisure . . . but small variety of reading, their minds being shut up in a few authors, as their bodies were in the cells of their monasteries'.

efficient causes alone. Formal and final causes were the business of meta-physics, not physics. Indeed, he protested,

> the handling of final causes, mixed with the rest in physical inquiries, hath intercepted the severe and diligent inquiry of all real and physical causes, and given men the occasion to stay upon these satisfactory and specious causes, to the great arrest and prejudice of further discovery.[25]

In other words, introducing final causes into natural philosophy polluted, corrupted, distorted and diverted it. Final causes had no place in science.

Believing that the idea of a telos – a purpose, end, or final cause – had no place in science helped transform natural philosophy into something like modern science. It worked. Separating water into its constituent elements and assuming their properties changed on account of immediate (or efficient) causes was a better way of understanding it than assuming water was itself a constituent element that was drawn, by a final cause, to the space between earth and air.

For some, where science pointed, reality followed. If natural philosophy was indifferent to final causes, then that was because nature was. As Baruch Spinoza put it in his *Ethics*, seventy years after Bacon, '[N]ature has no particular goal in view, and . . . final causes are mere human figments.'[26] The real challenge came when this was applied to humans. Certainly, humans were material beings changed by various efficient causes. But they were also clearly goal directed, aware of themselves, aware of time, exercising agency, capable of rational thought and inclined to plan. Absent final causes from humans, and they became *mere* animals, or *mere* machines, or *mere* vehicles programmed for genetic survival, or *mere* information.[27]

Many demurred from such conclusions, and not just the religious. They pointed out that just because the methods of science bracketed out final causes, that didn't necessarily mean there were no final causes; no telos to

---

25 *The Advancement of Learning*, II.vii.7.

26 Spinoza, *Ethics*, Appendix.

27 In reality, many of those who liked to denounce final causes altogether (including for humans) often smuggled them in under the cover of darkness (e.g. survival, reproduction, progress), but this need not distract us here.

which humans, life or even nature itself was ordered. Perhaps, as Bacon had originally suggested, this was simply the business of metaphysics rather than physics.

Either way, regardless of whether there was indeed a purpose or ends to humans or to life itself, it was simply not within the remit or the capacity of science to discern it. Science, including the science that led ultimately to the decoding of the human genome, succeeded precisely by bracketing out final causes. But that meant that when 'scientific advancement' ran into the question of final causes – which it did spectacularly in the case of the human genome – it found itself in need of disciplinary help. Science alone could not answer the questions about the ends that scientific progress posed.

Soldiers and astronauts

This might appear to be the point at which religion steps in or, more accurately, where the conversation provoked by human genome editing finally and justifiably lands on an issue that is of particular and longstanding interest to religious thought. But it is not – quite.

Although the need for human genome editing to grapple with questions of purpose or ends seems unavoidable, and the inability of science alone to answer those questions is similarly clear, that does not necessarily mean we need to go straight to religious or metaphysical ideas for 'answers'. There are other, more specific ways in which we can respond to the question, which can be illustrated with a few contemporary examples.

One is war. The interest of the military in human genetic editing will surprise no one. Humans have long been the weakest link in the military chain, 'the rate-limiting factor in the conduct of war' as one paper on the use of CRISPR technologies for military enhancement put it.[28] The ability to genetically edit out such weaknesses is too tempting to ignore.

There is a great deal for science fiction to get to work on here – indestructible, emotionless, cyborg-strength soldiers and the like – but such dystopian fears are a distraction from the more immediate and realistic possibilities at hand. The shift towards asymmetrical warfare and the

---

28 Marsha Greene and Zubin Master, 'Ethical issues of using CRISPR technologies for research on military enhancement', PubMed, National Library of Medicine https://pubmed.ncbi.nlm.nih.gov/29968018 (accessed 17 November 2023).

danger of biohazards has left the army exploring the military potential of thermal imaging genes found in reptiles[29] and of genetically engineered resistance to biological attacks. Already it is known, for example, that reduced expression of one gene (capillary morphogenesis gene 2 or CMG 2) 'correlates strongly with lower susceptibility to anthrax'. Perhaps CRISPR-Cas9 can help create soldiers immune to terrorist bioweaponry?

When framed in this 'defensive' way (as opposed to the aggression of cyborg-soldiers) and also placed in the context of the vaccination programmes that are already mandatory for service members, the prospect of such gene editing is a little less frightening, if no less ethically questionable. However frightening or ethically dubious the prospect may be, though, the point is that the question of whether gene modification of this kind is acceptable is rendered comprehensible by the immediate framework of the 'ends' in which it is posed. We know what soldiers are for. We know what they need to achieve, what their end or purpose is. It is within this framework that we can evaluate the legitimacy or otherwise of the genome modification in question.

You can make the same point with a second example: space travel. Elon Musk has repeatedly directed the world's attention to the alleged need to move to Mars and beyond. We know that the technical challenges of getting there are enormous, but the human ones are no less significant. In reality, it is hard to see how humans – oxygen-breathing, short-lived, earth-bound, fragile, social creatures that we are – could ever withstand the physical and psychological demands of such a venture. To take one example, it is estimated that a return trip to Mars (not including any time on the planet itself) would expose any courageous space traveller to a dangerously high level of radiation; way more than half of NASA's lifetime cap for its astronauts. Ordinary humans may not be able to stand this, but perhaps modified ones could?

At first, this sounds as much like science fiction as cyborg-soldiers, but there is ongoing research into the way in which gene therapy might 'enhance radioresistance via the translation of exogenous and engineered DNA repair and radioprotective mechanisms' into the human genome.[30]

---

29 See E. O. Gracheva et al., 'Molecular basis of infrared detection by snakes', *Nature* https://www.nature.com/articles/nature08943 (accessed 17 November 2023). We didn't say there was no science fiction in this!

30 Franco Cortese et al., 'Vive la radiorésistance! Converging research in radiobiology and biogerontology to enhance human radioresistance for deep space exploration and colonization', Oncotarget https://www.oncotarget.com/article/24461 (accessed 17 November 2023).

Some species of bacteria, like tardigrades, are resistant to radiation, and researchers have found that 'human cells with tardigrade genes added were able to suppress x-ray damage by about 40%'.[31] The point here, as with biohazard-resistant gene modification for the military, is not to say that the editing in question is necessarily good or right. Rather, it is to point out that it is only because we have some idea of what objective we are trying to achieve that we are able to adjudicate on it. We know what an astronaut needs to be able to do, what she or he is *for*, and so we can take a view on the legitimacy or otherwise of gene modification to help them achieve it.

This is more or less the position that Sheila Jasanoff, a leading figure in Science and Technology Studies, arrives at in her book on the life sciences, *Can Science Make Sense of Life?*[32] The question of what life *is*, she argues, cannot be disentangled from the question of what is life *for*, and to understand what life is for necessarily entails conceiving it in its wider social, linguistic, cultural, moral and metaphysical contexts. Sometimes the process of this contextualisation is straightforward. We instinctively recognise the legitimacy of gene therapy that treats cancer or severe degenerative diseases because we instinctively understand that being alive is a necessary good for human beings. In a similar (but not identical) way, we can see the good of gene therapy that restores people's vision because we understand the good inherent in seeing clearly.[33]

However, when we are faced with questions about enhancing human capacities, the question of whether these are indeed goods to be pursued invariably runs into the wider question of what context we are talking about, what ends we should be seeking. Why do we *want* to be more intelligent, more confident, more resilient, thermal-sighted, radioresistant, etc.?

In certain specific cases, the situation we find ourselves in – such as fighting in a war or travelling to other planets – might help us answer those questions, because they supply us with an idea of the objectives or purposes we are seeking to achieve. We know what a soldier or an astronaut is there

31 Sarah Betancourt, 'Gene therapy may help astronauts going to Mars resist deadly radiation', *The Guardian* https://www.theguardian.com/science/2018/apr/07/gene-therapy-may-help-astronauts-going-to-mars-resist-deadly-radiation (accessed 17 November 2023).

32 Sheila Jasanoff, *Can Science Make Sense of Life?* (Cambridge: Polity, 2019).

33 Importantly, however, we also recognise that this good is not an alternative to the wider social responsibility of adjusting to and supporting those with blindness or indeed dwarfism.

to do. But what about when we don't have those specific contexts to guide us, when we broaden the perspective to consider humans *in general*, rather than humans-as-soldiers, or humans-as-astronauts, or athletes, or workers, etc.? In doing that, we are faced with the kind of question that, though meaningless to science, is central to so much religious thought: what are humans for?

What are humans for?

There is no single 'religious' answer to this question. Indeed, as we have been at pains to emphasise throughout this book, there are no religious *answers* to any of the questions raised in this book. The book is an attempt to explain where and why there might be particularly important, urgent and fruitful areas of dialogue between science and religion in the twenty-first century, and to outline what they might look like. Dialogue does not mean that science raises problems that religion then 'solves' (whatever that might mean). True dialogue is not a Q&A; human genome editing is not the kind of activity that is amenable to straightforward answers, and to think that religion is simply a way of solving ethical problems shows an emaciated understanding of what it is.

Like the other topics covered in the book, what human genome editing does is draw science onto traditionally religious territory that it is, by definition, ill-equipped to navigate. In the process, we can begin to see the potential for profitable dialogue. That being so, this chapter ends not with an answer, still less *the* answer, but with a perspective that might inform and enrich this conversation, and help us chart a path through the complexities before us.

At one point in Sophocles' play *Antigone*, the chorus poses a question about the human race that is oddly similar to the one posed by Psalm 8 in the Hebrew Bible. 'Among the many wonders of the world / Where is the equal of this creature, man?' the chorus asks.[34] The implicit answer is that there is no equal, and a little later on, Haemon, son of King Creon, offers a

---

34 These lines are from Seamus Heaney's rendition, *The Burial of Thebes*, c. line 415. Other translations tend not to phrase these lines as a question, which tends to suggest that Heaney was deliberately drawing out the parallel with Psalm 8.

kind of answer why. 'Father, the gods implant intelligence in humans. / Of all our properties, that is the supreme one.'[35]

This has proved a remarkably popular view in Western thought, including among many Christian thinkers, which has regularly invoked reason as *the* quintessential human characteristic.[36] If this indeed were the case, it would constitute a strong argument for gene-augmented intelligence. Just as soldiers are for fighting and astronauts for exploring space, humans are for being intelligent, so we should seek to enhance that in whatever safe way we can.

The psalmist's question sounds similar – 'What are human beings that you are mindful of them, mortals that you care for them?'[37] – but is marked by a subtle difference. The question is embedded within a song or prayer to God, marked by praise and a sense of awe. This is not an abstract enquiry and is not answered with an abstract virtue but by a poem that places humans in a network of relationships. 'You have made them a little lower than the angels . . . You made them rulers over the works of your hands . . .'[38]

Notwithstanding the Christian thinkers who have sanctified it, intelligence is not much lauded, or even mentioned, in the New Testament (no doubt to the delight of Christianity's cultured despisers). The Greek word *sunetos* is sometimes translated as 'intelligence', but it occurs only four times and then usually in a negative formulation.[39] The writers of the Hebrew scriptures and the New Testament did value *wisdom* highly, but wisdom was not a matter of raw intelligence or logical reasoning so much as its application to the goal of a virtuous, godly life.

This is a goal that no humans achieve but which is understood to be reached by Jesus, who is described by Paul as the last Adam, the kind of

---

35 This translation is from Richard Emil Braun's translation for the Oxford University Press Greek Tragedy series. Heaney prefers to translate the word as 'reason'.

36 As we note in another chapter, it is this view of humans – as marked out by intelligence and reason, accompanied by the attendant view that reason can be deconstructed into processing information – that underlies the belief that superfast processing equates to super-intelligence, which equates to super-humanity, i.e. that AI will one day surpass humanity.

37 Psalm 8:4. This translation is from the NRSV. Others tend to prefer the singular, such as the ESV: 'what is man that you are mindful of him, and the son of man that you care for him?'

38 Psalm 8:5–6.

39 For example in Matthew 11:25 ('At that time Jesus said, "I praise you, Father, Lord of heaven and earth, because you have hidden these things from the wise and learned, and revealed them to little children"') or 1 Corinthians 1:19 ('For it is written: "I will destroy the wisdom of the wise; the intelligence of the intelligent I will frustrate"').

complete human that the first Adam singularly failed to be.[40] Jesus is the model of full humanity, the person to follow, to emulate, to become. Jesus' fullness, completion, or 'perfection' as it is sometimes rendered, is not marked by intelligence, still less by appearance, but by the kind of life he lives. For a short collection of books and letters, the New Testament references and endorses a truly remarkable range of virtues and patterns of life marked by goodness.[41] But above them all, it is love that is foundational to Jesus' words and actions. As Paul says, 'The only thing that counts is faith expressing itself through love.'[42]

To live a full or perfect human life is to love, and to love is to know, enjoy, preserve and celebrate the object of love, even to the point of giving all one has for its sake. Love is characterised by self-gift, the willingness to sacrifice whatever I have or am – even to the point of my life – so that your good is brought to fullness. 'Greater love has no one than this: to lay down one's life for one's friends.'[43] If Christianity has any succinct answer to the question of what humans are for, it is to love God and their neighbours, practically, expansively, expensively.

This perspective on the ends or purpose of human existence helps orient us in the face of the kind of question that lurks behind the promise of gene editing, namely, in the words of one newspaper headline, 'How far should we go with gene editing in pursuit of the "perfect" human?'[44] If perfection is conceived as possessing certain attributes or characteristics, such as intelligence, strength or confidence to a great degree, then we might make an argument for gene editing for those qualities.

---

40 1 Corinthians 15:45–7.

41 On a recent reading of the New Testament, we noted the following virtues: attentiveness, blamelessness, clear-mindedness, comfort, compassion, confidence, consideration, contentment, conviction, discipline, endurance, faithfulness, fellowship, generosity, gentleness, godliness, goodness, grace, hard work, harmony, helpfulness, holiness, honesty, honour, hopefulness, hospitality, humility, integrity, justice, kindness, love, maturity, meekness, mercy, modesty, mutuality, obedience, patience, peace, perseverance, persistence, purity, respect, reverence, righteousness, sacrifice, self-control, self-denial, seriousness, service, sincerity, soundness, strength, submissiveness, sympathy, temperance, thankfulness, trust, truthfulness and wisdom. We are bound to have missed some.

42 Galatians 5:6.

43 John 15:13.

44 The question asked by an article in the *Observer*. Robin McKie, 'How far should we go with gene editing in pursuit of the "perfect" human?', *The Guardian* https://www.theguardian.com/science/2023/feb/05/how-far-should-we-go-with-gene-editing-in-pursuit-of-the-perfect-human (accessed 17 November 2023).

If, however, human perfection is not a matter of personalised abilities, but the willingness to love the *other*, then gene editing of this nature is rather less important.[45] Because humans do not need to be excessively intelligent, strong, confident, still less tall, far-sighted or good-looking, in order to love. Indeed, at least according to some New Testament motifs, it is those who are weaker, poorer or more vulnerable, like the widow with her mite, who are often better able to give themselves away for the good of the other, 'for my power is made perfect in weakness'.[46]

If human beings ultimately find their purpose and fulfilment in love, and love involves the gift of the self to and for the other, it becomes harder to see how genetic editing could improve humans, still less perfect them.

Back to playing God

We began this chapter by pointing out that the phrase 'playing God' is often deployed in the context of human genome editing in particular, and that it is distinctly unhelpful. 'Playing God' imposes an unwarranted zero-sum game on an issue that cries out for interdisciplinary nuance, and then it unhelpfully maps that opposition directly onto the clichéd conflict between science and religion. Ultimately, no one's good is served by this. In reality, as we have seen, genetic editing is an area in which we are more or less compelled to 'play God'. The real question is what kind of God we should be imitating.

One of the many things that He Jiankui was criticised for was the fact that he had achieved his ambitions by creating clones. Cloning has a particularly elevated place in the pantheon of human anxieties, and the reason why is instructive. Melodramatically, we envisage clones in the same way as we do cyborg-soldiers, indistinguishable ranks of only partially human beings, equipped with all our capacities except compassion and kindness. This, however, is simply our familiar knee-jerk dystopianism. As many people like to point out, not least biologists, clones are no more

---

45 'Of this nature' because none of these qualifications around the kind of 'perfection' we should be pursuing affect the kinds of goods, regarding disease and disability discussed earlier in the chapter, that we *should* be pursuing. Recognising human perfection in love and gift, even in weakness, is not a reason to refrain from intervening to help the health of those who need it. We are grateful to Madeleine Pennington for this clarification.

46 2 Corinthians 12:9.

indistinguishable, characterless or scientifically suspect than identical twins. Nature clones people all the time. Why shouldn't we?

The root of the anxiety lies not in the fact of genetic similarity, however, but in the status of the being that is created. Identical twins are, we would hope, born to parents who want and love them, even if they didn't expect or plan for them. After all, no self-respecting parent values their twins less than they would a single child. The issue around cloning is not the content of the genetic material but its context; not, to reference Sheila Jasanoff, what the life sciences create but what they create for.

Would a genetically engineered clone be valued, known and loved in the way human twins are? Will editing the genome create humans that are better capable of loving one another, and the creation they are placed in? Is the vision of perfection that is motivating us one in which the human organism is augmented to be able to do what it already does, only quicker and more efficiently? Or is it one where true perfection, true fullness, is characterised by self-gift? If the question central to genetic editing is what kind of God we should be playing, these are the kinds of question we will need to ask.

Ultimately, Christian thought does not consider the human genome sacred or inviolable any more than it considers nature sacred and unalterable. Nature is continually changing, by its nature. Our very position in creation is precisely to recognise that malleability, that possibility, and to exercise the right kind of control over it; as a creature among other creatures, but one that has a unique responsibility to represent God's love to creation. We are there to play God, not to avoid doing so.

Postscript

Science has periodically promised to completely remake humanity. In the early nineteenth century, Auguste Comte, philosopher and founder of sociology, developed what he considered to be the 'science of mankind' that would liberate humanity from its theological and metaphysical darkness, and lead to the 'gradual and slow improvement of human nature'.[1] A century later, eugenicists, working in the shadow of Darwinism, thought they could purify and strengthen the human stock by breeding out weakness and 'imbecility' in order to leave only healthy specimens to reproduce. Fifty years after that, Soviet cosmonauts became emblematic not only of Russia's technological superiority in the early Cold War but also of a new stage of history, a new age in which a new humanity had finally transcended its limited, earth-bound existence.

These were all, quite clearly, religious aspirations, born of the Christian salvation narrative that provided the backdrop against which the new science was operating. We may be on the cusp of a similar quasi-salvific moment. Indeed, some of the chapters in this book suggest we are already there. This is most clearly the case in the quest for scientific immortality, in our newfound ability to edit the human genome, and in the breathlessness with which developments in AI are greeted. To quote the inimitable Ray Kurzweil, 'We're going to get more neocortex, we're going to be funnier, we're going to be better at music. We're going to be sexier . . . We're really going to exemplify all the things that we value in humans to a greater degree.'[2] If that isn't a vision, albeit a painfully individualistic and possessive vision, of the new creation, it's hard to know what is.

Although these are the most obvious examples, they are not the only ones. The quest for a new humanity is visible in our pharmacological ability to treat mental ill health and free our species from the troublesome burdens

---

1 Comte, *Positive Philosophy*, II.113.
2 Quoted in John Wyatt and Stephen N. Williams (eds), *The Robot Will See You Now: Artificial intelligence and the Christian faith* (London: SPCK, 2021), p. 135.

of the human condition. It is discernible in our epidemiological capacity to immunise against the kinds of pandemic that have plagued humanity through history. It is even there in the background of our perennial discussion of aliens and our own post-Earth future.

Even those topics we have discussed that clearly aren't about humans transcending their historic limitations still pose questions about the boundaries of the human 'territory'. At what point does human life begin to merit the protection we like to think it deserves? That question, never easy, becomes more complex still as science peers ever further into the womb and offers the unborn the same medical attention as it does the born. And then, of course, there is the very different, but curiously similar, question of where the boundary between humans and other animals lies, how permeable it is, and what that means for our fellow species. Time and again, the contours and limits of human nature and the human condition are probed and pulled.

The fact that that particular discussion about animals revolves around the ancient, originally theological, concept of personhood is an indication of the way in which these conversations edge into the territory of science and religion. Just as zoology and, in particular, primatology invite discussion of personhood, so other disciplines catalyse similar conversations. The quest for scientific longevity, even immortality, asks questions about human temporality, about the actual meaning of eternal life, and about the possibility, or necessity, of transformation. The quest for alien intelligence invites reflection on human uniqueness and what, if any, significance that has. The astonishing development in AI demands reflection on the centrality of human embodiment, contingency and vulnerability. Pharmacology poses questions about the meaning and ultimately the source of health and of ill health. Genetic engineering provokes questions about human ends, perfection, weakness, and about what human qualities and characteristics we should value. The newfound ability to look into the womb and heal during pregnancy provokes questions about whether and how (ab)normality, rationality, viability, sentience or existence are fundamental to the dignity of being human. Even the success of vaxxing and rise of anti-vaxxing, and the religious dimension it has unfortunately taken, poses questions about the balance of state power, mutual responsibility and human freedom.

Religion doesn't answer these questions. Indeed, at the risk of repeating ourselves, these questions do not *have* answers, in the same way that most scientific questions have answers. But that is precisely the point. The questions that are posed by science, in all these areas, have moved onto a territory that doesn't admit answers, in the scientific or mathematical sense, but rather demands perspectives that draw on the kinds of worldview that all humans have, even if they don't know it.

Those perspectives are often already embedded in the language we use to describe the matter in hand, as we have also emphasised throughout this book. As we observed earlier, the words we use to name and describe something invariably locate, categorise and value the thing that is named. How you describe something determines what you think it is and also, therefore, how you should respond to it. A language is a form of life, and how we talk about issues of AI, abortion, gene editing and mental ill health will often predetermine what we conclude about them. As much as anything else, this book is a plea to retain an open and multi-voiced language, which retains humanistic, ethical and spiritual layers when talking about these things, rather than collapsing everything we say into simplistic, positivistic vocabulary.

In the same vein, if there is one take-home message from this book, it is that single answers to the ultimate question of what a human is are almost always inadequate. 'No single picture of the human will exhaust the true depth of ourselves.'[3] Historically, it has been our propensity to allow only singular answers to the question of the human – we are *only* material, or *only* spiritual, or *only* evolved, etc. – that has stoked science and religion conflict. That risk remains a live one in the twenty-first century: humans are only information, or only genes, or only neurochemicals, or only animals. If the science and religion conversation achieves anything, as it seeks to leave behind the models of competing explanations and of 'non-overlapping magisteria' in favour of what we might call 'human entanglement', it is to draw attention to the inexhaustible and unfathomable richness of that ancient question, what a piece of work is a [hu]man?

---

3   From p. 142 above.

Index

193

Index

Christian libertarianism 65–6, 69, 70, 73–4, 75

Christian nationalism 66–8, 69–71, 73–6

cloning 188–9

Clough, David 81

community, resurrection and 28–30

consciousness 103–5

Copernicus 35, 43

Covid-19 pandemic: mental health deterioration 132–3; vaccine hesitancy 52–3, 56–62, 64, 65–6, 67–8, 71, 73

Crowe, Michael J. 40

cryonics 15–16, 24

Darwin, Charles 82, 83

Davies, Paul 1, 43, 51

de Waal, Frans 94

death *see* eternal life

depression *see* mental health

disability 158–9, 162, 163–4, 175–80

Drake, Frank 37

dualism, body–soul/mind 109–10, 112, 113, 117

dwarfism 177–8

Einstein, Albert 2

emotional intelligence, of animals 84–5

emotions 82, 104

ends (final causes, purposes) 174–88

eternal life 13–32; and the body 118–19; enthusiasm (or lack of) for 22–5; religious promise of 13–14; science of immortality 15–22; scientific immortality vs Christian resurrection 25–30; unattractiveness of, without transformation 30–2

ethical judgements, basis of 154–5, 167

extra-terrestrial life 33–51; Christ and other planets 41–2; human (in) significance and 43–51; probability of 37–8; the search for 33–9, 51;

as a threat (or not) to Christian belief 39–41, 44, 48–9, 51

Fermi Paradox 38

Galileo Galilei 6–7, 169

Gallup, Gordon 83

gene editing 168–89; ethical issues 172–4; 'playing God' metaphor 168–71, 188–9; purposes of 174–80, 182–8, 189; rise of 171–2; somatic vs germline modification 172–3, 176

genetics, ageing and 18–19

God: existence of 8; human specialness conferred by God's choosing 45–8; personhood of 86–8; sovereignty of 26–7, 63

'Goldilocks' stars and zones 36

Goodall, Jane 84

Gould, Stephen Jay 4–5, 153

Gregory of Nyssa 161

happiness *see* mental health

Happy the elephant 77–8

Harari, Yuval Noah 93, 107, 152–3, 155, 163

Hauerwas, Stanley 160

Hawking, Stephen 106–7, 111

Hawking–Harari attack (of AI on humanity) 108–9, 110–13

Hays, Richard 159–60, 161, 166

He Jiankui 169–70, 173–4, 175, 188

health 149–52, 158–9, 162, 163–4, 175–80; *see also* mental health

Hobbes, Thomas 110, 112

Hoyle, Fred 2–3, 43–4

human genome *see* gene editing

humanism, anthropocentric vs theocentric 48–9, 51

humans, nature and significance: AI and 99–101, 105–8; animals and 80–6; extra-terrestrial life and 43–51;

Index